THE WITCHES OF FIFE

THE WITCHES OF FIFE:

Witch-hunting in a Scottish Shire, 1560–1710

Stuart Macdonald

TUCKWELL PRESS

First published in Great Britain in 2002 by
Tuckwell Press
The Mill House
Phantassie
East Linton
East Lothian EH40 3DG
Scotland

Copyright © Stuart Macdonald, 2002

ISBN 1 86232 146 9

British Library Cataloguing in Publication Data

A catalogue record for this book is available
on request from the British Library

Typeset by Hewer Text Ltd, Edinburgh
Printed and bound by Bell & Bain Ltd, Glasgow

For my parents

David and Helen Macdonald

Contents

Tables and Graphs

Maps

Abbreviations

APS   *Acts of the Parliaments of Scotland.*

EMEW   Ankarloo, Bengt, and Gustav Henningsen. *Early Modern European Witchcraft: Centres and Peripheries.* Oxford: Clarendon, 1990.

KS   Kirk Session.

PBK   Stevenson, William, editor. *The Presbyterie Booke of Kirkcaldie: Being the record of the proceedings of that Presbytery from the 15th day of April 1630 to the 14th day of September 1653.* Kirkcaldy: James Burt, 1900.

RPC   *Register of the Privy Council of Scotland.*

SBSW   Larner, Christina, Christopher Hyde Lee, and Hugh McLachlan. *A Source Book of Scottish Witchcraft.* Glasgow: Sociology Department, University of Glasgow, 1977.

STACUPR   Kinloch, G.R. ed. *Selections from the Minutes of the Presbyteries of St. Andrews and Cupar 1641–98.* Edinburgh: Abbotsford club, 1837.

SWHDB   Scottish Witch-Hunt Data Base Project. Created by Stuart Macdonald. The Scottish Witch-Hunt Data Base exists in MS ACCESS format and is available to researchers upon request.

SYNFIFE   Kinloch, George R.. *Selections from the Minute of the Synod of Fife.* Edinburgh: Abbotsford Club, 1837.

Acknowledgements

The seeds of this project began in the fall of 1981. At that time I was doing a course with Ted Cowan on the renaissance and reformation periods in Scotland. A paper presented by a visiting scholar to faculty and students on the Scottish witch-hunt raised several questions which I later explored in an essay. The result was an abiding interest even before reading Christina Larner's *Enemies of God*. In using the *Sourcebook of Scottish Witchcraft* in researching the essay I kept thinking that there were so many other ways I wanted to sort the data. The idea that this information should be put back on a computer never quite died. When I decided to begin doctoral studies on a part-time basis in 1987, that idea became my area of interest and research. The original concept of doing some kind of quantitative study gradually faded as Ted Cowan and other members of the history department at Guelph suggested other possibilities. The results follow.

From those years to the present, many debts have been incurred. This project by its very nature has always relied on the work of other historians and academics, as well as input from others of a specialized nature. The academic work is cited throughout. Still it seems important to note that without the work of Christina Larner, Christopher Hyde Lee, and Hugh McLachlan in compiling the *Sourcebook*, and without the careful work of those who have transcribed and published so many of the documentary sources, any attempt at analysing the witch-hunt in a region as large as Fife would not have been possible. Three parishes (Culross, Tuliallan, and Newburgh) became part of the study after some of the initial research had been completed. I am indebted to Michael Wasser for his generosity in sharing with me information on the cases from Newburgh, including notes relating to a documentary source which could not readily be photocopied and mailed from Scotland. Richard Bensen's chronological information in the Appendix to his thesis *South-West Fife and the Scottish Revolution* provided information on early cases in Culross.

This project also involved specific technical expertise as to what computer software might be best used in organizing and presenting the data. That task was especially difficult because of the ever-changing requirements of hardware and the development of newer, possibly better, software. To everyone who ever tried to help me find or set up the software, I extend my thanks. Special thanks go to Ian Macdonald, my brother, for helping to design the computer database which is the core of the SWHDB project and to Donald Mercer who taught me how to use spreadsheets. Wendy Taxis donated her time to compile Appendix C. I would also like to extend my thanks to the Aberdeen and North East Scotland Family History Society for allowing me permission to use two of their 'County/Parish maps' as the basis for the parish maps used in this book.

Doing Scottish history in Canada is always a challenge. I would like to extend my thanks to the librarians at the University of Guelph for their patience and assistance in obtaining various books and articles for me. Special thanks also to the librarians at Knox College for assisting me in accessing the collection in the Caven Library. The research trip taken in the summer of 1994 to Edinburgh, Glasgow, St. Andrews, and the various communities in Fife was vital to this project. It would not have been nearly as profitable without the assistance of the staff at the Scottish Record Office (now the National Archives of Scotland), the National Library of Scotland, Edinburgh University Library, the Special Collections Department of the University of Glasgow Library, and the Muniments Department of St. Andrews University. Thanks to them all. The local libraries in Fife were extremely welcoming and put their collections readily at my disposal. I would like to extend my appreciation to the staff of the Kirkcaldy District Library and the Kirkcaldy Town House, the Carnegie Library in Dunfermline, and the David Hay Fleming Library, St. Andrews. Special thanks also to Elizabeth Ewan and David Mullan, who graciously gave of their time while on their own research trips to Scotland to make the arrangements to have documents I needed photocopied and mailed to me in Canada, and even helped with some of the transcribing. The trip was also personally rewarding, thanks to the company of those whom I met along the way or who provided me with somewhere to stay. My thanks to Ted Cowan for accommodation in Glasgow and Roger Mason for meeting with me while I was at St. Andrews. A special thanks to my friends at David Horn House, Edinburgh, July 1994, with whom I shared many laughs and ideas (and even watched the world Cup final – *Italia*!).

I would like to extend my thanks to the following for their generous financial support over the years: the Cameron Doctoral Bursary of the Presbyterian Church in Canada which generously contributed to the research trip to Scotland and to an extended study leave for the writing of my thesis in May and June of 1996; the congregations of Centreville, Grace, Millbrook, and St. Andrew's, Cobourg for allowing me to use my yearly study leave towards graduate studies; David and Helen Macdonald; and, my current employer, Knox College, for study leave to edit and finish the thesis and this book. Special thanks go to my wife, Alison Kneen, for understanding, financial contributions, and mostly for taking care of our family while I was raiding archives and consuming pints in Scotland. As grateful as I am for the financial support, there have been times when the interest and moral support of friends and colleagues have been invaluable. To all, many thanks. I would especially like to note two friends who died before the research was completed: Mr. Stan Watson and the Rev. Dr. John MacMurray. Both Stan and John always offered interest and encouragement. Their support was deeply appreciated.

The history department at the University of Guelph has been extremely supportive. My original advisor, Ted Cowan, continued to support my research after taking a new position as Professor of Scottish History at the University of Glasgow and was gracious enough to offer comments on later drafts. I hope he is pleased by the results. I would like to express thanks to Ronald Sunter for stepping in as my advisor and helping to complete this project, and to the members of the committee, Linda Mahood and Hans Baaker, for their contributions. Thanks also to Brian Levack and R. Quaife.

To Meaghan, Brendan, and Alison, thank you again.

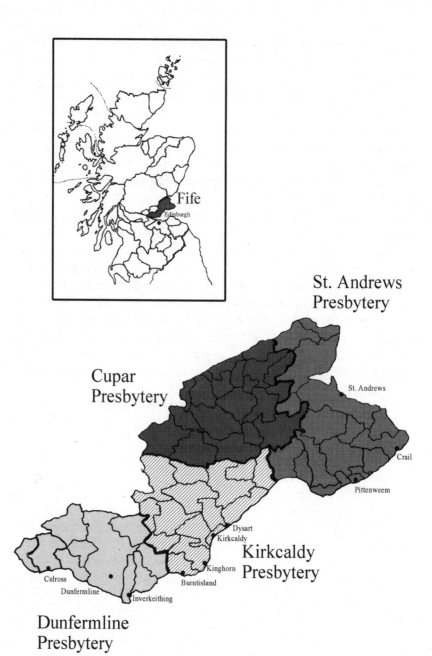

St. Andrews
Presbytery

Cupar
Presbytery

St. Andrews

Crail

Pittenweem

Dysart
Kirkcaldy

Kirkcaldy
Presbytery

Culross
Dunfermline

Kinghorn
Burntisland

Inverkeithing

Dunfermline
Presbytery

Fife

Edinburgh

Map 1 – Overview: parishes and presbyteries in Fife

Introduction

The actors stood in costume and talked casually. The audience sat on the sides of the hill, some licking ice creams. Everyone waited. As the time approached, the cast took their positions. A jailer guarded the woman who hunched over by the side of the pulpit. A figure with a flowing beard and ministerial robe approached the pulpit. The play began. It was an imaginative recreation of a stray piece of information which we know from the historical records (and which we will discuss later), namely that once in St. Andrews John Knox 'spoke against a witch' prior to her execution. Our modern concerns and questions were voiced by one character in the play, a citizen of the town, who challenged Knox's reading of scripture. All the time the woman sat by the side of the pulpit, hunched over and seemingly unaware of the events which were transpiring. The audience applauded at the end of the play, then moved off into the pleasant summer afternoon to enjoy the rest of the day.*

Plays and stories about witches seem strange. Historical dramas, however well presented, struggle to get us to imagine ourselves in a time when people believed in (and feared) the local witch. Like ghost tours and haunted walks, they seem more recreational, glimpses of part of a distant past which we do not understand. Yet interest in the witch-hunts of early modern Europe is on the increase. Along the coast of Fife, in villages like Culross and Pittenweem, historical markers and pamphlets now include the fact that some women were executed as witches within these burghs. Still the reality of what happened the night that Janet Cornfoot was lynched in the harbour is hard to grasp as one sits in the harbour of Pittenweem watching the fishing boats unload their catch and the pleasure boats rising with the tide. How could people do this to an old woman? Why was no-one ever brought to justice for the action? And why would anyone defend such a lynching?

---

* The play, *Moses Law*, was written by David Kinnaird and performed by members of the Heritage Events Company, Stirling, in the summer of 1994. I am indebted to members of the cast for discussion and to David Kinnaird who answered several of my questions by correspondence.

The task of the historian is to try to make events in the past come alive and seem less strange. This is particularly true in the case of the historian dealing with the witch-hunt. The details are fascinating. Some of the anecdotes are strange. The modern reader and researcher find it hard to imagine illness being blamed on the malevolence of a beggar woman who was denied charity, not on germs and bacteria. It is difficult to understand the economic failure of a sea voyage being attributed to the village hag, not bad weather. Yet for all that may appear strange, there are elements within these stories which we can understand. Fear. Tensions between neighbours. Poverty, and various attitudes towards poverty and those who are poor. The blaming of those 'outsiders'. Trying to find someone to blame for the difficulties of life seems, at times, to be a natural human trait. Trying to explain the crimes we fear most, be it supposed attempts at taking over the government or child molestation or economic control by small groups (ethnic, bankers, unions), as part of an evil conspiracy has not changed since the seventeenth century. In our own times it is often difficult to discern the underlying patterns. Our political views, religious beliefs, and economic opinions can all be used to name one part of our community as the cause of the problem or the enemy.

Witch-hunting was similarly related to ideas, values, attitudes and political events. It was a complicated process, involving religious and civil authorities, village tensions and the fears of the elite. The witch-hunt in Scotland also took place at a time when one of the main agendas was the creation of a righteous or godly society. Civil and religious authorities may have fought over some of the areas of jurisdiction and the meaning of these terms, but there was at least some consensus that this was the kind of society which should be built. As a result, religious authorities had control over aspects of the lives of the average person which seem every bit as strange to us today as might any beliefs about magic or witchcraft. That the witch-hunt in Scotland, and specifically Fife, should have happened at this time was not accidental. This book tells the story of what occurred over a period of a century and a half and offers some explanation as to why it occurred.

The structure is relatively simple. We will begin by discussing what we already know about the European and Scottish witch-hunts. In Chapter 2, the historical and geographic patterns of witch-hunting in Scotland will be described. This is significant, not only for Fife, but for studies of witch-hunting in other regions of Scotland. The following chapters begin with an overview, then move to tell the story of the witch-hunt in each of the four presbyteries into which Fife was divided. Chapter 8 will summarise the findings of these chapters, and suggest that the picture which has emerged challenges some established understandings of the Scottish witch-hunt, in particular the role played by judicial torture. The witches of Fife will be the topic of Chapter 9. Chapter 10 will look at how different groups in society participated in witch-hunts and will place witch-hunting within the overall agenda of the creation of a godly society.

In order to understand witch-hunting in Fife, we have to understand this drive to create a godly society. The Reformation changed the dynamics between the clergy and common people. The beliefs and behaviour of the common people mattered, whether it was their sexual behaviour or their seeking of charms and incantations in order to protect themselves from disease. Church discipline was used to try to alter both belief and behaviour. It is the main argument of this book that witch-hunting developed naturally out of this concern. It was the clergy, not other members of the elite, who were primarily concerned with eradicating witchcraft from the parishes of Fife. This concern was not so much with the Devil but with all acts of charming, curing, slanderous speech, or 'heretical' belief which were included under the term 'witchcraft'. In order to obtain the confessions which were required in order to have a suspect taken to a secular trial, sleep deprivation was used. Sleep deprivation, not the application of direct physical torture, was the dominant method used to gain confessions and maintain the witch-hunt. The Devil makes only a few appearances in Fife, and, as we shall see, often folk beliefs about fairies seem to be more important than diabolic theory. The reality was that the victims of this aspect of the attempt to create a godly society were often those who lived on the fringes of the society. Women, and particularly women who were old and poor, were the primary suspects.

The witch-hunt is a fascinating topic in its own right. It also needs to be recognised that by studying the witch-hunt we gain a greater understanding of the nature of society in Scotland in the period from 1560 to 1710. It is a lens through which we can view such different areas as village life, the functioning of the legal system, and the activity of the church. Further, it is hoped that such a study will shed some light on how we as a society have persecuted those considered to be on the 'outside'. Those defined as being on the outside may no longer be old women called witches, yet today there are still people defined as outsiders. Seeking someone to blame may not be as distant as we had hoped.

CHAPTER ONE

Scottish and European Witches

Janet Brown. Beatie Dote. Lilias Baxter. None are names which auto-matically lead us to remember a story about Scotland's past. None are names likely to be glorified by Hollywood stars in a big budget movie. Sometimes we don't even have a name but only a passing reference that a 'witch' was tried and executed in a particular parish in Scotland. In other situations we know of these women only in relation to their spouse. The 'wife of Thomas Wanderson'. The 'wife of John Crombie'. Names. And yet it is through these names that an important part of the Scottish past can be told. This is part of Scotland's past which until recently has been ignored. In a historical literature dominated by discussions of reformers and covenanters, the politics of the Stewart monarchy, and the looming crisis of the parliamentary union with England, there has been little room to discuss the fate of old women who were seen by their communities as witches.[1] Yet in the seventeenth century itself concern about witches was widespread, affecting all levels of society from the parliament to the national church, from Edinburgh to the Orkney islands. Indeed, Scot-land's witch-hunt was only part of a much broader concern which included almost every corner of Europe.

Lilias Baxter who fled her home in Dysart, Fife when an accusation of witchcraft was levelled against her was one of only thousands of women who found themselves accused of the crime of witchcraft in the three hundred year period from approximately 1450 to 1750. Estimates vary as to how many women found themselves in this situation, as well as how many were executed. The earlier estimates of nine million women executed have been replaced with the more moderate estimates of approximately 110,000 accused, and between 40,000 and 60,000 ex-ecutions throughout Europe.[2] In most of Europe the accused were primarily women, although in Estonia, Finland and Iceland the majority of the accused were male. The predominance of women among those accused as witches has become one of the major questions in the study of the European witch-hunt. Accusations could fall against a solitary witch, or an entire region could be swept up in a fervour of fear. One of the most famous witch-hunts was the one which occurred on the soil of what is now the United States of America at Salem, in Massachusetts. Salem, while sharing many features of other witch-hunts, had its own unique qualities. What is particularly noteworthy was the role played by adolescent girls in the accusations, as well as the relative lateness (1692). It is hunts such as Salem, or the events surrounding the trial of the North Berwick witches (1590–91) in Scotland, where the hunt moves out in a serial fashion from one accused to another, which have gripped the popular imagination. Yet accusations of witchcraft often were made against troublesome neighbours, or older impoverished women who survived by begging and knowing various charms and cures.

Historians have struggled to explain what occurred over these three centuries. Early writings attempted to explain the entire witch-hunt across all of Europe. The title of Hugh Trevor-Roper's influential 1967 essay 'The European Witch-craze of the Sixteenth and Seventeenth Centuries' is very revealing.[3] At a time when few regional studies existed the essay covered Europe over two centuries. The term 'witch-craze' also suggested we were studying abnormal human behaviour, a 'craze' something like Beatle-mania, not beliefs, values, or social systems. Historians also struggled to deal with the popularity of the theories of Margaret Murray who had earlier in the century posited that the witch-hunts had been directed at organized covens of a pre-Christian pagan religion.[4] Single causes for witch-hunting were put forward, causes which ranged from the effects of hallucinogenic substances (for example, ingested from wheat that had particular types of mould), to the shock of syphilis being introduced into Europe, to a cunning and successful plot by the political oligarchies of Europe to deflect criticisms of themselves onto the supposed witches.[5] These outbreaks of persecution could be seen as the last outbreaks of mediaeval superstition until it was shown that one of the large mediaeval witch-hunts had, in fact, never occurred. Massive persecution of witches was not a product of the mediaeval period, but an early modern phenomenon.[6]

While historians continued to suggest broad themes and adopt interesting approaches in order to study witch-hunting in early modern Europe,[7] more and more of the studies came to be done on particular geographical regions of Europe. This was in many ways not surprising. While early writers could paint in broad brush strokes, any attempt to prove these arguments as either correct or incorrect required more modest aspirations and a greater concern for detail. Europe was simply too large a field of enquiry. Historians naturally began to study the witch-hunt within particular regions. Works on Germany, France and Switzerland, Salem, Massachusetts, Spain, England and Scotland all appeared in the 1970's and early 1980's.[8] Regional studies demonstrated the kinds of resources that were available and raised important themes. A pivotal point came with the publication in English in 1993 of the collection of essays *Early Modern European Witchcraft: Centres and Peripheries,*[9] key parts of which had originally been published in Swedish six years previously. The essays in this volume, as well as others which appeared elsewhere, have been central in demonstrating the variety of experiences across Europe and its colonies.[10] Regional studies continue to challenge our conceptions of the dynamics and forces behind the European witch-hunt.

Another major contribution to the study of the European witch-hunt has been the realization that historians must distinguish between the preconditions for witch-hunting and the triggers that caused a particular region to begin seeking out and executing 'witches'.[11] Brian Levack has identified the preconditions (the factors needed before witch-hunts could occur) as: a new conception of what a witch was; increasing social tensions; and, changes in legal and religious systems. At the same time he argued it was essential to go beyond these

> general causes of the hunt and explore the specific circumstances and events that triggered individual witch-hunts, for the European witch-hunt was really nothing more than a series of separate hunts, each of which had its own participants.[12]

Earlier historians had felt compelled to try to explain every detail of the witch-hunts, from the intellectual pre-conditions to why a particular woman in a particular village found herself accused. This distinction between the preconditions and the triggers which caused a witch-hunt to break out in a particular region at a certain time, has given historians more freedom to focus on specific themes and study them intensely. For example, Stuart Clark's recent book *Thinking with Demons,* is an excellent study of the ideas in Europe in the early modern period and their relationship to witch-hunting, while Ian Bostridge explores the decline as a mainstream force of the idea of witchcraft in *Witchcraft and Its Transformations.*[13] On the other hand, recent studies such as the current one, have been more concerned about the form which a particular witch-hunt took. Neither approach is better, but they are different and that difference needs to be understood and respected.

Finally, the study of the European witch-hunt has necessitated the adoption of a distinction between the cultures of the elite and the cultures of the general populace. For example, Richard Kieckhefer challenged historians to distinguish clearly between the learned theories, popular traditions and actual practice of witchcraft in Europe.[14] His clear distinction between elite and popular cultures, as well as consideration of how they interacted, allowed Kieckhefer to see that the population at large was far more interested in village problems and sorcerers than any demonic theory.[15] Similarly, Carlo Ginzburg in *The Night Battles: Witchcraft and Agrarian Cults in the Sixteenth & Seventeenth Centuries* demonstrated that the concerns of the interrogators and the concerns of those accused as witches were markedly different.[16] This distinction has become the working understanding of almost all historians working in the area of European witchcraft. To give but a simple example: what precisely was understood by the term 'witch'? For those who lived in the villages and burghs, the word would have many meanings, but a witch was usually considered to be someone who knew various charms and cures, someone who could heal and harm. The witch was both a valued and a feared member of the community. There were various popular understandings of the witch, but generally the witch was welcomed as long as she used her power for good (as a white witch) and not to do harm (black witchcraft). It was those with more education and power who gradually changed this idea, arguing that all witchcraft, whether white or black, was destructive to the community. It was also the elite which introduced the idea that to be a witch one had to have gained one's power from the Devil. Witches thus became, at least in the eyes of some among the elite, the shock troops of a demonic conspiracy intent upon overthrowing society. If we are to understand the witch-hunt at all we need to recognise how different these understandings were.

The study of the European witch-hunt, while moving in various directions, has coalesced around these themes: the importance of studying particular regions; the distinction between pre-conditions and triggers (although different terms may be used); and the acceptance of distinctions between elite and popular cultures, as well as the importance of their interaction. No new consensus as to the meaning or 'causes' of the hunt has emerged. Works of sweeping scope, such as Carlo Ginzburg's *Ecstasies: Deciphering the Witches' Sabbath* (1991) and Stuart Clark's *Thinking with Demons* (1997) continue to raise new questions.[17] There are now many general historical surveys which give a fuller background to the events of Europe during these three centuries.[18]

The study of Scottish witches has been part of this larger study of the European witch-hunt. It is estimated that there were 1,337 executions for witch-craft in Scotland, although this figure may have a margin of error of 300 either way.[19] The number of people known to be accused of witch-craft stands at over 3,100 and although new cases are being discovered the increase is relatively modest.[20] While the topic was of considerable interest in the nineteenth century and into the early twentieth century,[21] few serious books were published before the results of Christina Larner's research appeared, first in articles, and finally in her book *Enemies of God* which was published in 1981.[22] *Enemies of God* remains a milestone, both in its contribution to Scottish history and the broader European understanding of the witch-hunt. In her writings, Larner stressed that it was the ruling elite who 'controlled and manipulated the demand for and supply of witchcraft suspects'.[23] She also suggested that witch-hunting was an idea before it became a phenomenon, and suggested that, in practice, witch-hunting was equivalent to woman hunting. To illustrate and demonstrate these themes Larner discussed the geographical and chronological patterns of witch-hunting, the dynamics of witch-hunts and the process that led from accusation to condemnation, the belief system, and offered some conclusions. She argued that in many ways what we were witnessing was the results of the 'Christianization' of Scotland and the subsequent suppression of popular beliefs. As a 'political ideology' Christianization meant, in practice, the suppression of deviance, an activity in which the nobility, as much as the clergy took part:

> The pursuit of witches was an end in itself and was directly related to the necessity of enforcing moral and theological conformity. The fact that a high proportion of those selected in this context as deviants were women was indirectly related to this central problem.[24]

Witches were indeed, as the title stated, perceived to be enemies of God and of the godly state. While individual ideas put forward in *Enemies of God* will be challenged within this book, it is important to note what a vital contribution it and Larner's other writings made and continue to make.

As members of the elite leave behind books, tracts, letters and other written documents, their values and fears tend to be the easiest for historians to deduce. It is far more difficult to study the values and attitudes of those who may not have been able to write, or whose writings have not been preserved. To even begin to study what documents may exist it is necessary to know where and when witch-craft accusations occurred in Scotland. Christina Larner's contribution in this area was a project conducted with the contribution of research assistants Christoper Lee and Hugh McLachlan and a grant from the Scottish Social Science Research Council. The project involved searching the central government records and codifying all of the known cases of witchcraft allegations in Scotland. The result, *A Sourcebook for Scottish Witchcraft* (1977)[25] gave researchers a valuable tool which not only added to the number of cases previously known through George Black's *A Calendar of Cases of Witch-craft in Scotland*,[26] but organised and standardized the information. The work done since Christina Larner opened the field in such a significant way has been, until recently, somewhat limited. The current book represents the first regional study at a village, parish or shire level to be done for Scotland.[27] Only one of the major hunts, apart from the North Berwick trial, has been investigated. Brian Levack's 'The Great Scottish Witch Hunt of 1661–62' serves as a model of how the study of a major hunt can be conducted.[28] This hunt involved over 660 individuals, making it the largest hunt in Scottish history. Levack argued that this hunt was a turning point, coming as it did after the end of the English occupation. Those accused generally continued to fit the stereotype of the traditional witch (old, widows, quarrelsome) despite the fact that one of the driving dynamics of the hunt was the activity of the witch-prickers, including the infamous John Kincaid. Michael Wasser has taken a different approach, looking at a period when relatively few cases occurred and tried to determine the role which some members of the judicial elite played in stemming witch-hunting during this period.[29] Various aspects of the Scottish witch-hunt are being actively studied by historians and the results of this research should soon reach publication.

A consensus has emerged in the literature on Scottish witchcraft, which gives us a general picture of the nature and shape of the witch-hunt in Scotland. Scotland had a major witch-hunt, even in European terms, in which the main victims were overwhelmingly women. Several major peaks of intense hunting have been recognised. The witch-hunt in Scotland is understood as more 'continental' than that which affected England, largely as a result of the use of judicial torture and the pervasive notion of the demonic pact. Elite interest in the latter has been distinguished from the common people's interest in *malefice,* or the harm caused by the suspected witch. The central government is understood to have restrained regional witch-hunting. There is still some question as to which group among the elite were the most enthusiastic witch-hunters, although at the moment the role of the local nobility has been emphasized. This study like all studies, began with an awareness of these themes and certain assumptions. The main ones included: the belief that it was the nobility, in particular the local lairds who were the major witch-hunters among the elite; the suspicion, after the initial runs on the database had been conducted, that torture would not be a factor in all cases; the assumption that witch-prickers would be key; and, the

expectation that Satan would be a dominant player in witchcraft confessions after 1610. On this final point, research for an essay done during
my Masters in 1981 on the initial phase of the witch-hunt had led me to
argue that the idea of the demonic pact had taken some time to spread
throughout Scotland after its introduction in the 1590's. A period of
about twenty years was assumed as adequate for this to have occurred.
One way to test these themes is through an intensive study of one
particular region, a task to which we will turn after re-examining the
shape of the witch-hunt in Scotland. We will discover how many of these
assumptions have proven incorrect.

Notes

1. Gordon Donaldson, *James V-James VII* (Edinburgh: Oliver & Boyd, 1965) makes only passing references to the subject. This reference occurs in the context of the political strife between Francis Stewart, Earl of Bothwell and James VI and the former's imprisonment as a suspected sorcerer in 1590 (p. 191). Donaldson attributes the decline in witch-hunting prior to 1638 to the 'restraint' of the bishops, p. 354. The word 'witch' does not even appear in the index of W. Croft Dickinson *Scotland from the Earliest Times to 1603* 3rd edition revised by Archibald A.M. Duncan (Oxford: Clarendon 1977). More recent surveys have devoted space to the topic.
2. Brian P. Levack, *The Witch-hunt in early Modern Europe* 2nd ed. (London: Longmans, 1995), 24–25. Robin Briggs, *Witches and Neighbours: The Social and Cultural Context of European Witchcraft* (New York: Harper Collins, 1996; New York, Viking, 1996), 8.
3. H.R. Trevor-Roper, 'The European Witch-craze of the Sixteenth and Seventeenth Centuries', in H.R. Trevor-Roper, *Religion, the Reformation and Social Change and other Essays by H.R. Trevor-Roper*, 2nd ed. (London: Macmillan Press, 1972). Peter Burke has argued that this article summarized what was known at the time it was written just as an explosion of new themes and interpretations emerged. Peter Burke, 'The Comparative Approach to European Witchcraft' in Bengt Ankarloo & Gustav Henningsen, *Early Modern European Witchcraft: Centres & Peripheries* (Oxford: Clarendon, 1990): 435.
4. Margaret Murray, *The Witch-cult in Western Europe* (Oxford: Clarendon Press, 1921). Though discredited among academics, this thesis continues to thrive in popular circles, in particular among those wishing to make connections between early-modern witches and neo-pagans today. See, for example, Margot Adler, *Drawing Down the Moon: Witches, Druids, Goddess-Worshippers, and other Pagans in America Today* Revised edition (Boston: Beacon Press, 1986); and Raymond Buckland, *Scottish Witchcraft: The History and Magick of the Picts* (St. Paul, Minn: Llewellyn, 1992). Penethorne Hughes, *Witchcraft* (Longmans, Green, 1952. Penguin, 1965) represents an earlier and learned defence of Murray's thesis. The weaknesses of the Murray thesis are most eloquently expressed by Norman Cohn in chapter 6 of *Europe's Inner Demons* (Sussex: Sussex University Press, 1975; Granada, 1976).
5. Marvin Harris, *Cows Pigs, Wars & Witches: The Riddles of Culture* (New York: Vintage, 1974). Geoffrey Quaife, *Godly Zeal and Furious Rage: The Witch in Early Modern Europe* (New York: St. Martins, 1987), offers a summary of these various positions and theories in his first chapter.

6. Richard Kieckhefer. *European Witch Trials: Their Foundations in Popular and Learned Culture, 1300–1500* (Berkley: University of California Press, 1976), ix, 16–18. Norman Cohn, *Europe's Inner Demons* (Sussex: Sussex University Press, 1975; Granada, 1976), Chapter 7.

7. Julio Caro Baroja, *The World of the Witches* (1961) translated by O.N.V. Glendinning (Chicago: University of Chicago, 1964). Keith Thomas, *Religion and the Decline of Magic: Studies in Popular Beliefs in Sixteenth- and Seventeenth-Century England* (London: Wiendenield & Nicolson, 1971; Penguin, 1982). Alan Macfarlane, *Witchcraft in Tudor and Stuart England* (London: Routledge K. Paul, 1970). The anthropological work which was particularly influential was E.E. Evans-Pritchard, *Witchcraft, Oracles and Magic among the Azande* (Oxford: Clarendon, 1937). Also, J.R. Crawford, *Witchcraft and Sorcery in Rhodesia* (London: Oxford University Press, 1967), Edward Geoffrey Parrinder, *Witchcraft: European and African* (London: Faber and Faber, 1963).

8. On Germany, H.C. Erik Midelfort, *Witch Hunting in Southwestern Germany, 1562–1684: The Social and Intellectual Foundations* (Stanford: Stanford University Press, 1972). On France and Switzerland, E. William Monter, *Witchcraft in France and Switzerland: The Borderlands During the Reformation* (London: Cornell University Press, 1976). On the Basque region of both France and Spain, Gustav Henningsen, *The Witches Advocate: Basque Witchcraft and the Spanish Inquisition (1609–14)* (Reno: University of Nevada, 1980). On England, Macfarlane *Witchcraft in Tudor and Stuart England* (1970). On Scotland, Christina Larner, *Enemies of God: The Witch-hunt in Scotland* (London: Chatto & Windus, 1981). While Salem seems to have a literature all its own as part of American history, several works are worth noting from this period: Paul Boyer & Stephen Nissenbaum, *Salem Possessed: The Social Origins of Witchcraft* (Cambridge, Mass.: Harvard University Press, 1974); John P. Demos, *Entertaining Satan: Witchcraft and the Culture of Early New England* (New York: Oxford University Press, 1982.); Richard Weisman. *Witchcraft, Magic and Religion in 17th century Massachusetts* (Amherst: University of Massachusetts Press, 1984); and, Richard Godbeer, *The Devil's Dominion: Magic and Religion in Early New England* (Cambridge: Cambridge University Press, 1992).

9. Ankarloo and Henningsen, *Early Modern European Witchcraft*.

10. The regional studies in *Early Modern European Witchcraft* include Bengt Ankarloo, 'Sweden: The Mass Burnings (1668–76)'; Francisco Bethencourt, 'Portugal: A Scrupulous Inquisition'; Kirsten Hastrap, 'Iceland: Sorcerers & Paganism'; Antero Heikkinen & Timo Kervinen, 'Finland: The Male Domination' ; Jens Christian V. Johansen 'Denmark: The Sociology of Accusations'; Juhan Kahk 'Estonia II: The Crusade against Idolatry'; Gabor Klaniczay 'Hungary: The Accusations and the Universe of Popular Magic'; Maia Madar, 'Estonia I: Werewolves and Poisoners'; and, Hans Eyvind Naess, 'Norway: The Criminological Context'. There were also two interpretive essays directly related to these regional studies E. William Monter, 'Scandinavian Witchcraft in Anglo-American Perspective' and Peter Burke, 'The Comparative Approach to European Witchcraft'. Other regional studies of note include, Susanna Burghatz, 'The Equation of Women and Witches: A Case Study of Witchcraft Trials in Lucerene and Lausanne in the Fifteenth and Sixteenth Centuries' in *The German Underworld: Deviants and Outcasts in German History* ed. Richard J. Evans (London: Routledge, 1988), 108–140; Marijke Gijswist-Hofstra, 'Witchcraft in the Northern Netherlands' in *Current Issues in Women's History* ed. Arina Angerman (London: Routledge, 1989), 75–92; Annabel Gregory, 'Witchcraft,

Politics and 'Good Neighbourhood' in Early Seventeenth-Century Rye.' *Past and Present* 133 (Nov. 1991): 31–66; Ruth Martin, *Witchcraft and the Inquisition in Venice 1550–1650* (Oxford: Basil Blackwell, 1989); Robert Muchembled, 'The Witches of Cambrésis: The Acculturation of the Rural World in the Sixteenth and Seventeenth Centuries,' in *Religion and the People, 800–1700* ed. Jim Obelkevich (Chapel Hill: University of North Carolina Press, 1979), 221–276 ; Jonathan L. Pearl, 'Witchcraft in New France in the Seventeenth Century: The Social Aspect.' *Historical Reflections* 4 (1977):191–205; J.A. Sharpe, 'Witchcraft and Women in seventeenth-century England: some Northern evidence' in *Continuity and Change* 6 (August 1991):179–199; Irene Silverblatt, *Moon, Sun and Witches: Gender Ideologies and Class in Inca and Colonial Peru* (Princeton: Princeton University Press, 1987); and, Janet A. Thompson, *Wives, Widows, Witches & Bitches: Women in Seventeenth-Century Devon* (New York: Peter Lang, 1993). A new study of English witchcraft has recently been published. J.A. Sharpe, *Instruments of Darkness; Witchcraft in England 1550–1750* (London: Hamish Hamilton, 1996).

11. Brian P. Levack, *The witch-hunt in early modern Europe,* 3.

12. Ibid., 3.

13. Stuart Clark, *Thinking with Demons: The Idea of Witchcraft in Early Modern Europe* (Oxford: Clarendon, 1997). Ian Bostridge, *Witchcraft and Its Transformation c.1650–c1750.* (Oxford: Clarendon, 1997).

14. Kieckhefer, *European Witch Trials*, 3.

15. Ibid., 105.

16. Carlo Ginzburg, *The Night Battles: Witchcraft and Agrarian Cults in the Sixteenth and Seventeenth Centuries* (1966), trans. John Tedeschi and Anne Tedeschi (Baltimore: John Hopkins University Press, 1983).

17. Carlos Ginzburg, *Ecstasies: Deciphering the Witches' Sabbath* (1989) trans. Raymond Rosenthal (New York: Pantheon, 1991).

18. Quaife, *Godly Zeal* (1987). Levack, *The witch-hunt in early modern Europe* (1987, 1995). Geoffrey, Scarre, *Witchcraft and Magic in Sixteenth- and Seventeenth-Century Europe* (New Jersey: Humanities Press International, 1987). Joseph Klaits, *Servants of Satan: The Age of the Witch Hunts (*Bloomington: Indiana University Press, 1985). Anne Llewellyn Barstow, *Witchcraze: A New History of the European Witch Hunts* (New York: Pandora, 1994). Robin Briggs, *Witches and Neighbours* (1997).

19. Larner, *Enemies*, p. 63.

20. Christina Larner, Christopher Hyde Lee, & Hugh McLachlan, *A Source Book of Scottish Witchcraft* (Glasgow: Sociology Department, University of Glasgow, 1977). George F. Black, *A Calendar of Cases of Witchcraft in Scotland 1510–1727* (New York: New York Public Library and Arno Press, 1938). Black's list offered excerpts from cases in a roughly chronological order. The *Sourcebook* listed the cases by court level and coded certain basic information, such as gender, fate, and marital status. Dates and geographic data were given whenever known.

21. F. Legge, 'Witchcraft in Scotland', *The Scottish Review* 18 (1891), reprinted in *Articles on Witchcraft, Magic and Demonology* ed. Brian P. Levack. Vol 7, *Witchcraft in Scotland* (New York: Garland, 1992), 1–32, summarized interpretations to that point. In the same year J.W. Brodie Innes published a less than useful exploration of the subject in which he argued that hypnotism explained the witch-hunt. J.W. Brodie Innes 'Scottish Witchcraft Trials' in *Witches and Witch Hunters* (1891) ed. A.E. Green (Reprint by Menston, Yorkshire: Scholars Press, 1971). R.D. Melville, 'The Use and

Forms of Judicial Torture in England and Scotland,' *Scottish Historical Review* 2 (1905). W.N. Neill, 'The Professional Pricker and His Test for Witchcraft,' *Scottish Historical Review* 19 (1922). J.A. MacCulloch, 'The Mingling of Fairy & Witch Beliefs in Sixteenth and Seventeenth Century Scotland,' in *Folklore: The Transactions of the Folklore Society* xxxii (December, 1921). John Gilmore, *Witchcraft and the Church in Scotland*. (Ph.D. diss., University of Glasgow, 1948). On North Berwick, Margaret Murray, 'The 'Devil' of North Berwick,' *Scottish Historical Review* 15 (1918). Edward J. Cowan, 'The darker vision of the Scottish Renaissance' in *The Renaissance and Reformation in Scotland* ed. I.B. Cowan and D. Shaw (Edinburgh: Scottish Academic Press, 1983) and 'The Royal Witch-Hunt' in *The Sunday Mail Story of Scotland*, Vol 2., Pt 15(1988) are two of the better articles on the subject. Also, Margaret Carol Kintscher, *The culpability of James VI of Scotland, late James I of England, in the North Berwick witchcraft trials of 1590–91* (M.A. diss, San Jose State University, 1991). Mody C. Boatright, 'Witchcraft in the Novels of Sir Walter Scott', *University of Texas Studies in English* 13 (1933): 95–112. Stuart Clark, 'King James *Daemonologie*: Witchcraft and kingship' in *The Damned Art: Essays in the Literature of Witchcraft* ed. Sydney Anglo (London: Routledge and Kegan Paul, 1977). Isabel Adam, *Witch Hunt: The Great Scottish Witchcraft trials of 1697* (London: Macmillan, 1978). In many ways Adam's *Witch Hunt* is reminiscent of Marion Starkey's popular retelling of the Salem witch-hunt, *The Devil in Massachusetts: A Modern Enquiry into the Salem Witch Trials* (New York: Alfred A. Knopf, 1949). The poor books on Scottish witchcraft are voluminous, often written for the popular market in the hopes of feeding into the notion that Scotland was a uniquely superstitious place. Raymond Buckland, *Scottish Witchcraft*, explains how to become a witch. More bothersome than the how-to manuals and the obviously tourist-inclined pocket books, are those which make some pretension to scholarship, For example, Godfrey Watson, *Bothwell and the Witches* (London: Robert Hale, 1975); and, Ronald Holmes, *Witchcraft in British History* (Plymouth: Frederick Muller, 1974). Nicholas MacLeod, *Scottish Witch-craft* (Cornwall: James Pike, 1975) completely endorses Murray's thesis, arguing a relationship between witches and pygmies.

22. Larner, *Enemies of God*. Christina Larner, 'James VI and I and Witchcraft' in Alan G.R. Smith, ed. *The Reign of James VI and I* (London: Macmillan, 1973), 74–90; 'Two late Scottish witchcraft tracts: *Witch-Craft Proven* and *The Tryal of Witchcraft*' in Sydney Anglo, ed., *The Damned Art: Essays in the Literature of Witchcraft* (London: Routledge and Kegan Paul, 1977), 227–245. 'Crimen Exceptum? The Crime of Witchcraft in Europe' in *Crime and the Law: The Social History of Crime in Western Europe since 1500* ed. V.A.C. Gatrell, Bruce Lenman, and Geoffrey Parker (London: Europa, 1980), 49–75. Published posthumously, Christina Larner, *Witchcraft and Religion: The Politics of Popular Belief* (Oxford: Basil Blackwell, 1984).

23. The quote is taken from 'Crimen Exceptum? The Crime of Witchcraft in Europe'. See also *Enemies of God*, 22, 60.

24. Larner, *Enemies of God*, 102.

25. Larner, Lee, & McLachlan, *A Source Book of Scottish Witchcraft*.

26. Black, *Calendar of Cases*. Black list offered excerpts from case's in a roughly chronological order. The *Sourcebook* listed the cases by court level and coded certain basic information, such as gender, fate, and marital status. Dates and geographic data were given whenever known.

27. One other source of information is contained in the writing of local historians. James

Wilkie *The History of Fife: From the Earliest Time to the Nineteenth Century* (Edinburgh: William Blackwood, 1924) has a good chapter on witchcraft. The topic is also discussed in two recent local histories on Fife, Stephanie Stevenson, *Anstruther: A History* (Edinburgh: John Donald, 1989) and Eric Simpson, *Dalgety – The Story of a parish* (Dalgety: Dalgetty Bay Community Council, 1980).

28. Brian P. Levack, 'The Great Scottish Witch Hunt of 1661–62' in *Journal of British Studies* 20 (1984), 107. For the stereotype of the witch see p. 101–102 while the role of nobility versus clergy is discussed p. 96–97.

29. Michael Wasser, 'Law, Politics and Witchcraft: The Curtailment of Witchcraft Prosecutions in Scotland, 1597–1628' (Unpublished paper, 1996).

CHAPTER TWO

Village Tensions and Elite Fears:
The Patterns of the Scottish
Witch-Hunt

In 1597 Andro Man was accused of being an ally of Satan and a witch. He was one of the many individuals charged during the great hunt for witches which swept Scotland during that year. An old man who lived in Aberdeen, Andro claimed to have visited the fairy-queen over a period of sixty-years prior to his arrest and interrogation. Over the years he had attended many revels and feasts in the company of the elf-queen and others many of whom, like James V and Thomas the Rhymer, were 'deid men'. Andro Man received secret knowledge and power to heal as a result of his association with the queen of fairyland, yet it was claimed that his real master was a mysterious figure named Christsonday: 'The queen has a grip of all the craft, but Christsonday is the gudeman and has all power under God'. Christsonday – understood by Man's inquisitors as Satan in disguise – appeared as a stag alongside the elf-queen at revels, and had power such that he was able to show Andro the fires of hell. Andro Man was eventually executed for the crime of witchcraft.[1]

Seventy-five years later and at the other end of Scotland, Elspeth Thomson also found herself accused of witchcraft, a crime against 'the divyne law of the almightie god, set doune in his sacred word, especiallie in the 20th chapter of Leviticus and 18th chapter of Deuteronomie'.[2] Specifically, Elspeth was accused of a series of incidents that had taken place over a number of years. For example, seven years prior to her being charged it was claimed that after John Corsbie & Rosina Mcghies had neglected to invite her to either the birth or baptism of their child she had vowed to 'doe them ane ill turne and to cause them rue it'. After this curse Rosina fell ill and in a vision saw Elspeth and another accused witch, Janet McMuldroch, standing beside her ready to murder her and her child. Her husband's response was to go and take some thatch from above Elspeth Thomson's door and burn it before his wife, 'This being the ordinar course qrby your neighbours used to remove any seiknes which they

15

apprehendit to be laid on themselves or yr beasts by yor witchcraft'. This time the remedy failed, and the child died. John himself took sick and was only cured when Elspeth came at his invitation to his bedside, touched his body, and prayed to God to 'send him health'. Their troubles continued, however, when Rosina again became ill. Other accusations made against Elspeth included: casting a spell on a child's cradle which only failed to harm the child when the suspicious mother threw a dog in the cradle first (the dog 'immediately' lost the use of his back legs and had to be destroyed); causing the death of Donald McGhie after he accused her of being a witch; destroying the health of James McGhie after he refused to hire her for a day's work; and other acts of hostile magic directed against her neighbours. Long suspected as a witch, Elspeth Thomson was tried and executed in Dumfries in 1671.[3]

These examples represent only two of the more than three thousand cases where accusations of witch-craft were made throughout Scotland during the period from 1560 to 1758. Both cases are familiar, having become part of the secondary literature on the Scottish witch-hunt. What is more difficult to determine is how they – and other well known cases such as the Berwick trials of 1590, Bessie Dunlop, Alison Peirsoun and others[4] – fit within the larger reality which was the Scottish witch-hunt. This chapter will reassess the overall pattern of the Scottish witch-hunt using the data collected in Christina Larner, Christopher Lee & Hugh McLachlan, *A Source Book of Scottish Witchcraft* (1977)[5] and supplementing it with other relevant data and information. The focus will be on examining the chronology and the geography of the existing cases. In order to do this adequately, it will be necessary to use some tables, charts, and maps. Hopefully, the numbers and statistics will help us to gain insight into the experiences of Andro Man, Elspeth Thomson, and so many others, and allow us to position their individual narratives within a clearer picture of what occurred throughout Scotland during this period. A better understanding of the national scene will also help us to study the witch-hunt in the particular regions of Scotland.

As the major authority in the field, Christina Larner's analysis of the chronological and geographical pattern of the hunt serves as a vital starting point to any discussion. In *Enemies of God*, Larner divided the hunt into four basic categories based upon intensity: National hunts (1590–1; 1597; 1629–30; 1649; 1661–62) 'in which cases came from all over the non-Gaelic-speaking areas and even occasionally from the Gaelic areas of Invernesshire and Ross-shire'; 'almost national hunts' in which several regions would become involved; small panics; and isolated cases, in which individuals would be pursued for acts of *malefice* and not specifically for 'ideological non-conformity'. The smaller categories were always subsumed into the larger, so that the large national hunts included examples of each.[6] Larner illustrated the variation in the intensity of the hunt over time with a graph.[7] The most obvious factor for these variations, as noted by Larner, was the 'rise and fall of the level of official interest' in witch-hunting displayed by the elite.[8]

The geographical dimensions of the witch-hunt in Scotland were also explored by Larner. *Enemies of God* includes a map showing which areas of Scotland had intensive hunts, which had many cases, few cases or no cases.[9] The difference in intensity between the various regions of Scotland was discussed. In particular, Larner notes the general lack of witch-hunting in the Highlands:

> In the Highlands, especially those parts outside the Kirk session's, system and within the dominion of the clans there was no witch-hunting, or none that reached the records. Gaelic-speaking areas in general provided very few cases although Tain in Ross-shire was an exception to this . . . Towards the end of the 1661–2 hunt there were several cases in Strathglass in which the landlord used accusations of witchcraft as a means of evicting some unwanted tenants. On the whole, though, Gaelic patronymic names such as those of Mary Nein Goune Baike of Strathglass and Marion Nein Gollimichaell of Tain are rare in lists of suspects.[10]

This chapter will return to the entire subject of the Highlands and the witch-hunt.

The Scottish witch-hunt, according to both the map and text of *Enemies of God*, was centred on Fife, the Lothians, the eastern Borders and a small area around Aberdeen. Proximity to the centre of government is suggested as one possible explanation for this.[11] Larner also notes that within 'these general areas there were certain small towns and villages which appear again and again'. Tranent and Prestonpans in particular are singled out as two places 'which featured in both in the first witch-hunt and in all the major hunts', and Inverkeithing, Dumfries, and Aberdeen are also given examples of places with long records of involvement in the witch-hunt. Larner concludes:

> There seems to be a self-perpetuating element in witch-hunting. Where there were local memories of actual burnings it was relatively easy to stimulate them again.[12]

The prominence of fishing villages such as Bo'ness, Largs, and Pittenweem in the list of those places where witch-hunting was frequent is noted.[13] In assessing this pattern, Larner comments that there is no obvious link on a national level between famine, pestilence, war and other demographic disasters and the incidence of witch–hunting: 'Whether there may be at a local level is an issue yet to be explored'.[14] There is thus no obvious explanation for the witch–hunt which arises out of an examination of this data.

Christina Larner is the only author to have attempted to provide a comprehensive analysis of the witch–hunt in Scotland. It is under-standable, therefore, that her interpretation of the geographical and chronological dimensions has dominated the discussion since *Enemies of God* was published. For example, Ian and Kathleen Whyte have suggested that the prominence of East Lothian in witch–craft cases can be explained because of the 'close proximity to the justiciary in Edinburgh'. They concur in the notion that once an area had some experience of accusations for witch–craft, it was easier in future for a panic to begin.[15] Writing on Fife, Raymond Lamont-Brown argues that in 'no other place in Scotland were witches hunted with such fervour as in Pittenweem'.[16] In his survey of European witchcraft, *The Witch-hunt in early modern Europe*, Brian Levack has used statistics from Scotland, derived from the *Sourcebook*, to make the argument that witches were more likely to be executed if tried in the regions than by the central government.[17]

What has gone largely unnoticed in the statements made since *Enemies of God* was published, was the tentativeness and limited nature of the discussion within the book itself of the geographic and chronological patterns of the Scottish witch–hunt. Two suggestions for further study in as many pages should alert us to the reality that an author is valiantly exploring new territory – not that extensive research has answered all possible questions.[18] Among the simple questions *Enemies of God* did not address was the variation in witch–hunting between particular shires. Put simply, which shire witnessed the most cases? Which shire had the least? The map in *Enemies of God* failed to note that Ayrshire was an area with a substantial witch–hunt. Despite the fact that any discussion of the shape and nature of the Scottish witch–hunt must at least begin by dealing with the list of known cases, the *Sourcebook of Scottish Witchcraft* has remained a virtually untapped source of information and material since the publica-tion of *Enemies of God*.

One reason for reluctance on the part of historians to use the *Sourcebook* may have arisen from the cautions and warnings made by both Larner and Bruce Lenman.[19] Both raise valid points. The *Sourcebook* does have many drawbacks. Information is incomplete, infuriatingly inadequate in terms of data on social class and position, irregular, and at times duplicated. It must be used with great caution, particularly in those areas where large quantities of data are unknown, especially in terms of the 'fate' of those accused and the number of executions.[20] One area where the *Sourcebook* is quite good, however, is in the area of chronology and geography. There are many instances when the precise date is missing, yet only in 47 cases do we not know the year. Similarly, there are only 105 cases for which we have no geographical information whatever. We can currently position 89% of the cases within a particular shire.[21] To begin the re-examination of the pattern of the Scottish witch-hunt it was necessary to re-enter the data contained in the *Sourcebook* on a computer database, standardize some of the information, and then begin to analyse it. (For a detailed discussion of the *Sourcebook*, the creation of the *Scottish Witch-hunt Database* and a discussion on geography and the creation of the maps, see the Appendices.)

Chronology

A re-examination of the chronological patterns of the Scottish witch hunt (See Graph 1) makes it clear the extent to which witch-hunting in Scotland was a seventeenth-century phenomenon. Graph 1 is similar to the one found in *Enemies of God* (the one important difference will be discussed in a moment). The major hunts, or 'peaks', can clearly be seen: 1590; 1597; 1629–30; 1649–50; 1658–59; and, 1661–62. It is important to remember that Graph 1 portrays the number of 'cases', not the number of witches. Some individuals appear more than once: for example, Elspeth Thomson, whose story has already been told, is listed twice in the *Sourcebook* under different spellings. That same year another Elspeth Thompson's name appears in Banff, again twice.[22] The opposite is also true: one case may represent many individual accused witches. References to 'many witches', 'some witches', 'a great number of witches', or some similar phrase, makes any attempt at accurate quantification impossible. Graph 1 attempts, in a minor way, to take account of these 'multiple cases' by noting when they occurred and taking some estimate of their significance by assuming that each multiple case involved two additional witches (noted in black on Graph 1). The preponderance of these cases in 1649 is worth noting. The dominance of cases in the seventeenth century is apparent.[23]

Another problem in trying to portray the Scottish witch-hunt on a graph relates to the 1590s. This decade saw the first major persecution of supposed witches in Scottish history; however, it was not until 1597 that government regulations required a commission before a local witch could be executed.[24] The result is that we have no idea how many witches may

19

have been brought before local courts prior to the enforcement of this regulation. The rather mysterious comment that 'a great number of people' throughout Scotland were executed for witch-craft in 1597 only adds to the confusion.[25] What was meant by a great number? What regions were involved? Christina Larner attempted to take the poor quality of the records into account by noting the estimates in a dotted section above both 1590 and 1597.[26] Any estimate is problematic, particularly when we are dealing with such imprecise phrases as a 'great number'. The difficulty comes in regard to the data graphed in *Enemies of God* for 1597. The graph shows 200 known cases with another 100 estimated, for a possible total of over 300. The *Sourcebook* however records only sixty-one cases in 1597.[27] An additional twenty-two have been added as a result of the intensive research on Fife.[28] That there were cases in this year of which we have as yet no record is certainly true: the issue becomes the size and extent of these cases. It is in the estimate of the extent of the witch-hunt in Scotland that Graph 1 differs significantly from the one found in *Enemies of God*.[29]

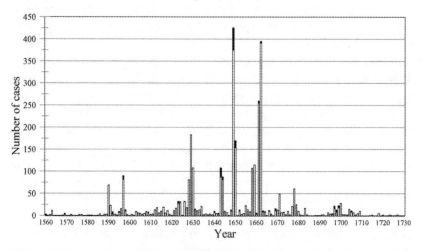

Graph 1 – Cases of Witchcraft in Scotland, 1560–1730.
Source: Scottish Witch-Hunt Data Base (SWHDB)

Our concern for the major years of persecution distorts our understanding of the period. As the graph makes clear, Scotland was not always in the midst of a great witch-hunt. Indeed, it is the major hunts which stand out as somewhat unusual, arising unexpectedly and being short-lived. Larner suggests that the most obvious 'immediate causal factor' for these variations was 'the rise and fall of the level of official interest in the apprehension and conviction of this particular type of criminal'. As such, the political events with which she associates these events are to be considered as 'pegs rather than explanations in themselves'.[30] Yet, we still need to consider what factors may have contributed to 'the rise and fall' of elite interest in persecuting witches.

The timing of the major hunts coincides closely with significant events, some political, some intellectual and social, of which we are already aware. The royal initiative and possible political motives of the events of 1590 and North Berwick kirk have been thoroughly explored.[31] The 1629–30 outbreak parallels a major 'continental witch panic'.[32] Persecutions began in 1649 shortly after the radical Presbyterian faction took power in January of that year.[33] The increase in interest in 1658 and early 1659 coincided with the collapse of English authority within Scotland, and was followed, after a period of judicial paralysis, by a severe persecution at the time of the Restoration in 1660.[34] Certainly other significant political events occurred in Scotland, notably the National Covenant (1638) and Bishop's Wars (1639–40), with there being no contiguous increase in witch-hunting. Still, the reality is that significant political events coincided with witch persecution. A political event has also been seen as significant in the decline of witch-hunting. The sparseness of cases from the 1650's is usually explained by the leniency of English judges,[35] during the period of Cromwellian occupation. This could have been the result of distrust and an unwillingness on the part of the occupying authorities to strengthen the power of the kirk. Indeed, Geoff Quaife has suggested the occupation marked something of a pause or an interlude between the hunts of 1649–50 and 1658–62.[36] The possibility of a link between these political events and witch-hunting needs to be considered carefully.

Geography

When we move from considering the chronology of the Scottish witch-hunt to the geographic distribution of the cases, different issues emerge. Our concern is no longer with attempting to understand the pattern over time, but with discerning why a particular region of Scotland had a higher incidence of witch persecutions than another particular region of Scotland. Table 1 catalogues, in order from highest to lowest, the number of cases in each Shire of Scotland throughout the entire period. It was in Haddington (East Lothian), that the most intense witch-hunting took place. Edinburgh and Fife also witnessed severe hunts. Surprisingly Linlithgow (West Lothian) did not experience such intense persecution.

The varying intensity of the witch-hunt in Scotland is obvious from this information and from Map 2. It comes as no surprise that certain areas produced far more witches than did other areas; however, what must be recognised is that these patterns defy simplistic interpretation. Proximity to the national capital does not seem to have been a factor.[37] Linlithgow, closer to the central administration than Aberdeen, Perth, Berwick, Lanark, Ayr, Dumfries and Fife, was not a major centre of the witch-hunt. Kinross, squeezed between Fife and Perth, witnessed only eight cases. Similarly, Kincardine and Selkirk remained minor players, though surrounded by Shires in which the witch-hunt was far more severe.

Map	Shire	no.	Map	Shire	no.
1	Haddington	520	19	Moray	43
2	Edinburgh	325	20	Bute	42
3	Fife (SBSW)	280	21	Caithness	35
	(SWHDB)	(420)			
4	Aberdeen	158	22	Inverness	35
5	Ayr	127	23	Clackmannan	32
6	Berwick	125	24	Kirkcudbright	32
7	Perth	118	25	Dumbarton	21
8	Lanark	116	26	Selkirk	21
9	Linlithgow	101	27	Shetland	19
10	Dumfries	99	28	Banff	10
11	Peebles	79	29	Kinross	8
12	Forfar	74	30	Wigtown	8
13	Renfrew	69	31	Sutherland	5
14	Ross	65	32	Argyll	3
15	Orkney	50	33	Kincardine	2
16	Stirling	48		Unknown	317
17	Roxburgh	47		other	6
18	Nairn	46		Total	3089

Table 1 – Witchcraft cases in Scotland listed by shire, 1560–1760.
Map number refers to the codes on map 2.1. Highland areas are included in the following shires: Ross, Nairn, Moray, Caithness, Inverness, Sutherland, and Argyll.
Source SWHDB; see Appendix B for details.

Although the intensity of the witch-hunt varied from place to place, cases appeared in all of the Shires of Scotland – including the Highland Shires. The Highlands were never a major area of witch persecution. It needs to be stated, however, that certain areas of the Lowlands could make similar claims. These cases also come from a wider area of the Highlands than has been recognised.[38] As can be seen by Map 2, cases occurred in different parts of the Highlands, including the West coast and the Isle of Skye. So far no cases have been located in the Outer Hebrides. Still, it needs to be recognised that the characterization of the Highlands as an area where the witch-hunt did not occur is far too simplistic. (Nor, if one reads closely, is this what Larner said.)

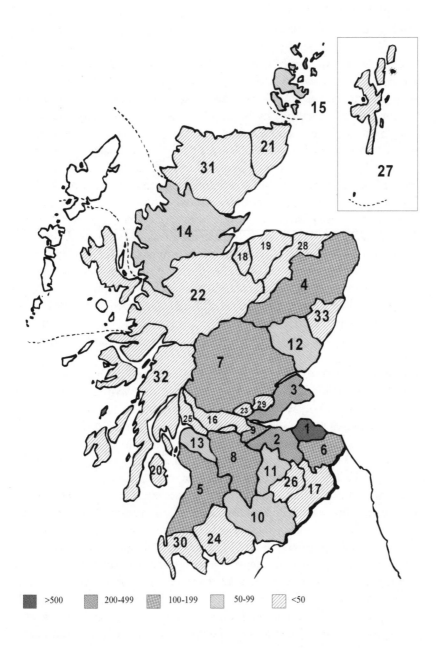

Map 2 – Scotland, 1560–1760. Witchcraft cases by shire.
Numbers refer to the codes as listed in Table 1.

Chronology and Geography

While a separate analysis of chronology and geography is very enlightening it must be remembered that such a separate analysis is somewhat
misleading: witchcraft accusations did not occur in time or place, they
occurred in a time *and* a place. This more complex task of combining the
when and the where of each case gives us a far more complete picture of
the hunt. Within the study of the European witch-hunt, various attempts
have been made to combine these two axes, yet no one model or
approach has won consensus.[39] Nor is a particular approach immediately
obvious. With which axis, time or place, do we begin? What unit of time,
year or decade, should we use? Are Shires an appropriate level at which to
study the phenomenon, or should we move 'down' one level to that of
parishes? The answer to the latter question is, of course, 'yes': parishes are
a better level to study the witch-hunt than shires. Unfortunately, the data
are such that this is, for the moment at least, impractical for Scotland in its
entirety. Choices must be made. The unit of 'year' seems most practical,
yet even here attempting to represent this within a chapter poses some
difficulties, unless one wants to leaf through 200 maps. We will take a
brief look at each of these two axes, beginning with the shires of Scotland,
in order to develop a clearer sense of how they shed light on the Scottish
witch-hunt.

If we begin by looking at a specific 'place' and examine how the witch-
hunt occurred within that place over time, the complexity of the Scottish
experience becomes readily apparent. Persecutions in Haddington seem
to have arisen abruptly and often involved many individuals. There are
isolated cases spread out over the entire period from the 1560's to the
early 1700's, but it is the major hunts which are so dramatically evident.
The cases in Edinburgh are also focused on specific hunts (1661 in
particular), although not to the same extent as was the case in Haddington. On the other hand, Fife shows a broader spread and a much lower
intensity of accusations. Only one year witnessed more than fifty cases in
Fife, compared to four years in Haddington. This approach works well
for regional comparisons or regional studies but is not particularly helpful
to our understanding of the overall shape of the Scottish witch-hunt.

The second axis, 'time', brings a sharper focus to our study. Several
realities begin to emerge as we look at which areas were affected in any
given year. For example, there is no obvious rhyme, reason, or rationale
to the location of witchcraft cases from year to year in the period from
1616 to 1620, a period which witnessed no national hunt. Only in two of
the years were there more than ten cases throughout the entire nation:

nineteen cases in 1616; and, eleven in 1618. Orkney produced ten cases in 1616, Ayr seven in 1618, Shetland five again in 1616, but in all other shires the cases were less than a handful. This pattern of five or fewer cases occurring in any given shire in a particularly year is not restricted to this five year period. In the previous fifteen years only in one year, 1613, were there more than five cases in any shire (Perth had nine cases in that year). During the 1620's the number of cases intensified prior to the major outbreak of persecution in 1629. It is important to stress that, to use Larner's categories, individual witches and 'small panics' springing up without apparent pattern was normal throughout the course of the entire witch-hunt in Scotland.[40]

While many years witnessed small numbers of cases spread throughout Scotland, other years witnessed major national hunts. Maps 3 and 4 illustrate the national hunt of 1649 and 1650 respectively. To place these accusations in context, there were no cases in 1647 or 1651, and only isolated cases in different Shires in the years 1645 and 1646.[41] (The years 1643 and 1644, years of national crisis, did see significant witch-hunting, 56 and 67 cases respectively; yet only one case in either year came from Haddington.) The focus of the persecutions along the Fife-Lothians axis is dramatically demonstrated by the maps. After serious persecution in this region, 'aftershocks' rumbled out to affect other regions of Scotland. A similar focus on Haddington and Edinburgh can be seen in 1661, with the persecution broadening to other areas of Scotland in 1662. The differences between these national hunts and other accusations of witchcraft are noticeable.

When we examine the geography of the Scottish witch-hunt on a yearly basis the difference between the great national hunts and the persecution that took place at other times becomes very apparent. Indeed, there seem to have been two witch-hunts going on concurrently in Scotland during this period; the one driven by village tensions (as in the case of Elspeth Thomson); the other by elite fears, which resulted in the persecution of otherwise harmless individuals like Andro Man. The former was erratic, unpredictable, moved from area to area, and generally involved isolated individuals (or a small group of individuals) who had already been named by the community as a witch. The accusations involved actions of *malefice*; the laying on and removal of illness, the interference with reproduction of humans and livestock, and other displays of hostility to one's neighbours.[42] The latter, the great hunts, were focused in particular areas and coincided with times of particular tension within the Scottish elite or times when political purposes could be served through persecution.

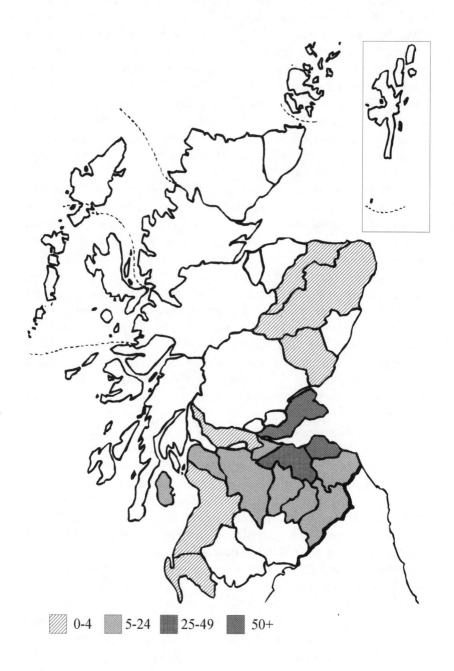

Map 3 – Scotland, 1649. Witchcraft cases by shire.

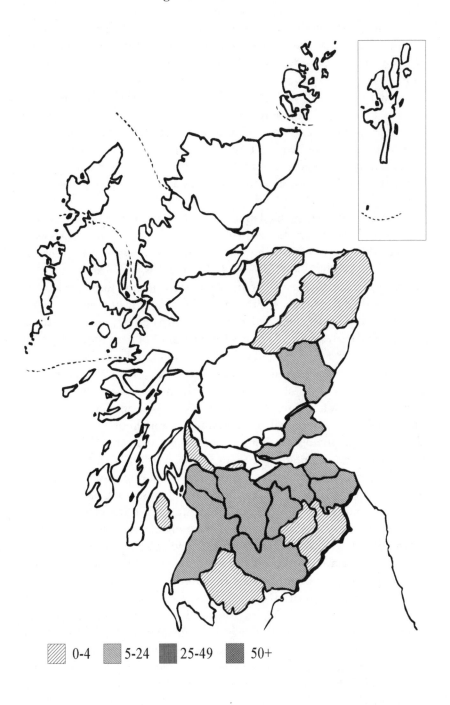

Map 4 – Scotland, 1650. Witchcraft cases by shire.

This neat characterization of the witch-hunt into two categories is far from perfect and at the moment is more suggested than proven. There was obviously overlap within and between these two witch-hunts: elites must always be involved even in isolated cases for witch-craft to be deemed a crime dealt with by the judicial process; those condemned as witches during the great hunts were in many cases individuals already suspected as 'witches' by their community.[43] Still the different dynamics which seem to exist require further exploration and explanation. An intense study of one region may shed further light on the inter-relation-ship between the cases of isolated witches and the outbreaks of major panics.

The information contained in the *Sourcebook* and refined in the *Scottish Witch-hunt Database* can also be used to test the theory, advanced by Geoff Quaife, that there was an intimate connection between the hunts of 1649–50 and those which occurred after the Cromwellian occupation ended. As Quaife succinctly stated: 'Military occupation suspended rather than abolished the hunt'.[44] If this were the case, it seems fair to assume that we should see this reflected in the regional patterns: put simply, those in a particular area picked up in 1659 and 1661 where they left off in 1650, persecuting the same individuals. Yet, this is not at all what we see. The 1649 hunt was extremely focused, especially in Haddington (107 cases) and Fife (45 cases), and then spread through the lowlands. (See Maps 3 and 4). When cases 'resumed' in 1658 – ignoring for the moment that accusations against witches continued throughout the 1650's, in-cluding a large, mysterious hunt in 1652 and a hunt in 1655 involving twelve cases in Caithness – the focus was in Ayrshire with 55 cases and Clackmannan with thirty-one. Haddington only becomes a major player the next year in 1659 with fifty-three cases. Fife saw no cases, and was only a minor player in the 1661 and 1662 hunt and, as we shall see, within the shire these involved parishes that heretofore had not been involved in any significant way with witch-hunting. Haddington was the main player in both 1661 and 1662 (93 and 99 cases respectively), but other areas not involved in the period prior to the English occupation became intensely involved.[45] An examination on the national scale does not preclude that individuals accused in 1650 who escaped prosecution because of the changes brought about by the English occupation might not have been accused again once the Scottish judicial system was back in place. Such cases certainly happened. But on a national scale, the links between the hunts of 1649–50 and those which followed the English withdrawal are not as direct as one might suspect.

Our discussion of chronology and geography has shown how complex the Scottish witch-hunt was. Still, this information can help us in several ways. First and foremost, it can serve as a basic foundation for any regional study. We will only be able to understand the whole once we have come to understand the regions better; yet, we must have some tools to assist us in our regional studies as well as a sense of how the particular region we are studying fits into the whole. So, for example, studies of the witch-hunt in the Highlands can now proceed with a better sense of the overall picture of the witch-hunt in Scotland. Secondly, we can use this information to critique some of the current understandings of the Scottish witch-hunt.

The patterns that we have described cast doubt on the role of judicial torture as the key determining factor in witchcraft persecution in Scotland. There is no question that it may have played a role in the major national hunts. Its role in the cases involving isolated witches or in small panics is less clear. Even in years where the hunting was at an intense, national level one would expect to see a concentration of cases greater than that in 1649 (Map 3) and far greater than that found in 1650 (Map 4). This is a subject to which we shall return in great length in chapter eight. For the moment, however, it is important to recognise that the national pattern does not support the notion that the use of judicial torture was the main driving force behind the Scottish witch-hunt. The pattern is more compatible with the notion of travelling witch-finders who may have served to confirm the suspicions of local communities that particular individuals in their midst were indeed witches.

Andro Man was a victim swept up in a major witch-hunt which occurred throughout Scotland. Elspeth Thomson was someone caught in events of a more local nature. It is important that we recognise these differences. Village tensions existed throughout, and when combined with concerns and fears of the elite, produced wide-scale witch-hunting. To understand better how this occurred we will turn our attention to a particular region of Scotland, namely Fife, examine the chronological and geographical patterns and tell the story of the individual women and men who found themselves accused as witches or accusing others.

Notes

1. MacCulloch, 'The Mingling of Fairy and Witch Beliefs in Sixteenth and Seventeenth Century Scotland', 235–36. Andro Man appears as case no. 2302 in the SBSW. See also *Spalding Club Miscellany* VI, 117–125.
2. Cited in A.E. Truckell, 'Unpublished Witchcraft Trials – Part 2' in *Transactions of the Dumfries-shire and Galloway Natural History and Antiquarian Society* (1976), 103.
3. Ibid., 103–106. Elspethe Thomsone appears as case no. 588 in the SBSW. Case 838 also appears to be a reference to the same Elspeth Thomson (at a different court level).

This case is very well known. The above description comes from the court records, as quoted in Truckell. Christina Larner discussed this case at length, in chapter 10 'Two Classic Cases' in *Enemies of God*, 120–33. Innes MacLeod also refers to the case in *Discovering Galloway* (Edinburgh: John Donald, 1986), 173.

4. There are several cases which have become common to the literature. Baroja, *The World of the Witches* discusses Bessie Dunlop, Alison Piersoun, and the North Berwick cases, 125–28. The North Berwick case has, of course, received the most extensive treatment. Margaret Murray cited many cases from Scotland. Nicholas Macleod's *Scottish Witchcraft* gives a brief 'tour' of some cases from different regions of Scotland.

5. Larner, Lee, and McLachlan, *A Source Book of Scottish Witchcraft* (Glasgow, 1977). For a detailed description of the *Sourcebook* and how it has been used in this thesis, please see Appendix B. The abbreviation SBSW will be used throughout the footnotes to refer to this source.

6. Larner, *Enemies of God*, 61–62. Larner admits the line between a small and large panic cannot really be 'drawn with any precision'. She suggests the line is somewhere around ten cases.

7. Ibid., 61. The graph is good although no citation exists as to what data it is based upon; however, it is obviously based upon data from the SBSW.

8. Ibid., 60. Chapter 6 includes an excellent discussion of elite interest and activity in all of the major hunts. In this sense the chapter does give a 'Chronology', as the title suggests, but primarily in terms of the major hunts.

9. Ibid., 81. No indication is given in *Enemies of God* as to what information this map is based upon. However, it does seem plausible that Table 11, SBSW, 248 is the source. It is important to note that only 62% of the cases contained in the SBSW are represented in this table.

10. Ibid., 80.

11. Ibid., 80.

12. Ibid., 82.

13. Ibid., 82.

14. Ibid., 83.

15. Ian & Kathleen Whyte, *Discovering East Lothian* (Edinburgh: John Donald, 1988), 48–49.

16. Raymond Lamont-Brown, *Discovering Fife* (Edinburgh: John Donald, 1988), 60.

17. Brian Levack, *The witch-hunt in early modern Europe*, 2nd ed., 96. This chapter has avoided factoring in the number of individuals executed, simply because these statistics are so incomplete.

18. Larner, *Enemies of God*, 82–83.

19. Bruce Lenman's review of *Enemies of God*, *Scottish Historical Review* (1979) 197–200; Larner, *Enemies of God*, 38–39; see also, Larner, 'The Crime of Witchcraft in Scotland,' in Larner, *Witchcraft and Religion: The Politics of Popular Belief*.

20. Brian Levack, *The witch-hunt in Early Modern Europe*, 2nd ed., 96, uses the information from the SBSW to discuss central versus local execution rates. The NK category – fate 'Not Known' – is extremely large. Levack's argument that the witch-hunt was 'dramatically higher when unsupervised local authorities heard witchcraft cases than when judges from the central courts did so,' seems plausible. However, this conclusion is based on only 402 cases where the fate is known out of a possible 1929 in the relevant sections of the SBSW. This is only a small sample of the 3069 cases listed in the SBSW. Given the sample size, caution needs to be taken. We simply don't have enough data at this point to pursue this argument forcefully.

21. Cases with no year, see SBSW, 50–53, 230–32. As the SBSW is organised chronologically according to Court Level, those cases with no geographical references are scattered throughout. They are easily accessible in the computer database created for this project. As stated in the text, at present 89% of the cases have been placed within a Shire – up significantly from the 62% represented in Table 11 of the SBSW, 248.
22. Cases 600 & 834 in the SBSW involve an individual in Banff.
23. The same point was made in a graph which appeared in Geoffrey Parker's introduction to 'The European Witchcraze Revisited' in *History Today* (November 1980): 24, which compared the appearance of the witch-hunt in several different European countries.
24. Larner, *Enemies of God*, 62.
25. SBSW, case no. 2293. The original source of this information is the *Chronicles of Perth*.
26. Larner, *Enemies of God*, 61.
27. SBSW, 9–10, 61, 175–80.
28. The Scottish Witch-Hunt Data Base project. The abbreviation SWHDB will be used throughout the footnotes..
29. Larner, *Enemies of God*, 61; Lenman, *SHR*, 198. Commenting on the SBSW, Lenman wrote: 'what is more troubling by far is the probably serious underestimate that total provides, for it must be greatly reduced by the absence of records for the period of the great witch-hunt of 1590–7 and the general lack of information in privy council records.' It should be remembered, however, that estimates of numbers in the European witch-hunt have generally moved lower, rather than higher. Any numbers for this period must remain, until more local records are profitably mined, only estimates.
30. Larner, *Enemies of God*, 60.
31. Julio Caro Baroja, *The World of the Witches*, 125–28. The North Berwick case and James VI's interest in witchcraft, of course, have received the most extensive treatment: E.J. Cowan, in *The Sunday Mail Story of Scotland*, Vol. 2, Pt. 15, 406; Stuart Clark, 'King James's *Daemonologie*.' References to other works appear in the notes to chapter 1.
32. Larner, *Enemies of God*, 60.
33. No study as yet exists on the 1649 witch-hunt. It should be noted that there are a large number of cases with no specific date from both 1649 and 1650. Still, the SBSW records one case in February 1649, two in March, three in April, fifteen in May, and by June the hunt was in full course. SBSW, 13–14, 113–19, 151–52, 158–71, 195–200. (There were no witch-craft cases recorded in 1647, and only 10 in 1648.) The timing seems suggestive, to say the least.)
34. Brian Levack, 'The Great Scottish Witch Hunt of 1661–62', especially 93–97, 107–108, has done an excellent analysis of the events of these years.
35. Ibid., 91, 92, 93.
36. Quaife, 119.
37. Ian and Kathleen Whyte, *Discovering East Lothian*, 48–49. Larner, *Enemies of God*, 80.
38. Larner, *Enemies of God*, 80.
39. Alan MacFarlane, *Witchcraft in Tudor and Stuart England*, made extensive use of cartography to demonstrate the dynamics of the witch-hunt within the county of Essex in England. By noting which particular villages produced accusations at the Essex Assizes in a given decade, MacFarlane was able to demonstrate the rise and fall

of prosecutions and which particular villages were affected. Gábor Klaniczay, 'Hungary: The Accusations and the Universe of Popular Magic,' in EMEW, 225, 231 takes a slightly different approach. He includes a standard chronological graph, but then notes when the particular counties of Hungary experienced the first witch-trials. Klaniczay's approach is interesting but would produce some odd conclusions for Scotland: Moray (1560), a shire with only a moderate level of witch-hunting would appear at about the same time as Haddington (1563), the shire with the highest number of cases. Edinburgh, another area of very intense witch-hunting, did not have its first case until 1572, four years after Forfar, another area of only moderate persecution. Antero Heikkinen and Timo Kervinen 'Finland: The Male Domina-tion,' EMEW, 325 show the different incidents of witch accusations in three different periods in Finland, while in the same collection Bengt Ankarloo 'Sweden: The Mass Burnings (1668–76)', EMEW, 301, maps the spread of indictments in a particular area of Sweden over a two year period. There are similar maps in Boyer and Nissenbaum, *Salem Possessed*, 34, 84, 85, 95, 118, 127, based upon and adapted from the work of other historians of the Salem witch-hunt. This list is by no means exhaustive. These different approaches illustrate the reality that there is no set pattern or approach to the entire topic of the chronology and geography of the witch-hunt in any given region or throughout Europe.

40. SWHDB.

41. The following information can be constructed from the data in the SBSW: 1645: Bute (1); Edinburgh (3 – including one multiple case, 'certain witches'; Fife (4); Moray (1). 1646: Edinburgh (1); Fife (3); Lanark (1) Moray (2).

42. A.E. Truckell, 'Unpublished Witchcraft Trials'; 'Unpublished Witchcraft Trials – Part 2.' All of the cases in both articles involve some form of *malefice*.

43. The continued strong belief which existed among common people and many in the elite, even during the last English witch-craft case, has been ably demonstrated through a close reading of Phyllis Guskin, 'The Context of Witchcraft: The Case of Jane Wenham (1712)' in *Eighteenth Century Studies* 15 (1981): 48. When the elite-controlled judicial machinery ceases processing witches or dealing with witchcraft as a crime then even isolated witches cannot be hunted – except by lynch mobs. Brian Levack's investigation of the 1661–62 hunt found that many of those accused fit the traditional stereotype of the witch. Levack, 'Great Scottish Witch Hunt', 102.

44. Geoff Quaife, *Godly Zeal*, 119.

45. See Appendix D.

CHAPTER THREE

The Witch-Hunt in Fife

No regional study of a witch-hunt exists for Scotland. Instead, we have an extremely good overview of the national situation in *Enemies of God*, studies of particular hunts or peak years, and discussions of some of the more dramatic and famous cases. This chapter and the chapters following will attempt to remedy this situation by exploring how a witch-hunt developed over this period in particular areas of Fife. The style will primarily be narrative. This is a story that first needs to be told before we begin to analyse its meaning. In the telling, several factors will hopefully become clear. One is the central importance of the presbyteries as the local geographic unit in which most witch-hunting occurred. Only on rare occasions did hunts cross presbytery borders. We will see how these specific presbyteries functioned in publicizing information, in becoming involved in cases that came to them from the parishes, and in the process of the witch-hunt itself.[1] After exploring these themes over the next five chapters, we will then summarize in chapter 8 our discussion in terms of what drove the witch-hunt in Fife and specifically the role played by judicial torture.

One of the purposes of this section is to show the fragmentary nature of the evidence from which we must attempt to understand the events of these years. In telling the story of the witch-hunt in these particular regions the various sources of information and the nature of what we know, and in many cases do not know, will become clear. While in some circumstances we have a great deal of information, in others the paucity of detail is noteworthy. The names of those listed in commissions gives us little information; but even here we can attempt to determine what was occurring, or the links with other commissions at about the same time. The nature of the sources is one of realities with which historians need to grapple. Too often answers are demanded which simply cannot be given because of the fragmentary nature of the evidence. We do not know enough to answer questions about social class. Even marital status is rarely noted. As this is the first attempt at a regional study in Scotland, it is important to give a picture of the nature of the evidence which exists.

The narrative form has also been chosen in order to show both the strengths and weaknesses of the arguments presented. It is possible in a thematic study to emphasize or choose the examples that support one's arguments. By giving as complete a picture as is possible, it is hoped that this temptation will be avoided. It is, however, still necessary to tell the story in a particular way. This study will tell the story of the witch-hunt as it developed in each of the four presbyteries of Fife. Presbyteries were chosen because their boundaries, more than any other geographic feature, seems to be important in the development of the witch-hunt. One could argue that this choice ends up proving itself: or, to put it another way, because we have used sources from presbyteries and sessions, and organized the discussion around their boundaries, have we given an importance to these bodies which they might otherwise not have? This chapter will discuss the chronology and geography of the Fife witch-hunt and will make the case for the importance of presbytery boundaries. We will see how localized witch-hunting tended to be in Fife. Throughout the following five chapters, evidence will be given through the narrative of the role which church courts played in the witch-hunt – a role which has not been adequately recognised up to this point in the historical literature – and of the way in which presbyteries served as a clearinghouse for information, as well as active agents of witch-hunting

It is difficult to give a clear picture of Scottish institutions and how they operated throughout the sixteenth and seventeenth centuries. The presbyterian system of church government was not created at a particular moment. While the theory of presbyterianism was laid out in the *Second Book of Discipline* (1578), the actual processes by which these various courts operated were not codified until near the end of our period.[2] One of the struggles of this period was over which form of church government, presbyterian or episcopalian, would be established in Scotland. Less concern was given as to how the system should operate. It is still helpful to make some generalizations about how church courts in Scotland in this period operated.

Fife was divided into parishes. Each parish was governed by a session which was moderated (chaired) by the minister, and was comprised of other significant members of the community, such as the burgesses or the local lairds. Sessions tended to meet weekly. From their records it is clear that their main interest was church 'discipline' or the moral behaviour of all of the people who lived within the geographic bounds of the parish. Sessions imposed fines and penalties on those found guilty of breaking the rules of behaviour established by the church. All of the sessions in a particular geographic area were governed by a presbytery, which was made up of representatives from each of the sessions. Presbyteries also met weekly and tended to deal with the same kinds of issues as the local sessions. They too were concerned with guaranteeing that the behaviour within the bounds was moral and godly. Only ministers attended presbytery until 1638, while after this ordained elders were also permitted to attend. Witchcraft, charming, celebrating Christmas or Yule, and other activities deemed contrary to the will of God were seen as the business of these courts. This belief in the enforcement of morality on the community arose out of the kirk's understanding of its place in the world. As Jane Dawson recently explained:

> If the Church . . . was something which could be heard, touched, and seen by everyone, then its life on earth could also be assessed and judged by the rest of the world. The earthy insistence that the corporate body of the Church was a physical reality brought with it a pronounced emphasis upon discipline . . . Since that body was real and easily identifiable, its conduct was under constant scrutiny.[3]

As everyone in the community was deemed to be part of the church, discipline was a reality for all in the parish. The local secular authorities generally supported these goals, and, again in Dawson's words, 'the establishment of a Reformed community'.[4] Advice on how certain matters should be dealt with was sometimes sought from the superior regional court, the Synod, or from the national court, the General Assembly.

It is difficult to determine the exact processes and procedures of the sessions and presbyteries in this period. The minutes are brief and state what was done and what was decided, not always how. Still, in cases involving witchcraft the presbytery functioned similar to a pre-trial hearing. Witnesses appeared and gave testimony. Suspects were interrogated. Judgement and sentences were pronounced. Cases involving charming or slander could be dealt with entirely by the church court, and the sentence imposed in these situations usually involved some act of public repentance before the entire community. More serious punishments, including the execution of a witch, were outside the jurisdiction of the church courts. In these cases a commission to put the suspect to a secular trial was required. Often the evidence, and in particular the confession, gathered by and before the session or presbytery were used to obtain a commission to put the suspect to trial.

The Scottish legal procedures at this time were not simple. Various courts had intersecting jurisdictions. In an article on how the court system in

Stirlingshire actually functioned, Stephen J. Davies describes how ten different kinds of courts intersected, overlapped and operated. Many of his conclusions seem to hold true for Fife. Davies discovered witchcraft cases before church courts, the Court of Justiciary, burgh courts, and commission of significant local individuals established by warrant of the Privy Council. He does not mention any cases appearing before Sheriff's courts or Franchise courts.[5] Most of the women we will be discussing in Fife appeared before church courts or were dealt with by special commissions which were granted by the Privy Council. There are only a few cases where the Court of Justiciary was involved. Church courts should have referred 'very grave 'moral' offences such as bestiality, sodomy, incest or flagrant adultery to the civil courts as well as most witchcraft cases' to the secular courts.[6] The process in Fife was sometimes less precise. Church courts were, as Davies noted, 'by far the most active branch of the legal system'.[7]

The chronology and geography of the Fife witch-hunt

Fife, the shire which contains the various burghs, parishes and presbyteries, lies on a peninsula north of the capital city of Edinburgh. The shire is surrounded on three sides by water: to the north by the Firth of Tay, to the east by the sea, and to south by the Firth of Forth. Water was one of the most efficient means of transport at this time, and the coasts of Fife included many busy seaports and trading burghs. The main centre of religious life in Scotland during the medieval and into the early modern period was St. Andrews, the seat of the archbishop and later bishops, as well as the home of reformers and sessions. Many of the principal martyrs of the early Scottish Reformation, men like Patrick Hamilton and George Wishart, were executed at St. Andrews and it was some of the local Fife nobility who responded to Wishart's execution by murdering Cardinal Beaton and taking control of his castle. Fife was an area where support for the early stages of the Reformation could be found. Later there was also support for dissenters from the church which was established after the Reformation. The courts and structures of the reformed church – sessions, presbyteries, and synods – were established relatively early and effectively in this area, helped in part by the proximity to one of the great centres of education at St. Andrews University.

Economically, Fife was a mixture of agriculture, commerce, craft and some craft industries. Trade flowed from ports such as St. Andrews, Kirkcaldy, Crail, Burntisland, Inverkeithing and Culross. Along the South coast of Fife, coal and salt were industries of note. While clearly a region, Fife was not isolated from outside events, plagues, famines, wars, or the ideas of this period. Fife was certainly not isolated from the witch-hunt. The witch-hunt began early in Fife, and lasted into the early eighteenth century. It would be helpful to be able to note the changes over this period in population, agriculture, trade, urban growth and other social and economic factors. Comparisons to other regions of Scotland would also be enlightening. While work in these areas continues, we do not at the moment have extensive or detailed information on Fife in this period.[8]

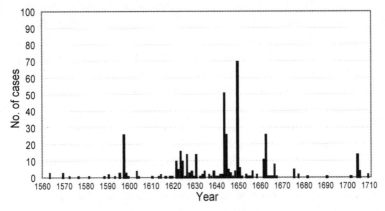

Graph 2 – Cases of witchcraft in Fife, 1560–1710

In order to effectively study witch-hunting in this region of Scotland, it is necessary to determine the communities from which the suspects came. Most of those accused of witch-craft in Fife can be placed within particular areas of the shire – if not an actual burgh or village, at least within a presbytery. There are exceptions. The *Booke of the Universal Kirk* notes four women delated for witch-craft in 1563 by the Superintendents of Fife and Galloway.[9] Aleson Piersoun of Byre-hill was accused in 1588 and appeared before the High Court. (There is no direct evidence that she was tortured.) Her confession included the fact that she had been taken by 'ane lustie mane, with mony mene and wemen' to a mystical place where there was much piping and dancing and merriment. The key to her being named a witch may lie in the fact that she had a knowledge of healing, learned from an uncle. She was charged with 'dealing with charmes, and abusing the commoun people thairwith, be the said airt of wichcraft'. Although apparently only nineteen, she was found guilty and executed.[10] In 1623 Thomas Greave was also executed, after appearing before the Court of Justiciary charged with witchcraft.[11] Finally, there is a notation in the Acts of Parliament during the large witch-hunt in 1649 that 'some witches' were executed in Fife.[12] The other accused witches can be placed within a particular presbytery.

The chronology of the witch-hunt in Fife corresponds to the chronology of the Scottish witch-hunt as a whole. While the witch-hunt in Fife occurred over a long period with cases extending from 1563 to 1709 (See Graph 2) the vast majority of the cases occurred in the seventeenth century, in particular in the fifty-year period from 1620 to 1670. The peak years were in 1649 (70 cases), 1643 (51 cases) 1644 (26 cases) and 1597 (26 cases). All of these years were years of major witch-hunts on a national scale. Fife's most significant contribution was to the hunt in 1643 when its total of fifty-one cases represented more than half of all cases in Scotland (87). Interestingly, Fife contributed only slightly to the massive witch-hunt of the period 1658–59 and 1661–62 with a total of 37 cases, the majority (26) of which occurred in 1662. Another thing to note is the number of instances of individual cases, or small groups of cases, a pattern which continues throughout the period.[13]

The geographical distribution of cases is equally fascinating (see Map 5). The intense concentration of cases in the south-west, centred on Culross, Dunfermline and Inverkeithing, with another concentration in the parishes of Kirkcaldy and Dysart, is noticeable. In sharp contrast, the Tay coast of Fife was not a major area of witch-hunting. Pittenweem, often picked out as a formidable area of persecution,[14] produced 28 cases, in contrast to 51 for Inverkeithing, 44 for Culross, 39 for Dunfermline, 36 for Kirkcaldy and even 22 for St. Andrews.[15] While proximity to Edinburgh may have been a factor in the concentration in the south-west of Fife, it does not explain why the parish of St. Andrews produced more witches than Wemyss, or why Collessie produced more than Abbotshall. It is also worth noting the number of parishes in which no known cases of witchcraft accusations occurred, parishes such as Kingsbarns, Elie, Cameron, and Kettle. Population density may have been a factor, although given our lack of knowledge of population distribution in this period, this is difficult to either prove or disprove. Topography does not seem to have been a factor.

When we move away from the consideration of the pattern over time and the geographical concentration to consider the shape of the witch-hunt on a year-by-year basis, several realities come into clearer focus. The first is that while categories such as national hunt or isolated witch may be helpful, it is more difficult to effectively categorize those instances which fall in between. Witch-hunting was an irregular process. There were many years in which no accusations of witchcraft occurred in Fife. Indeed, accusations came in only 61 of 150 years in the period from 1560 to 1710, and most of these, as already noted, in the fifty years between 1620 to 1670. Witchcraft accusations were also very localized.

There were many years when cases occurred in only one parish (37 of 61) or in two parishes in different presbyteries (7 of 61). Rarely did these ever involve enough individuals to be considered a 'large panic' as discussed in the previous chapter. Many of these incidents involved an isolated witch. To give but a few examples: Euphame Lochoir was accused in the parish of Crail in 1590 (the year of the royal witch-hunt); William Hutchen of Kinghorn, a weaver by trade, was brought before the presbytery of Kirkcaldy for charming in 1636; and, Elspeth Kirkland was accused as a witch by Bessie Lamb in Aberdour in 1681.[16]

Fife witnessed significant witch-hunting in many of those years when major persecutions occurred throughout Scotland. The year 1649 saw more cases in Fife than any other. Next in intensity was the hunt which spanned the two years, 1643 and 1644 and involved 51 and 26 cases respectively. Fife was also dramatically affected by the witch-hunts of 1597 and 1662. What is important to note is how focused these hunts were within a particular presbytery. The hunt which took place in 1649 occurred primarily within the bounds of the presbytery of Dunfermline (see Map 6). With the exception of the cases involving Elspeth Seath, Helen Young and Helen Smith which began in Balmerino in 1648 and carried on into 1649, an isolated case in Dysart, and thirteen cases in the parish of Burntisland (which borders Dunfermline Presbytery), the remaining cases, many of them involving an undetermined number of individuals, took place within the bounds of the presbytery of Dunfermline. In other words, 55 of 70 cases came from one presbytery. Similarly, in 1597, the 26 known cases occurred in two presbyteries, St. Andrew's and Kirkcaldy. Given the general lack of records for the 1590's this might seem to be an exception. Yet, in 1662 a similar pattern emerged. All of the 26 cases in Fife occurred in the presbytery of Cupar with two exceptions: two cases in Forgan (St. Andrews Presbytery) which borders on Cupar Presbytery; and, an isolated case in Culross (see Map 10). The exception to this idea that the major hunts tended to have a focus in one particular presbytery, was the witch-hunt which took place in 1643 and 1644. This hunt involved three of the four presbyteries (see Map 14). While the parish of Dunfermline (18) had the most cases in 1643, Culross (9), also in the presbytery of Dunfermline, was affected. Crail (6), Pittenweem (5) and Anstruther (3 cases, each of which involved more than one individual) all from St. Andrews Presbytery were also affected. Finally, the hunt affected three parishes in the presbytery of Kirkcaldy– Kinghorn (2), Markinch (1) and Dysart (1) – and became even more intense in this presbytery the following year, 1644, with 5 cases occurring in Dysart. In no year did cases appear in all four presbyteries in Fife.

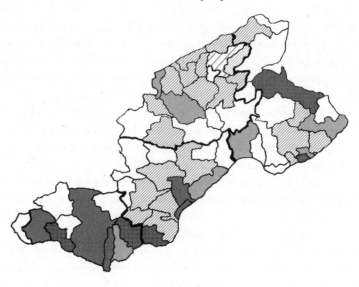

1-4   5-14   15-29   30-59

Map 5 – Fife, 1560–1710. Cases by parish.

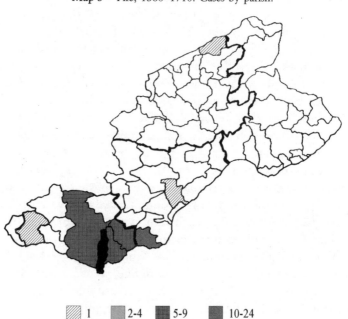

1   2-4   5-9   10-24

25+

Map 6 – Fife, 1649. Cases by parish.

Between what we can identify as the years of major witch-hunting and the cases of an isolated individual, are the years when we discover cases of two accused, three accused, or more; the types of cases referred to as 'small panics'.[17] Here too, these cases seem to be focused in particular areas, areas which developed a history of witch-hunting. In many cases the area which had a history of witch-hunting was a particular parish. For example, the six accusations of witchcraft in Inverkeithing in 1621 were followed by a much larger hunt within the same parish two years later.[18] Inverkeithing witnessed an even larger hunt in 1649. The latter hunt has often been blamed upon a particular ecclesiastical crisis, sparked by the minister Mr. Walter Bruce.[19] Yet, such a discussion needs to take place against an awareness of the fact that Inverkeithing was the only parish in Fife to produce on its own as many accusations of witchcraft as it did in 1623.[20] The links between hunts are often difficult to determine.

Attempts to establish patterns or organize the witch-hunt are difficult. In Fife, terms such as 'large panics' are not particularly helpful. There were few years apart from the national hunts when more than ten individuals were involved. Seen from above and looking at a national

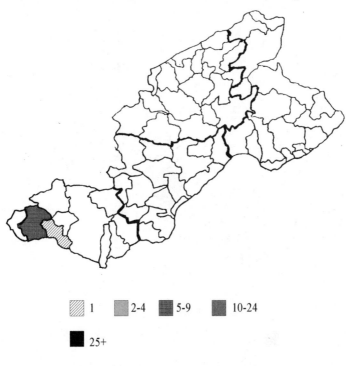

| ▨ 1 | ▨ 2-4 | ▥ 5-9 | ▨ 10-24 |

■ 25+

Map 7 – Fife, 1624. Cases by parish.

41

scale, such categories may seem reasonable. Seen from below, watching how accusations move from parish to parish, these same categories seem less helpful. The situation was very complex with a mixture of all shapes and sizes of hunts. What does seem apparent is that presbytery bound-aries were important. Cases were not spread all over Fife, but tended, as in the major hunts, to be contained within a particular presbytery. There were five years in which small hunts were contained within a particular presbytery. For example, in 1624 the neighbouring parishes of Culross and Torryburn, saw nine cases and a single case respectively (see Map 7). This pattern was repeated in the other four years. The presbytery of Kirkcaldy experienced such small hunts in 1626, 1627, and 1638. In Cupar Presbytery in 1646 Jonet Mitchell and Marie Mitchells of the parish of Kilmany were slandered as witches by Grissel Thomson, who appears to have been from the neighbouring parish of Cupar. Thomson had, by this point, been executed. Fortunately for Jonet Mitchells and Marie Mitchells, the presbytery ruled that, as neither had ever been accused prior to this, it was unfair to debar them from communion, based solely upon the accusation of one witch. They were cleared of the accusation.[21]

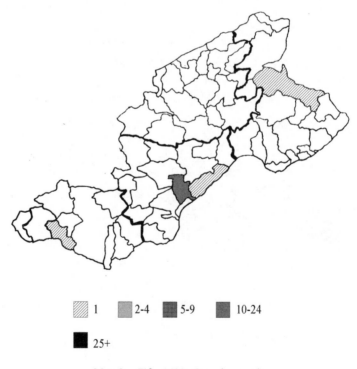

1 2-4 5-9 10-24

25+

Map 8 – Fife, 1630. Cases by parish.

While witch-hunting tended to be localized, occurring in a single parish or presbytery, there are exceptions to this even in years when there was not a major hunt underway. At times cases appeared in parishes in two different presbyteries. The year in which the most cases of this sort appeared was at the very end of the witch-hunt in Fife, 1704, when 6 accusations occurred in Torryburn (Dunfermline presbytery) and 7 occurred in Pittenweem (Kirkcaldy presbytery). In 1621 cases were scattered from Crail (1) in St. Andrew's Presbytery to Kirkcaldy (2) in Kirkcaldy Presbytery to Inverkeithing (6) and Culross (1) in Dunfermline Presbytery. In 1630 (see Map 8) isolated cases in St. Andrews and Torryburn, bracketed a major outbreak in the presbytery of Kirkcaldy, focussed on Dysart (11 cases) and including another case in the neighbouring parish of Wemyss. Similar patterns occurred in 1642, 1645, 1648, and 1656. The importance of the presbytery bounds in terms of witch-hunts is inconclusive when we simply look at the pattern from year to year, yet of all the geographical factors which could be examined– topography, proximity to Edinburgh, inland versus sea–it comes closest to giving a shape to the witch-hunt. We will, therefore, study the witch-hunt as it occurred in each of the four presbyteries. We will consider whether or not it is a useful level at which to study the witch-hunt. Were there features of the presbytery which contributed to witch-hunting? What role did it, and indeed other church courts, play? In order to investigate these and other questions, we turn over the next chapters to a narrative of the witch-hunt, beginning with the presbytery of Cupar.

Notes

1. Gilmore's thesis *Witchcraft and the Church of Scotland* (Glasgow, 1948) explored these themes. The data he used came from records from across Scotland, most of which were available in printed form. Gilmore's interest was to try to describe how each court level (General Assembly, synod, presbytery, kirk session) dealt with allegations of witchcraft. The result, while at times fascinating, can be rather repetitive. Gilmore's concern was with the institution's response to the issue of witchcraft. The current study is more interested in the actual cases themselves, at whichever church court level they were pursued. The geographic boundary of the presbytery is used both in order to focus the discussion and because the results of the research have shown that this was an important geographical unit in the history of the witch-hunt in Fife.

2. A. Ian Dunlop, 'The Polity of the Scottish Church 1600–37,' *Scottish Church History Society Records* 1 (1958): 161–84, attempted to determine how the church courts worked by looking closely at one period. Michael F. Graham, *The Uses of Reform: 'Godly Discipline and Popular Behaviour in Scotland and Beyond, 1560–1610* (New York: E.J. Brill, 1996), studies both discipline and how it was implemented in greater depth.

3. Jane E. A. Dawson, ''The Face of Ane Perfect Reformed Kyrk': St. Andrews and the Early Scottish Reformation,' in *Humanism and Reform: the church in Europe, England and Scotland 1400–1643: essays in honour of James K. Cameron*, ed. James Kirk (Oxford: Basil Blackwell, 1991), 421.

4. Ibid.,427. Graham, *The Uses of Reform*, 147. Graham also gives a definition of church discipline and speaks of the role played by the secular authorities on p. 1.

5. Stephen J. Davies, 'The Courts and Scottish Legal System 1600–1747: The Case of Stirlingshire,' in *Crime and the Law: the Social History of Crime in Western Europe since 1500*, ed. V.A.C. Gattrell, Bruce Lenman and Geoffery Parker (London: Europa, 1980), 120–54.

6. Davies, 'Scottish Legal System,' 131.

7. Ibid., 149.

8. Ian D. Whyte, *Scotland Before the Industrial Revolution: An Economic & Social History c.1050 – c. 1750* (Harlow: Longmans, 1995), has produced an important survey of the current state of information on Scottish social and economic history in this period. One simple demographic fact we do not have an answer for is whether the national population in the seventeenth century grew or declined, 113.

9. Cases 2214, 2215. The editorial decision was made in working on the SWHDB to place two of these women in Fife and two in Galloway. Original source, Alexander Peterkins, ed. *The Booke of the Universal Kirk of Scotland* (Edinburgh: Edinburgh Publishing company, 1839), 44.

10. Case 13. Robert Pitcairn, *Ancient Criminal Trials in Scotland* Vol. 1, (Edinburgh: Bannatyne, 1833), 162–165. Where precisely 'Byrehill' was is unclear. Hugo Arnot, *A Collection and Abridgement of Celebrated Criminal Trials in Scotland* (Edinburgh: G.W. Smellie, 1785; Reprint, Edinburgh, 1885), 390.

11. Case 139.

12. Case 3081. *Acts of the Parliament of Scotland*. vol 6, part 2, 463.

13. Data for graph and text derived from the SWHDB.

14. Larner, *Enemies of God*, calls attention to Pittenweem as an area where intense study could be done, 82. Brown, in *Discovering Fife*, 60, argues it was the worst place for witch-hunting in Scotland. Pittenweem's reputation can be explained by the lateness of some prominent cases and the pamphlet war that ensued: *A Just Reproof to the False Reports and Unjust Calumnies in the Foregoing Letters, A True and Full Relation of the Witches at Pittenweem to which is added . . .* and *An Answer of a Letter from a Gentleman in Fife to a Nobleman, CONTAINING A Brief Account of the Barbarous and illegal Treatment, these poor Women accused of Witchcraft, met with from the Bailies of Pittenweem and others, with some Observations thereon; to which is added, An Account of the horrid and Barbarous Murder, in a Letter from a Gentleman in Fife, to his Friend in Edinburgh, February 5th, 1705*, all date from 1704/5 and are collected in D. Webster, *A Collection of Rare and Curious Tracts on Witchcraft* (Edinburgh, 1820). The folk song, 'Burn the witch of Pittenweem', may have further added to the notoriety of the parish.

15. SWHDB.

16. Euphame Lochoir (3134), Mark Smith, *A Study and Annotated edition of the Register of the Minutes of the Presbytery of St. Andrew's, volume 1* (Ph. D. diss., University of St. Andrews, 1985), 51; William Hutchen (3134), *The Presbyterie Booke of Kirkcaldie* (PBK), 92. Hutchen's case will be discussed further; Elspeth Kirkland (2936) William Ross, *Aberdour and Inchcolme: Being Historical Notices of the Parish and Monastery in twelve lectures* (Edinburgh: David Douglas, 1885), 332.

17. Again, on these categories, see the discussion in the notes to chapter 2.

18. Larner, *Enemies of God*, 61–62.

19. William Stephen, *History of Inverkeithing and Rosyth* (Aberdeen: G&W Fraser, 1921), 440–41. Richard A. Bensen, *South-West Fife and the Scottish Revolution: The Presbytery of Dunfermline, 1633–52* (M.Litt diss., University of Edinburgh, 1978), 175–79, 185–86. Both are correct in attributing to Bruce a major role in this hunt. This case will be discussed in greater detail later. Larner notes one possible link between the Inverkeithing hunts, *Enemies of God*, 61.

20. The SBSW lists 22 cases in Inverkeithing in this period, however there is significant duplication. Many of the accused fled and are listed both when warrants are listed for their arrest as fugitives and upon their apprehension. Fifteen individuals can be identified. This was still more than in any other single parish in Fife in a given year outside of a wide-spread panic year. Cases 965–86. The primary source for this information are the commissions contained in the *Registers of the Privy Council* (RPC), v. 13, 181, 192–193, and 230.

21. G.R. Kinloch, ed., *Selections from the Minutes of the Presbyteries of St. Andrews and Cupar, 1641–98* (Edinburgh: 1837), 104. Hereafter, STACUPR. See also Gilmore, *Witchcraft and the Church of Scotland,* 127–28.

CHAPTER FOUR

The Witch–Hunt in the Presbytery of Cupar

Cupar Presbytery, made up of parishes along the Tay coast and the north central area of Fife, was never an area of intense witch-hunting yet those cases we have from this presbytery remain among the most puzzling and fascinating. The presbytery was established in 1591 and in this period contained nineteen parishes. One of these parishes, New-burgh, was not erected as a separate parish until 1632.[1] The area is fairly hilly, having the Lomond hills near Falkland and many steep slopes near the Tay coast. Cupar was the central burgh and apart from Falkland, which featured a royal hunting palace, the only village or town of significance.

Early witchcraft accusations in the presbytery of Cupar: 1590–1655

The first case of suspected witchcraft in the presbytery of Cupar appeared in March of 1590, prior to the outbreak of the royal witch-hunt of that year. The only record of the incident survives in the records of the presbytery of St. Andrews where it is noted on March 16 that 'Androw Melvin, James Melvin and Thomas Buchanan' were to visit the parish church of 'Ebdie' to examine Nans Murit, a suspect for witchcraft.[2] No further reference is made to the case. The area of Newburgh witnessed its first case in 1610 when the widow Grissell Gairdner was accused of various acts of laying illness on people and animals. The minister in the case stated that Grissell had been suspected as 'ane wicket woman and ane sorcerer' for fourteen years. Indeed it seems she had been arrested in the 1596–97 period and only escaped being executed, as others apparently were, because of the intervention of her husband. It is unclear what led to the accusations against her at this particular time, but they included consulting with the Devil and one charge of murder by witchcraft. Grissell was executed. She was sixty years old.[3]

The next known information in this presbytery comes from church courts. The minutes of the Synod of Fife recommended in 1645 that members of the presbytery of Cupar 'intimate in their several kirks, that

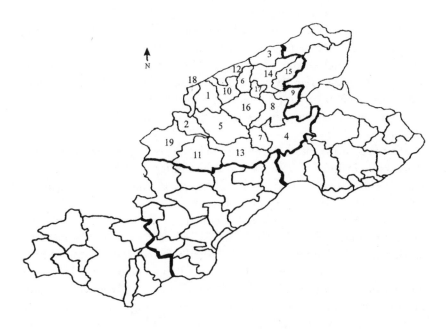

Map 9 – The parishes in Cupar Presbytery.

The presbytery of Cupar

Parish	code	Parish	code
Abdie	1	Falkland	11
Auchtermuchty	2	Flisk	12
Balmerino	3	Kingskettle	13
Ceres	4	Kilmany	14
Collessie	5	Logie	15
Creich	6	Monimail	16
Cults	7	Moonsie	17
Cupar	8	Newburgh	18
Dairsie	9	Strathmiglo	19
Dunbog	10		

Bessie Cuper and Jeane Buchane, fugitives from the discipline of the Kirk, suspect for witchcraft within the parish of Creice, that thei may be found out if thei be in the province'.[4] Such information given before the Synod served notice to the other presbyteries as well, both in regards to these particular women and to the fact that suspected witches had been discovered within the bounds of the Synod. Both women were unsuccessful in their flight, though their eventual fates are not recorded. What is recorded is that in February 18, 1647, David Barclay, a portioner of Luthrie, appeared before the presbytery of Cupar saying he has brought Bessie Cupar 'and hir daughter,' both of whom were suspected as witches, out of Lothian. After asking what he should do with the fugitives, Barclay was informed that he should present them before the session of Creich the next Sunday.[5] It is worth noting how effective church courts were in circulating information about suspected witches.

Later that same month, February 1647, the presbytery appointed three individuals, including Walter Greig the minister of Balmerino, to speak with Bessie Cupar and try to bring her to a confession in regard to witchcraft. Their attempt to bring her to a confession having failed, the presbytery moved to have three members of the court approach the magistrates of Cupar for 'ane ward howse quherins she might be keipt till farder tryelle'.[6] Matters were delayed, then referred to the synod of Fife, as also were the cases of 'sindrie others lying under the sclander of witchecraft and not yet cleared', and the resolution of this case remains unclear. The last reference has the presbytery writing to Lord Annandale regarding this matter, and a case of incest.[7] (This sort of uncertain resolution to a case will become only too frequent in our discussion of Fife.) There is no indication the presbytery ever succeeded in having Bessie Cupar incarcerated.

Jean Buchane's name appears in the records under quite different circumstances. John Spindie, a merchant of Dalkeith wrote to the presbytery in July 1647 to state that he had married Jean Buchane, but under the name of Jean Patersone. He asked that she might be cleared of any suspicion of witchcraft, 'that he might have hir for his wife'. The presbytery asked that a certificate of marriage from the minister of Dalkeith be produced, after which they would give an answer.[8] Little can be made of this fragmentary excerpt. Still it seems reasonable to assume that even though Bessie Cupar and Jean Buchane were eventually apprehended, neither was executed.

While the presbytery could be zealous in hunting witches, it could also serve as a place where those accused as witches might seek to clear their name. In 1646 two women from the parish of Kilmany, Marie Mitchells and Janet Mitchells, appealed to have the accusations made by Grissel Thomson tried before the presbytery.[9] Little is known of the accuser, other than the fact that she had already been executed as a witch. It is not known in which parish in the presbytery of Cupar she was executed, nor when.[10] This lack of information proved a problem for the presbytery itself. After Marie and Janet Mitchells' request that their names be cleared, the presbytery noted that nothing could be found 'in the clerk's books in the process concerning Grissel Thompsone or Janet and Marie Mitchell'; still, they knew that Grissel had 'spake something' and asked George Thomsone, who was going to the 'Commission of the Kirke' and was to investigate further to see what should be done.[11] This seems to have been a very important issue at the time. A minute of the Synod of Fife from October 6, 1646 notes that the matter of what to do with someone who has been accused by a confessing witch with no other suspicions was still being considered by the General Assembly.[12] On December 31st, George Thomsone reported that he had made enquiries and the opinion was

> that it was verie hard to keip young weomen under sclander, and to marre their fortune in the world, and debar them from the benefite of the Kirk, quher ther is nothing but the delatione of one witche, without any sclander befor, or anye other pregnant presumptione before or since.[13]

The danger of Marie and Janet Mitchell's strategy in asking for any accusations of witchcraft against them to be tried should not be underestimated. Despite the fact that there had been no indication that either woman was a witch and the seeming recognition that the testimony of an accused witch was not reliable, the presbytery still ordered both women to appear publicly before their congregation. At that time the congregation was to be informed that 'nothing was found against them saffe onlye that quilk that wretche spak, and how cruell a thing it was, upon so weake a groune, to keip them under so foul a sclander' – then told if anyone knew anything else about either they had two weeks in which to declare it. If no further evidence appeared, both woman would cease to be debarred from the 'benefite of the Kirk'.[14] To try to clear one's name was a difficult strategy; to continue to live under an unanswered accusation as a witch seems to have been even more difficult.

The next cases to appear in the presbytery occurred in 1649 in Balmerino and Monimail. The events surrounding Elspeth Seath, Helen Young and Helen Small will be discussed in chapter 8. Along the coast of Tay in Newburgh, Katherine Key was accused as a witch in 1653. Katherine first appeared before the session charged with cursing the minister because he had denied her communion, a charge which she denied. However others claimed to have heard this curse. Then various allegations of acts of evil or *malefice* against her neighbours were produced, affecting livestock and people. One charge was particularly noteworthy:

> 3. That the minister and his wyfe haveing purpose to take ane chyld of theiris from ye said Katharine which she had been nursing, the chyld wold sucke none womans breast, being only ane quarter old, bot being brought back againe to the said Katherine presently sucked her breast.[15]

After another dispute a little later, the child died. Katherine was summoned before the session to answer all of these allegations. In part suspicion fell upon her, it was noted, because 'her mother before her was of evil bruit and fame'. Despite numerous witnesses who testified to various acts of *malefice* and the unanimous sending of the matter to the presbytery, obtaining commissions to try witches was difficult at this time because of the English occupation. In May of 1655 Katherine was found guilty of cursing the minister. Further information about her witchcraft was sought, but none received.[16] The *Sourcebook* lists two other cases from this part of Fife which occurred during the English occupation but no further information has been located.[17] All of the cases so far discussed have involved isolated witches, or small groups of witches. That was to change with the hunt which occurred following the restoration.

The witch-hunt of 1661–62

The witch-hunt of 1661–62 is unique within the presbytery of Cupar. This was the only time when more than two parishes were involved. It was also the only occasion when so many individuals were accused. Indeed, during the great witch-hunt which extended throughout Scotland in these years only these parishes in Fife and the parishes of Aberdour and Culross in Dunfermline Presbytery were involved. What is particularly frustrating, given the exceptional character of the hunt, is how little we know about it. Our sources are almost all central government sources which record the commissions granted for various individuals to put to trial those suspected as witches. The records of the presbytery of Cupar are missing for this period. Parish registers and other local records seem to offer no help.[18] While the details may in places be scanty, we can at least map out the geographical spread of this witch-hunt which came to involve twenty-nine individuals.

Sometime in late 1661 Margaret Carvie and Barbara Horniman, both of Falkland, were imprisoned at the instigation of the parish minister and the magistrates. Six weeks later the women appealed to the Privy Council for their release, claiming that in the meantime they had endured 'a great deal of torture by one who takes upon him the trial of witches by pricking'. They proclaimed that, although their current situation was intolerable, they were innocent and no evidence to prove their guilt had been produced. The reply to their petition was an order from the Council for their release.[19] Whether that order was obeyed, is unclear. In November 1661, a commission was issued by the Privy Council to put to trial Katherine Kay and Margaret Liddell. It seems reasonable to assume that this was the same Katherine who was sought so persistently during the English occupation. The commission stated that these women had already confessed.[20] These may be the two unnamed women executed in Cupar sometime in November, noted by John Lamont in his diary entry; however, Lamont noted that these women had been accused by someone who had already been executed in Newburgh prior to this execution.[21] Though the details surrounding the origin are hazy, by November 1661 a hunt was underway.

Commissions were soon issued for other suspected witches from various parts of the presbytery. On January 23, 1662 commissions were issued for Margaret Dryburgh in Falkland; Margaret Bell, Elspeth Bruce, and Elspeth Seatoun in Abdie; Jon Dougleish and Jonet Edward in Flisk; Bessie Duncan in Creich and Jon Brounes and Agnes Brounes in Kilmany; and Issobell Page, Christian Anderson, Christian Bonar, Margret Philp, and Helen Wentoun in Newburgh.[22] According to the commissions, all fourteen had already confessed. The commissions for Abdie, Newburgh, Flisk and Creich all list Sir John Aitoun of that Ilk as the first named commissioner. Sir John Aitoun's name also appears as the first commissioner in a commission dated February 6, 1662 to try Elspeth Millar, Jonet Mar, Alison Melvill, Jonet Staig and Margaret Wishart. Again, all had confessed. To this basic information this commission included the additional phrase 'by entering into paction with the divell and otherwayes'.[23] This and the commission issued in November 1661 are the only commissions during this hunt in which reference is made to any pact with the Devil. Again, in a commission dated April 2, Aitoun's name was prominent among those designated to try confessed witches Elspeth Anderson of Dunbog, and Kathrin Black and Bessie Simson of Flisk.[24]

The final cases in this part of Scotland occurred in May, 1662. Two cases appeared in Forgan parish in the presbytery of St. Andrews, which borders the presbytery of Cupar.[25] Also, on May 19 the *Register of the Privy Council* records a plea by the heritors of Auchtermuchty to deal with

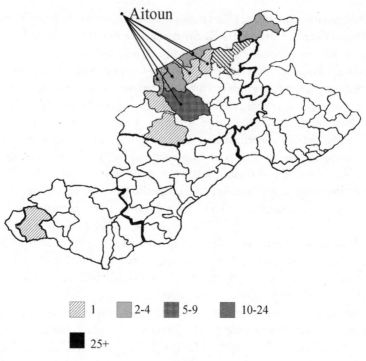

Map 10 – Fife, 1662. Cases by parish.

three individuals accused in a poisoning and an accused witch, Issobell Blyth. Commissions had been granted and the reports produced. The heritors were pleading that sentences be passed, as the cost of imprisonment and support of the prisoners was more than they could bear. The Privy Council ordered the prisoners to be brought to Edinburgh and put to trial.

The prominent place of Sir John Aitoun of that Ilk's name on the commissions of nineteen of the twenty-nine accused is striking. All of these parishes in which his name appears were in the central part of the presbytery close to the Tay coast (see Map 10). Falkland, Auchtermuchty, Collessie, Dunbog and Flisk witnessed their only cases during this period, a time of intense witch-hunting in other parts of Scotland. The role of a professional witch-finder during the early stages of the hunt in Falkland is suggestive. It is, however, equally fascinating to note that many parishes produced only a few cases. (The five cases from Collessie and the seven from Newburgh are the exception.) It seems fair to speculate that those whose names appeared in the commissions had already developed a reputation as witches within their communities. One of the first swept up in the hunt, Katherine Kay of Newburgh, certainly did. The dynamic which drove the hunt is unclear. Still, even with a witch-finder present, the selectivity of a few individuals in each parish is worth noting. Unfortunately, there are not enough details to explore the possible connections there may have been between the timing of this hunt and the restoration of the monarchy.[26]

Summary

The presbytery of Cupar witnessed only this one major witch-hunt. The other known cases all involve isolated witches or a few individuals. Witch-hunting in this area proved remarkably unsuccessful. There were only four known executions, a fact that should not be considered too seriously as we do not know the fate of the individuals in twenty-eight of the thirty-six cases. We do, however, know of several individuals who successfully fought an accusation of witchcraft. This was true whether they were under previous suspicion, as in the case of Elspeth Seath and Helen Small, or had no reputation as a witch, as was the case with Jonet and Marie Mitchells. The poor survival rate of the records for this part of Fife may in part be responsible for the low number of witchcraft cases in the region. But this is not the entire story. Distance from the central government in Edinburgh may have played a role. Whatever the explanation, the presbytery of Cupar was not an area which witnessed large scale witch-hunting.

Notes

1. *Fasti Ecclesiae Scoticanae*, vol 5 section on Cupar Presbytery, esp. 170. For convenience, those cases noted as 'Newburgh' prior to this date will still be located in that region in any mapping.
2. Smith, *A study and Annotated edition*, 41. Case 3090, SWHDB.
3. Case 131. Pitcairn, *Criminal Trials*, vol 3, 95–98. Cited here in Alexander Laing, *Lindores Abbey and Its Burgh of Newburgh* (Edinburgh, 1876), 219–222. The Justiciary Court record JC 26\7\1 gives details such as the role her husband played and her age. I am indebted to Michael Wasser for this information and his notes on this latter source.
4. George R. Kinlock, *Selections from the Minute of the Synod of Fife* (Edinburgh: Abbotsford Club, 1837), 142. Hereafter, SYNFIFE. Cases 2520, 2524 SWHDB. Bessie Cuper's name also appears in the records as Cupar. At one point, she is also referred as coming from the parish of Lithrie (April 1, 1647 Minutes, Presbytery of Cupar, St. Andrews University Muniments, Ch2\82\1).
5. Minutes of the Presbytery of Cupar, CH2\82\1. February 18, 1647; STACUPR, 107.
6. Ibid. February 25, 1647; March 4, 1647; STACUPR, 108.
7. Ibid. March 4, March 11, April 1, 1647; STACUPR, 110, 111.
8. Ibid. July 15, 1647; STACUPR, 116.
9. Ibid. November 26, 1646; STACUPR, 104–105. Also, Gilmore, *Witchcraft and the*

Church of Scotland, 127. Cases in the SWHDB: Marie Mitchells (2528); Janet Mitchells (2529); Grissel Thomson (2530). Numbers in brackets are the cases numbers listed in the SWHDB.

10. The only notation to Grissel is found here. Given that the presbytery searches its own records, it seems reasonable to assume she was from the presbytery of Cupar. The SWHDB lists her as being from the parish of Cupar, although this remains uncertain.

11. Presbytery of Cupar, CH2\82\1. December 3, 1646. This information was not excerpted in STACUPR. Further reference is made to George Thomsone during the meeting of December 10.

12. SYNFIFE, 148.

13. Presbytery of Cupar, CH2\82\1, December 31st; STACUPR, 106.

14. Ibid.

15. Case 2737 (duplicated as case 2735) quoted in Laing, *Lindores Abbey*, 224. Unless indicated otherwise, references are to the SWHDB.

16. Ibid., 223–27.

17. The cases were from 1656: Elspeth Scroggie (209); and, Agnes Pryde (210). The SBSW lists the source of this information as 'the Scottish Record Office hand list of processes.' It has not been possible to locate this list at the S.R.O. using this reference. No reference to these cases occurs in either STACUPR or the Manuscript of the Cupar presbytery minutes.

18. The presbytery minutes end in 1660 and do not exist again until 1693. The gap, obviously, covers this period. This gap would not be so serious were there any records from the affected parishes. Unfortunately there are no records from Abdie, Auchtermuchty, Creich, Collessie, Dunbog, Flisk, or Kilmany. The records of Falkland parish do exist (St. Andrew's Muniments, CH2\428\1) but no references in them to Barbara Horniman or Margaret Carvie were discovered. The Session records of Newburgh, which exist, contain evidence of other discipline cases at the time but no comments relating to suspected witches.

19. Robert Chambers, *Domestic Annals of Scotland,* vol. 2 (Edinburgh, W&R Chambers, 1858), 279.

20. Kay (1603); Liddell (1604) SWHDB. RPC, 3rd series, vol. 1, 90.

21. Two cases in the SBSW, as 2815 and 2816. G.R. Kinloch ed., *The Diary of Mr John Lamont of Newton, 1649–71* (Edinburgh: Maitland Club, 1830), 142.

22. Margaret Dryburgh (1623), RPC 3rd S. vol.1, 142–43. Margaret Bell (1625), Elspeth Bruce (1626), Elsepeth Seatoun (1627), Jon Dougleish (1621) and Jonet Edward (1622), ibid., 141. Bessie Duncan (1637), Agnes Brounes (1629) and Jon Brounes (1630), ibid., 142. Issobell Page (1633), Cristain Anderson (1635), Cristian Bonar (1636), Margret Philp (1634) and Helen Wentoun (1632), ibid., 142.

23. Margaret Wishart (1643), Jonet Staig (1644), Alison Melvill (1645), Jonat Mar (1646) and Elspeth Millar (1647), RPC 3rd Series, vol. 1, 154.

24. Elspeth Anderson (1674), Kathrin Black (1673) and Bessie Simson (1672), RPC 3rd series, vol. 1, 191.

25. Jonnet Annand (1692) and Elizabeth Clow (1693); RPC 3rd ser. vol. 1, 208. Isobell Blyth (1749). RPC 3rd ser. vol. 1, 209–210.

26. Levack, 'Great Scottish Witch Hunt,' 107–108.

CHAPTER FIVE

The Witch-Hunt in the
Presbytery of St. Andrews

Situated to the east of Cupar Presbytery, the presbytery of St. Andrews stretched along the entire east coast of Fife, including parishes along the shores of both the Firth of Tay and Firth of Forth. Throughout most of the period there were nineteen parishes in the presbytery.[1] As well as St. Andrews itself, other significant ports included Pittenweem, Crail, and Anstruther. This area saw some of the earliest sessions established and was one of the earliest functioning presbyteries in Scotland with records dating from 1587. The area was rich in commerce and contained St. Andrews, one of the major burghs at the time with an estimated population of 2,500 individuals in the years after the Reformation.[2]

Early years in St. Andrews presbytery: 1569–96

Witch-hunting began early in this area of Fife yet our evidence for what occurred in these years is very sparse and fragmentary. References are made in 1569 to the execution of the notable sorcerer Nic Neville, and the condemnation at the same time of William Stewart, Lyon King of Arms, for 'divers points of witchcraft and necromancy'.[3] It seems that William Stewart was hanged, while Neville was 'brunt'.[4] Thus, the first two individuals condemned in this presbytery were male, and one, William Stewart, of some rank. Coupled with these executions were others of unnamed witches in St. Andrews and Dundee.[5] Several cases of a political nature occurred throughout the period although we do not have specific dates. The Archbishop was called a witch as was Patrick Adamson and the curate of Anstruther.[6]

The name of John Knox finds itself attached to an execution in St. Andrews of an unnamed female witch in 1572. Knox's role in the incident seems to have been minor. According to his secretary:

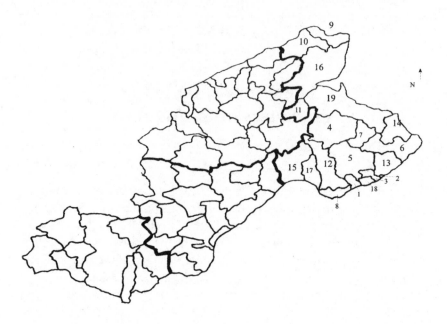

Map 11 – The parishes in St. Andrews Presbytery.

Parish	code	Parish	code
Abercrombie	1	Kemback	11
Anstruther Easter	2	Kilconquhar	12
Anstruther Wester	3	Kilrenny	13
Cameron	4	Kingsbarns	14
Carnbee	5	Largo	15
Crail	6	Leuchars	16
Dunino	7	Newburn	17
Elie	8	Pittenweem	18
Ferryport-on-Craig	9	St. Andrews	19
Forgan (St. Fillans)	10		

The 28 of Apryle thair was ane witche brunt in St Androis, wha was accused of mony horrible thingis, prowen. Being desyred that scho wold forgive a man, that had done hir some offence (as scho alledged), refused; then when ane vther that stude by said, gif sho did not forgive, that God wald not forgive hir, and so scho suld be dampned. But scho not caren for hell nor heawin, said opinlie, I pas not whidder I goe to hell or heawin, with dyvers vtheris execrable wordis. Efter hir handis were bound, the provest causeth

56

lift vp hir claithis, to see hir mark that scho had, or to sie gif sho had ony thing vpon hir I can not weill tell, bot thair was a white claith like a collore craig with stringis in betuene hir leggis, whairon was mony knottis vpon the stringis of the said collore craig, which was tacken from hir sore against hir will; for belyke scho thought that scho suld not have died that being vpon hir, for scho said, when it was taken from hir, 'Now I have no hoip of my self'.[7]

Knox's role in the matter seems to have been confined to his preaching a sermon against this witch, 'sche being set up at a pillar before him', a fact recorded, not by his secretary but by the diarist James Melville.[8]

While Knox's presence, even in a minor role, draws our attention to this case that presence should not obscure some of the more revealing details. What is clear is this woman was searched for the witches' mark yet from the description of the event it seems clear she was not being 'pricked'. A deformity rather than an insensate area on her body was what was being sought. The search was visual and when a white cloth was discovered, all attention seems to have then focused on this. Again, it is not clear what those interrogating this woman believed they had found. 'Craig' may refer to either a human or an animal neck; the modifier 'collore' is more difficult to decipher.[9] Was it something that looked like a collar that would go around someone's neck, yet worn between her legs? Was it some kind of animal neck wrapped in cloth and tied with many knotted strings? Two things seem clear. First, it was not understood to be a poppet or figure which could be used to torment others (as in the popular image of 'voodoo' dolls). Second, it was clearly interpreted as proof of the guilt which had already been ascribed to her. This was a woman 'who was accused of mony horrible thingis, prowen'. That proof included her unwillingness to forgive someone who had wronged her and her statement that she did not care if she went to heaven or hell. Her statement, 'Now I have no hoip of myself' when the collore craig was taken from her seems to have been interpreted as a confession that she was a witch. There is no notation that judicial torture was applied in this or other interrogations. Nor would such torture have been necessary. Her heretical views, her unneighbourliness, and the presence of the 'collores craig' seem to have been enough. She was condemned and executed.

Four years later in January of 1576 the case of Marjory Smyth appears in the records of the kirk session of St. Andrews.[10] Marjory was accused by Robert Grub of having layed her hands on Nanis Michel while she was giving birth and making Nanis ill. Marjory was called again to touch the sick woman. After she did Nanis became well. Marjory Smyth was also accused of harming cattle. When the 'kow gaif na milk' Marjory was suspected. Marjory Smyth does not appear to have been executed.[11] The next case in the presbytery again began before the kirk session at St. Andrews. Bessie Robertsoune was called before the session in 1581 for never coming to church or taking communion, and was also delated for witchcraft.[12] At the same time, Begis Dayes was called to appear for being 'at discention and hatred' with Bessie. Both were sentenced to be warned by the reader in church at the Sunday service, and were called to appear before the next session meeting. As is too often the case, no further notations can be found in the session Minutes.

Both of the cases which occurred in 1590 came prior to the major outbreak related to North Berwick. We have already noted a case from Abdie in Cupar presbytery. Accusations were also made against Euphame Lochoir in Crail. The notation in the minutes of the presbytery is brief:

> Forasmekill as Euphame Lochoir in Craill is suspect of witschcraft the presbyterie ordanis everie minister to try the same sa far as thai can and speaciallie the Session of Craill to be diligent in trying the sad matter.[13]

We do not know how diligent the session at Crail was; no other names, however, appear in regard to witchcraft within the presbytery's records for this year. The cases involving Nans Murit in Abdie and Euphame Lochoir in Crail occurred in March and May respectively – months before the panic that has come to be known as the North Berwick witch-trials occurred.

Several cases from the mid-1590s seem to be unconnected. In 1593 the presbytery asked Nichol Dalgleish, the minister at Pittenweem, to investigate the 'secreit and quyet dealing of Janot Loquohor' who was a suspected witch.[14] Jonet Lochequoir (note the different spelling) appears again two years later in a list of condemned witches in St. Andrews parish. Jonet, Elspeth Gilchrist, and Agnes Melvill were all referred to as condemned witches.[15] What is interesting is that the minute of the kirk session lists these names in passing. The concern is with those who have been consulting with these women. The consulters, Isobelle Anelle and others, were named and sentenced to make 'public humilia-tion' for their actions in consulting the condemned. At least in some of these cases it seems the women were seeking the 'witch' in order to obtain a cure for their spouse. All made the required repentance. It seems possible, perhaps likely, that Janot and Jonet were the same individual. This possibility is strengthened by the fact that Agnes Melville is known from the secondary literature as the 'witch of Anstruther' whose case dates from 1588.[16] This record in the kirk session minute of St. Andrews may signify a clearing up of all the consulting known to have taken place with various area witches who had previously been executed. No distinction was made in the mind of the session between curse and cure, between black and white magic.

The national hunt, 1597–98

The year 1597 has long been recognised as a year of a major witch-hunt which extended throughout the regions of Scotland. In Fife, this hunt affected the Presbyteries of Kirkcaldy and St. Andrews. (See Map 12) The events in the latter began in May of 1597 and surrounded a known warlock (the term is used in the original records) by the name of David Zeman. Zeman had been passing 'throughout the cuntrie to do curis' when he was apprehended and imprisoned. His imprisonment however had not prevented people from continuing to consult with and seek cures from him. In response, the presbytery sent two of its members, David Monepenny and James Melville, to go with the prior of Pitten-weem to put Zeman to the knowledge of an assize and also to try those who had consulted with him 'and with the rest of the witches'.[17] Two weeks later Melville and the prior reported 'that the bailzeis of Pitten-weime had confessit that thai had giwin license to Walter Gourlay to tak Zeiman to his sonne'. The presbytery was not pleased that an incarcerated warlock had been allowed by the bailies to visit someone's son! The bailies and Gourlay were ordered to appear before the next presbytery.[18]

The search for those who had consulted with Zeman continued, then spread to involve the other suspected witches. At the May 26 meeting of the presbytery the members were asked how diligent they had been in seeking out those who had consulted witches. A list was given of individuals from Crail, Kilrenny and Carnbee. Included in the list of those from Kilrenny was Beatrix Adie.[19] When Adie appeared along with Thomas Watson at the next meeting of the presbytery, it soon became clear that Adie herself was suspected as a witch:

> the said Thomas confessit that he passit to David Zeman hawing the milk tane fra his kow and desyrit him to go to Beatrix Adie and ask his kowis milk agane in godis name and so that milk was restorit agane.[20]

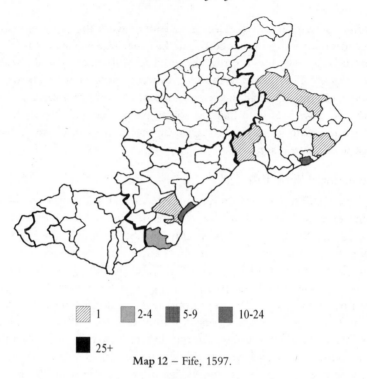

1   2-4   5-9   10-24

25+

Map 12 – Fife, 1597.

David Zeman's role in the eyes of the local populace as someone who could deduce who was responsible for a bewitchment was confirmed by the testimony of Walter Gourlay. He stated that he did not seek Zeman in order to make use of any cures, but to have him 'tryit whiddir giff ane Margaret Smyth at Balcormo Myln had bewitchit his sonne or not'. Zeman confirmed Gourlay's fears: Smith was the witch responsible for his son's illness.[21] Over the next two meetings others were also charged with consulting. One of these individuals, Catherine Smyth in Kilrenny, went to Zeman and again was told that it was Bettie Adie who was responsible for her troubles. She was told to confront Adie and ask for 'thair helth in godis name, quhilk shoe did and so became weill'.[22] As a result of this investigation David Zeman, Jonnett Willeamsoun, Jonnett Foggow and Beatrix Forgesoun were sent to an assize charged with various points of 'witchcraft, charmerie, consultation, and murther be witchcraft'; those found guilty of consulting were barred from the benefits of the church until they had shown repentance deemed acceptable by their various church sessions.[23] It seems reasonable to assume that those accused as witches were among those 'many witches' executed at St. Andrews around this time.[24]

The presbytery's concern quickly turned from specific witches and consulters in their midst to the behaviour of one of their members, Nichol Dalgleish, the minister of Pittenweem. On July 7 Dalgleish informed the presbytery that the crown agent had asked him for the extract of the depositions against the witches who had been burned at St. Andrews. On the advice of his session, he gave this information.[25] Two weeks later Dalgleish informed the same body that he had been 'chargit with letteris of horning' or been outlawed for supposedly withholding information on those accused as suspected witches, a charge which he denied.[26] Dalgleish's problems continued. The visitation of his session in October produced various allegations against him, including the suggestion that he was not diligent enough in seeking out the known witch Fritte Grutter within his parish. Fritte Grutter (or Cutter) had been known as a witch seven years prior to her death and been consulted by one Thomas Martin, a fact Dalgleish was charged with being aware of and yet doing nothing about.[27] Another charge levelled against him was holding back depositions against witches and thus the 'cloiking of that horrible syne'.[28]

Amidst their concerns regarding the behaviour of Nichol Dalgleish, the presbytery continued other action against witches. Suspected witches were discovered in the parish of Largo in early August and several ministers were dispatched to examine the accused women.[29] Later in the month a public fast and humiliation day was declared because of God's judgements evidenced in not only the 'pestilince and famine' affecting the presbytery, but 'also of the discoverie of the gryt empyre of the devill in this contrey be witchcraft'.[30] As concerned as they were for the growth of evil, the presbytery had certain cautions. On September 1, 1598 they appealed to the King for him to cease travelling around the country with a witch (apparently in order to determine who other witches might be). The witch being referred to was probably Margaret Atkin of Balweary, who was exposed as a fraud by the end of the year.[31]

The concern for witches within St. Andrews presbytery continued into 1598. In July of that year the presbytery began the search for one Patrick Stewart, alias Prich, who was suspected of being a witch. The formal accusation made in August against Stewart included no references to demonic pacts and indeed was fairly cautious. The charge was that Stewart had been involved in

> abusing and deceawing of the people, superstioun, scharming, professing of those thingis that giff they be done and practisit indeed is witchcraft.[32]

Popular belief in the power of such charms can be seen by the fact that at the same time the presbytery was considering the case of Patrick Stewart, one of the ministers, Nichol Dalgleish, asked the presbytery what penalty should be ascribed to those found guilty of seeking charms or cures. The advice was that those who consulted with known witches should 'satisfie as ane adulterer and the tym of continnowance to be according to thair repentance'.[33]

Indeed it was a confession by Alesoun Peirie in October 1598 that she had consulted with Geillis Gray, a suspected witch, which led to a very unique incident in Fife. Advice was sought by the laird of Lathocker. The presbytery desired more information and asked every minister to 'mak intimatioun of thair parochineris giff they had anything agains the said Alesoun and Geillis'.[34] These and subsequent actions by the presbytery seem to have been inadequate for the laird. Andrew Duncane, the minister at Crail, reported at the end of February 1599 that the laird had come and taken the suspected witch Geillis out of his custody 'and careit hir to his place of Lathocker and thair torturit hir, whairby now sho is become impotent and may not labour for hir living as sho wes wond'. Duncane sought advice on what should be done next.[35] Clearly the laird of Lathocker treated the suspect brutally and tortured her. What should be recognised, is that there is no evidence of a commission or that this torture was part of a judicial process. Even the presbytery seems taken aback by what occurred. (Given that they had participated in the execution of several accused witches the year previous, such a reaction is worth noting.)

Isolated cases: 1603–20

A brief lull in witch-hunting ended in October 1603 when the minister of Largo, Johne Auchinlek, asked the presbytery for assistance in examining a suspected witch. After a delay caused by weather, Janet Small appeared before the presbytery on December 15.[36] Janet confessed, claiming she had done all at the direction of Agnes Anstruther; unfortunately, the specific charges to which she confessed, all included in the delations, are not recorded.[37] Agnes was summoned to the next meeting, but failed to appear. Her husband did and claimed his wife was ill. Those in whom the presbytery was interested had also expanded to include Beatrix and Christen Traillis.[38] Christen apparently never appeared, but one week later Agnes, Beatrix and Janet were all 'confrontit and seweralie examined as ther particular depositionis bearis'.[39] The investigation continued, including the calling of a witness from the parish of 'Petmoge' to testify against Janet Small. In October of 1604, Janet was again being called to appear before the presbytery to answer charges.[40] Her fate is unknown.

The next indication of witch-hunting in this part of Fife comes over a decade later. In January of 1620 a commission was granted naming Margaret Wod, already in custody in Crail as a suspected witch. The commission noted that her guilt 'seems established 'by mony pregnant presumptionis, lykliehoodis, and circumstances of hir tryall and examinatioun'.[41] The same situation faced Marjorie Pattersone, an 'indweller' of Crail, four years later. Long suspected as a witch, she was held in the tolbooth. Named in both commissions are the bailies and a Sir James Lermond of Balcolmie.[42] A similar commission was granted against Margaret Callender to the bailies of St. Andrews and other individuals, in January, 1630.[43] The early period of the witch-hunt in this presbytery involved sporadic, generally isolated accusations against suspected witches.

A major hunt: 1643–45

The major hunt that affected St. Andrews Presbytery occurred in the period from 1643 to 1645. A major witch-hunt had begun in Dunfermline in January 1643. During this year the hunt spread throughout Scotland but the major area involved remained Fife. Our first indication that something significant was occurring in St. Andrews Presbytery comes in the minutes of the presbytery in August of 1643. The presbytery appointed three members to try to have the judge and bailies in Anstruther delay the execution of 'some witches' so that the appointed delegates may speak with them.[44] At the beginning of its next meeting, the presbytery stated:

> It is thought fitting, that ministers within this Presbyterie doe advertise the Presbyterie befor any witches with them be put to execution.[45]

The implication seems to be that the minister of Anstruther was at the very least aware of what was occurring in his parish. The presbytery wanted to become involved. Delegations were established at that same meeting, some to go to Anstruther Wester to witness the execution of 'some witches' and others to try to speak to witches who had been apprehended at Anstruther Easter and Crail.[46] This pattern was repeated at the next meeting, only this time those to be questioned prior to execution were from St. Andrews.[47] A delegation of three was again sent to Anstruther Wester to confer with those apprehended as witches. At the same time they were to give advice to the judge as to whether there was enough evidence against Isobell Dairsie for incarcerating and trying her.[48] Delegations were sent to St. Andrews to speak to the apprehended witches and 'sie if they can bring them to any confession'[49] and to Crail in order to give advice as to whether or not there was enough evidence to apprehend and try two suspected witches.[50]

Thus by early September, the presbytery of St. Andrews was involved in a full fledged witch-hunt, a witch-hunt which while not begun by the presbytery, clearly had its support and interest. The continual sending of delegations to try to bring witches to confession and/or give advice as to whether or not there was enough evidence demonstrates this interest. The way in which Isobell Dairsie's name enters the record gives support to the suspicion that the ministers were seeking through these inter-rogations to discover the names of other 'witches'. From the fragmentary evidence it also seems that Isobell was poor and without either means or family who would pay her costs while she was imprisoned.[51] The presbytery was aware that the forces let loose in this hunt had potential dangers including the naming of the innocent. At the September 6 meeting, the presbytery declared that it had been informed

> that ther be some quo slander these for witches, against quhom ther is neither presumption nor dilation, appoints such to be censured by the Sessions quher they remaine, as most notorious slanderers. As also ordaines such as conceales any presumption of any quho are apprehended, qhuen it shall come to light. They are apponted to be censured by Sessions also.[52]

That the latter concern, the withholding of information against suspected witches, was as serious as the potential slander of innocent women seems clear from an incident that occurred at the same meeting. A man was brought before the court and charged with riding upon the Lord's day. His claim that he was merely riding to communion was dismissed, as he was in fact riding in order to gain Lord Burghley's support in having his wife Margaret Balfour, who was one of the women held as a witch, set free. He was found guilty of breaking the sabbath and ordered to obey whatever punishment was determined by his session.[53] The presbytery also sought in January of 1644 to have the government grant a general commission for the 'apprehending trying and judging of such as are or selbe delated for witches within the sherrifdom'.[54] This would have allowed them to proceed to try and execute suspects without seeking commissions for each individual.

Delegations continued in the latter part of 1643 and into 1644 both to attend executions and give advice. In October one was sent to give advice at Anstruther Wester and attend executions in Crail.[55] In January a delegation went to meet with judges at Pittenweem, give advice regarding Christian Dote in St. Monans, and attend the execution of Isobell Dairsie[56] while in February another was sent to meet the judges at Silverdyke in relation to Margaret Myrton, to give advice regarding the watching of Christian Dote, as well as confronting some of those already suspected as witches.[57] In July a delegation attended the execution of some witches in Pittenweem.[58] The hunt continued throughout the year and into 1645, although the pace seems definitely to have shifted. By May of that year a suspect was imprisoned in St. Andrews whose last name was Sewis. The Synod's recommendation was that she be put to the knowledge of an assize.[59] In August, Jonet Wylie found herself accused in the parish of Largo.[60] In November the bailies and clerk of Pittenweem asked the presbytery's advice in the case of Christian Roch. Christian's suspicious behaviour had been the subject of rumour and conjecture (a *'fama clamora'*) for over twenty years. She was accused as a witch by three individuals who had been executed as witches. Also, the hangman had examined her and found 'two markes' on her body. The difficulty seems to have been that Roch's husband, Andro Strang, continued to fight to have her set free. Presbytery's advice was that she remain imprisoned until 'further tryell'.[61] Roch remained incarcerated for a lengthy period. In October of 1645, Andro Strang continued to plead that his wife be released. The presbytery's response, having seen the charges against her, was that she should be put to trial.[62] The final case from this period involved Androw Carmichael, a warlock from the parish of Dunino, who was incarcerated at St. Andrews. In contrast to Christian Roch, he was set at liberty on caution to return again if called.[63]

The hunt that swept through this presbytery in the period from 1643 to 1645 was clearly significant. Accurate numbers of those involved are impossible to ascertain. Still, we know that five parishes were affected in 1643, six in 1644 and two parishes in 1645. Executions occurred in 1643 in Anstruther-Wester, Crail, and St. Andrews of at least six individuals. The next year saw Isobell Dairsie executed at Anstruther-Wester, and an unknown number executed at Pittenweem. The presbytery served as a clearinghouse for information as well as being actively involved in trying to bring the accused to confession (and one assumes, name other witches). While the presbytery records give an overall sketch of the hunt which occurred in this period, local records for Pittenweem flesh out further details not recorded in the minutes of the presbytery. Before turning to those records, brief mention should be made of an accusation which emerged as a result of the witch-hunt. On February 21, 1644 an accusation against Alexander Baton appeared before the Presbytery. Baton had been accused of committing adultery by Bessie Mason, one of the witches from Kilrenny, an act which she claimed was the first cause of her slide into witchcraft. Baton had promised to appear to answer the accusation, but went instead to Edinburgh and stayed there until his accuser had been burned. Baton was ordered to appear at the next presbytery meeting. The incident eventually came to the attention of the synod of Fife.[64]

The burgh records from Pittenweem make it clear that the witch-hunt was well on its way by the time presbytery became involved in August. It is also clear that John Melvin the minister of Pittenweem was very aware of what was occurring. An excerpt from the meeting of July 31, 1643 is worth quoting at length:

> The quhilk day, for the better tryal of the witches presently apprehended, to the effect they may be the better watchit and preservit from information from their friends, it is ordanit that ane of the bailies or counsell sall ever be present at the taking off and putting on of the watches, three several times in the 24 hours, and sall injoyn the watches silence; and sall appoint the ablest man of the watch to command the watch until his return. The same day the bailies and clerk, or any twa of them, with concurrence of the minister, are ordainit to try and examine ye witches privately, and to keep their deposition secret, because heretofore, so soon as ever they did dilait any, presently the partie dilaittit got knowledge thereof, and thereby was presently obdurate, at least armit, for defence.[65]

There is a further reference to the watch from May of 1644, indicating that three constables and two watchmen were to be appointed every twenty-four hours. The number of watchmen and the isolation of the women and the demand for silence suggest that what was occurring was some form of waking or sleep deprivation. What is clear is that evidence was being gathered against incarcerated witches in such a manner that they were not to know or be able to defend themselves from that information.

Other information, including at least the names of the husbands and relations of those executed, can be found in the burgh records. An execution of an unspecified number of witches took place on August 8, 1643. Forty or fifty of the 'ablest young men of the toune' were put in arms for the execution.[66] Expenses for the executions soon came due. John Dawson paid £40 (Scots) to the burgh for the expenses involved in the execution of his wife. Thomas Cook paid £5 sterling for the execution of his mother Margaret Horsbrugh. Similar amounts were paid by John Crombie, Archbald Wanderson and Thomas Wanderson all for the execution of their wives.[67] In addition, a fine of fifty merks was levied on George Hedderick 'being found guilty of giving evil advice' to his mother-in-law Margaret Kingow, who was incarcerated as a suspected witch.[68] It is not specified what kind of 'evil advice' Hedderick had given, but the fact that such a fine was levied, combined with the earlier attempts to isolate the suspects from their friends, makes it clear that every attempt was being made to produce confessions and executions.

Another source gives us a final glimpse into the events in St. Andrews Presbytery during this witch-hunt. The source is the confession of Agnes Wallace in Crail, who confessed to being a witch in October, 1643:

> being in vard as ane vitch, vas demandit how long since sche entrit the Devillis service, sche ansuerit, that as sche thought about thrie or four and fourtie yeiris; for sche being as sche supposit, vea witchit be vmq Margaret Wood her mother . . .[69]

As has already been mentioned, a commission against Margaret Wood of Crail had been issued in 1621. Some of those implicated during the witch-hunt in 1643 were children of others previously accused as witches. At the same time, it should be noted that Agnes was not a young woman: she had, after all, been in the 'Devillis service' for forty-three or four years. It is unfortunate that the fragmentary evidence of this significant witch-hunt does not allow us to determine to what extent other suspects were similar to Agnes.

Later cases: 1650–1704

During the English occupation only one case, that of Maggie from St. Monans, is known. Maggie was accused of being in compact with the Devil and with doing many evil deeds. She was watched using a horn and goad in order to keep her awake in a successful attempt to get her to confess. Maggie was executed.[70] The great witch-hunt which occurred a decade later following the Restoration, affected only the border parish of Forgan within the presbytery of St. Andrews. In 1662 commissions were obtained to put Elizabeth Clow and Jonnet Annand, both of whom had confessed their guilt, to trial.[71] It seems reasonable, given the major hunt in Perth at the time and the fact that some of the same commissioners obtained other commissions to try witches in Perthshire,[72] to suggest this hunt had only a peripheral connection with the rest of the presbytery. In 1664 a commission was granted to try Margaret Guthrie of Carnbee. Guthrie had already been imprisoned in the tolbooth in Anstruther Wester and was, according to the commission, suspected as guilty. Her commission includes the notation that her confession should be voluntary, 'without any sort of torture or indirect meanes used to bring her to confession'.[73] The same formula again appears in the commission taken out against Isobell Key of St. Andrews in September 1666. Isobell was a prisoner in the tolbooth.[74]

A case which occurred in Crail in 1675 contained more information than was usually included in commissions. On July 21, 1675 Dr. Edwards the minister of Crail asked presbytery's advice in the case of Geilles Robertsone who had been imprisoned in that burgh as a suspected witch. A delegation was established to speak to her, which reported in August, and again in September, that she had not confessed. Considering her 'former confessions' and the fact that her daughter and the sister of her son–in–law have all testified against her, this seemed remarkable to the members of presbytery. None of Geilles' conversations were successful in clearing her name and she was considered to have been responsible for making at least one individual ill. The presbytery considered that there were sufficient grounds to gain a commission and appointed the minister to speak to the magistrates of the town. At this point, things bogged down. There were no actual magistrates in Crail. The presbytery's response was to suggest 'that it was a duetie incoment upon the honnest men of the toune to seik a commissioun, as is the use and custome in such caices quher ther is no magistrats'.[75] Edwards claimed to have obeyed the presbytery, but there is no indication that a commission was being sought before Geillis Robertson died in prison in December.[76]

Summary

The final cases to appear in this presbytery are unique enough to be worthy of a discussion of their own in chapter 9. In 1701, Elizabeth Dick of the parish of Anstruther Easter was accused of witchcraft.[77] Three years later a significant hunt occurred in Pittenweem. Suffice it for the moment to say that in the period 1704–05 accusations of witchcraft involving ten individuals occurred.[78] While the witch–hunt in St. Andrews Presbytery was very lengthy, extending from 1563 into the early eighteenth century, there were really only three hunts, 1597 (before the national hunt), 1643–45, and a final panic in Pittenweem in 1704. The other incidents involved isolated suspects or a handful of accused. While there is evidence of torture being illegally applied in one instance, there is no evidence of judicial torture having been a factor. Indeed, there are several incidents where the more effective technique of 'warding and watching' was effectively used in order to obtain confessions. The role of church courts in hearing cases, passing along information and otherwise contributing to the witch–hunt was significant in this part of Fife.

Notes

1. The *Fasti*, vol. 5, lists the parishes. Anstruther Easter was separated from Kilrenny in 1641. Cameron was divided from St. Andrews in 1646. Kingsbarns was 'disjoined' from Crail in 1632. Pittenweem did not officially become a parish until 1633,

although there is a record of ministers serving from 1588 on. None of these alterations are significant for the geographical study of this area.

2. The estimated population is from Jane Dawson, ''The Face of Ane Perfyt Reformed Kyrk', 414.

3. Cases 2219 and 2221. Chalmers, *Domestic Annals*, vol. 1, 60. Black, *Calendar*, 21.

4. Chambers, *Domestic Annals*, vol. 1, 60. Stewart's death is discussed in connection with that of a Frenchman who was hanged. It all depends on how one reads the reference: 'and a Frenchman callit Paris, wha was ane of the devisers of the king's death, was hangit in Sanctiandrois, and with him William Stewart, Lyon King of Arms, for divers points of witchcraft and necromancy.' Does the 'hangit' refer to both men, or only Paris?

5. Case 2220; for Dundee witches, 3087, SWHDB. –, *Diurnal of Remarkable Occurrents* (Edinburgh: Maitland Club, 1833), 145; Chambers, *Domestic Annals*, vol. 1, 60. Black, *Calendar*, 21.

6. Cases 3035 and 3032 respectively. The SBSW lists Gilmore's thesis in regard to both of these cases. Sharp was accused of being a witch in Kirkton's *History of the Church of Scotland 1660–79* (c. 1693), Ralph Stewart, ed. (Lewiston, N.Y.: Edwin Mellen, 1992), 45. Adamson, also a minister and later an archbishop, was charged with being a consulter of witches and his case investigated by both Session and General Assembly. David Calderwood, *The history of the Kirk in Scotland*, III, Thomas Thomson, ed. (Edinburgh: Wodrow Society, 1849), 176. Kirkton also accused the episcopalian curate of Anstruther of being a witch (case 3034): 'some suspect he medled with the devil, and he was known to have a brother that was a diabolick man.' Kirkton, *History*, 108.

7. Richard Bannatyne, *Journal of the Transactions in Scotland during the contest between the adherents of Queen Mary and those of her Son* (Edinburgh: J. Ballantyne, 1806), 339.

8. Rev. C.J. Lyon, *History of St. Andrews, Episcopal, Monastic, Academic and Civil*, (Edinburgh: William Tait, 1843), 338. J. Melville, *The autobiography and diary of Mr. James Melville*, ed. Robert Pitcairn (Edinburgh: Wodrow Society), 1842. 46. Knox's role in the matter was turned into a play entitled 'God's Law' which was performed in St. Andrew's during the summer of 1994.

9. *The Concise Scots Dictionary.* Maira Robertson, ed. (Aberdeen: Aberdeen University Press, 1987).

10. Case 2223. Source: St. Andrews Kirk session records, 1559–1600 in St. Andrews University Library, Muniments department; David Hay Fleming, *Register of the ministers and elders . . . vol. 1* (Edinburgh: Scottish History Society, 1889), 414. The date of this case has been corrected from 1575 to 1576. While the date of the minute does say 1575, this was obviously a scribal error because minutes for 1576 surround it on both sides.

11. Ibid. The SBSW lists her fate as Miscellaneous.

12. Case 2225. St. Andrews KS; Fleming, *Register*, 455.

13. Case 3091. Smith, *A Study and Annotated edition*, 51. St. Andrews Presbytery minutes Vol. 1., 1586–1605, St. Andrews Muniments..

14. Case 3092. Smith, 120.

15. Kirk Session Records, St. Andrews Muniments department, Sept 10, 1595. Also, Fleming, *Register*, vol 2., 800.

16. Stephanie Stevenson, *Anstruther: A history* (Edinburgh: John Donald, 1989), 117. She suggests Agnes Melville was the elder daughter of the late Andrew Melville, once reader at the church in Anstruther. Harry D. Watson, *Kilrenny and Cellardyke* (Edinburgh: John Donald, 1986), refers to Agnes as 'the witch of Anstruther', 37.

17. Zeman is case 3093. Presbytery meeting of May 5, 1597. Smith, *Annotated Edition*, 221.
18. May 19, 1597. Smith, *Annotated Edition*, 222.
19. Ibid., May 26, 1597, 222.
20. Ibid., June 2, 1597, 222–23.
21. Ibid.
22. Bettie or Beatrix Adie (3097) is mentioned twice by others. However, she is not included in the list of those given over to the assize by the June 9 meeting of presbytery. Meetings of June 9, June 16, Smith, *Annotated Edition*, 222–24.
23. June 9, 1597. Beatrix Forgesoun (3096); Jonnet Foggow (1597); Jonet Willeamson (3097). As no other location is known for these individuals, it is assumed they were from Pittenweem. The sentence for those found guilty of consulting was passed on June 30, 1597. Ibid., 224. Graham, *Uses of Reform*, 304, refers to Fogow.
24. 'Many Witches' (2294) in the SBSW. Original source is the Calendar of State Papers, PPS, v2, 739. The Kirk Session records for St. Andrew's do not list any cases of witchcraft from that parish. Kirk Session minutes, St. Andrews muniments.
25. July 7, 1597. Smith, *Annotated Edition*, 224.
26. July 21, 1597. Ibid., 228.
27. Fritte Grutter (3099). As Grutter was obviously dead by this time, she was never brought to trial. One of the few other details we do know is that she was poor. She apparently received 'toun almes' even though the session apparently knew of her reputation as a witch. October, 20, 1597. Smith, *Annotated Edition*, 242; also, October 6, 1597, 236.
28. Ibid.
29. August 3, 1597. Ibid., 229. Presbytery of St. Andrews, vol. 1, 82r.
30. August 17, 1597. Ibid., 231.
31. Fleming, *Register*, vol. 2, 800–01, footnote. Fleming makes the identification with Margaret Aitken.
32. Patrick Stewart (3100); July 20, 1598, Presbytery of St. Andrews minutes, vol. 1, f 93r; Smith, *Annotated Edition*, 271: August 3, 1598, 273.
33. July 13, 1598. Ibid., f 93r; Smith, *Annotated Edition*, 271; July 20, 1598, Ibid., f 93r; Smith, *Annotated Edition*, 272.
34. This case goes back to Black's *Calendar*. It is listed as 2312 in the SBSW. The date, however, is given as 1599, when the case appears a second time before the Presbytery. There is also some confusion as to which source is being cited. Black cites the source as the '*Register of St. Andrews Presbytery*'. The SBSW abbreviates this down to the 'Reg. St. And. Pres.' yet in the list of abbreviations, this abbreviation is said to refer to *Selections from the minutes of the Presbyteries of St. Andrews and Cupar 1641–98*, the Abbotsford Club volume which obviously covers a period far later. The printed source to look at is Smith, *Annotated Edition*, 283. October 6, 1598, Presbytery of St. Andrews Minutes, vol. 1, f95r.
35. February 22, 1599. Ibid., 96v; Smith, *Annotated Edition*, 290.
36. Case 3102. October 20, 1603. Smith, *Annotated Edition*, 376. December 8, 381. December 15, 382.
37. December 15, 1603. Presbytery of St. Andrews minutes, vol. 1, f120v. Smith, *Annotated Edition*, 382.
38. December 22, 1603. Smith, *Annotated Edition*, 383. Alexander Martyne's name is also mentioned as someone to be summoned, but it is clear from the next meeting he was

called as a witness. 'Siclyk compeirit Alexander Marene quhais depositioun is with the rest.' December 29, 1603. Beatrix Traillis (3104). Cristen Traillis (3105).

39. Ibid., 383. December 29, 1603.

40. January 12, 1604; January 26, 1604, Ibid., 385. October 11, 1604, 417.

41. Margaret Wod, (940). RPC. vol. 12, 412. The SBSW does include one case from 1618, that of Bessie Finlayson in Logie. The reference is to Ferguson's article on Bibliographic notes on Scottish witchcraft: John Ferguson, 'Bibliographical Notes on the Witchcraft Literature of Scotland,' *Proceedings of the Edinburgh Bibliographical Society* 3 (1884), Reprinted in *Articles on Witchcraft,* Vol 7, *Witchcraft in Scotland,* 87. Nothing related to Bessie Finlayson was discovered here.

42. Marjorie Pattersone (1022). RPC, 2nd ser. vol. 1, 108.

43. Margaret Callander (1310). *Register of the Privy Council,* 2nd ser. vol. 3, 426. Little is known of Callander, as her commission lists the commissioners, but then states that it is of the same date, 'tennour and subscriptiouns of the former' (a commission for Aberdeen witches). Some of the phrases, thus seem very formulaic, including the notion that the individual had 'long been suspected' of witchcraft.

44. Case 3107. August, 1643. STACUPR, 13.

45. August 16, 1643. STACUPR, 13.

46. Cases 3108, 3109, 3110. August 13, 1643. STACUPR, 13. It should be noted that some of these cases may be duplicates. Also, other names appear later in the records. These women might have been included at this point under the vague phrase 'some witches'. At the same meeting another delegation is sent to Leuchars to investigate some 'monuments to superstition' in the house of Pitcullo.

47. The two executed witches are cases 3111 and 3112. The apprehended witches, 3113. August 23, 1643. STACUPR, 13, 14.

48. Isobell Dairsie (3037 and 3040). August 30, 1643. STACUPR, 14. Gilmore, *Witchcraft and Church of Scotland,* 156, 397. The SBSW notes her location as St. Andrews.

49. Ibid. At the same meeting Presbytery asked Lord Burghley for orders to demolish the suspicious monuments.

50. Cases 3115, 3116. September 6, 1643. STACUPR, 14.

51. The judges asked Presbytery in October for advice on how Isobell 'salbe used in meate, drinke, sleepe, bead, and the lyke.' October 11, 1643. STACUPR, 15.

52. September 6, 1643. STACUPR, 14.

53. Margaret Balfour (2445). September 6, 1643. STACUPR, 14. The case is briefly mentioned in Lyons, *History of St. Andrews,* vol. 2, 18.

54. January 11, 1644. STACUPR, 17.

55. October 11, 1643. Delegation to Crail to attend executions and give advice. STACUPR, 15.

56. January 11, 1644. Presbytery of St. Andrews minutes, Ch2\MSdeposit\23, 48. STACUPR, 17. January 17, 1644. The delegation reported back that there was enough evidence to apprehend and try Dote. January 24, 1644. Delegation to attend execution of Isobell Dairsie at Anstrther; recommendation to put Dote on trial. STACUPR, 17–18.

57. February 7, Margaret Myrton (3042). Originally the accusation was one of consulting. Advice re: watching of Christane Done 'and her dyett of sleepe, bed, meate and drinks.' In Pittenweem, STACUPR, 19. February 21st. Myrton is charged with both consulting and being a witch. Six are appointed to a 'confrontation' with Christian Dote (St. Monans) Margaret Balfour (St. Andrews) and Bettie Dote (Crail) (3118). STACUPR, 19.

58. July 3, 1644. STACUPR, 22
59. Case 2521. SYNFIFE, 141.
60. Case 3121. August 7, 1644. The record says parish of James McGill. McGill served as the minister of Largo. STACUPR, 22.
61. Case 2482. November 7, 1644. STACUPR, 23.
62. October 1, 1645. STACUPR, 32. October 8, 1645. STACUPR, 33.
63. Case 3122. November 8, 1645. STACUPR, 33.
64. The executed witch is case 3119. February 21, 1644. STACUPR, 21. Also, case 2487. The source is SYNFIFE, 139. The Synod minutes repeat the charge and state that Alexander should be 'putt to his oath.'
65. David Cook, *Annals of Pittenweem,* 49.
66. Ibid., 49.
67. The 'wife of John Dawson' is a duplicate record, case numbers 2450 and 2451. Margaret Horsburgh (2454). Wife of John Crombie, Janet Anderson (2455). Wife of Archibald Wanderson (2472), and of Thomas Wanderson (2473). Ibid., 49–50.
68. Ibid., 49. Kingow is case 2453; her fate is not known.
69. Agnes Wallace (2466). The confession continues to list other names, but it is difficult to determine the context. She was sent to these various individuals, but whether to recruit them, or because her mother had been executed or because she was ill remains unclear. The confession is included in a footnote within John Lamont's diary, in the context of a general discussion of witchcraft in Fife. Lamont, *Diary,* 6.
70. Case 3218. J.E. Simpkins, *Examples of Printed Folklore concerning Fife . . . County Folklore,* vol. VII (London: Sidgwick & Jackson, 1914), 96.
71. Cases 1692 and 1693. RPC, 3rd Ser, vol. 1, 208.
72. There was a major witch-hunt in Perth in the year 1662, numbering 55 cases. The commissioners also received commissions to try Jonet Robe (1714), Jonet Martin (1713) and four others all from Perth, as well as Issobel McKendley (1708), Elspeth Reid (1707), and seven others, again all of whom the SBSW lists as being from Perthshire, 132–133. RPC 3rd Ser vol. 1, 208. The SBSW misses the name of Agnes Husone, also of Dunning parish. The parishes are listed in the commissions. Given the fact that there was also a major hunt in Cupar presbytery at the same time. Forgan was surrounded by witch-hunting.
73. Case 1836. RPC, 3rd ser, vol. 2, 165.
74. Case 1842. RPC, 3rd ser, vol. 2, 246.
75. Case 2903. The minutes are from July 21, August 18, September 11, September 15, 1675. STACUPR, 90–91. Also there is notation of this case in Gilmore, 138. While this discussion was occurring at Presbytery, there does not appear to be any references in the kirk session records. St. Andrew's Muniments, CH2\CRAIL\1.
76. Minutes of September 29, and December 27. STACUPR, 91.
77. Case 2976. Kirk Session records, CH2\625\2 St. Andrews Muniments, 246–47.
78. The names associated with this case include Isobel Adam (2998) a Mrs. White (2989), Margaret Jack (3127), Margaret Wallace (3126), Lillias Wallace (3125), Janet Horseburgh (3124), Janet Corphat or Cornfoote (3001, also duplicated as 2990), Nicholas Lawson (3000) – despite the name, a woman – Beatrix Laing (2998) and Thomas Lawson. The SBSW records two other cases of witchcraft in Pittenweem in 1709, but this author could not track down the references: Nicolas Lawson (872) and Betty Laing (873). The SBSW cites D\228, the Circuit Court Minute Book.

CHAPTER SIX

The Witch-Hunt in the Presbytery of Kirkcaldy

An area of rolling hills and coast, of coal fields and salt pans, the presbytery of Kirkcaldy sits in the centre of Fife, bordering on all of the other presbyteries and occupying the south-central sea coast. The presbytery included major burghs at Kirkcaldy, Burntisland, Dysart, and Kinghorn. Kirkcaldy was a significant trading port and burgh with an estimated population for it and the surrounding parish of over 3,000 people in this period.[1] The presbytery itself contained fifteen parishes. The only change within the presbytery in this period was the creation of the parish of Abbotshall in 1650, which brought together areas that formerly had been parts of Kinghorn and Kirkcaldy parishes. The presbytery itself dated its origins to 1593 although presbytery minutes survive only from the 1630's, with a major gap existing for the period from 1653 to 1688. The presbytery was united with Dunfermline Presbytery from 1692 until the close of the seventeenth century, a time of limited witch-hunting.[2]

The national hunt: 1597–98

Witch-hunting arrived in this area of Fife, seemingly out of nowhere, during the national hunt of 1597. In that year eighteen of the twenty-six known cases from Fife occurred in this presbytery: fifteen in Kirkcaldy, two in Burntisland and one in Abbotshall. (See Map 12) At the centre of some of the cases throughout Scotland was Margaret Atkin of Abbotshall,[3] also known as the witch of Balweary, whose career as a witch-finder was mentioned in Chapter 5. Also sometime during 1597 Janet Smyth of Burntisland was executed as a witch.[4] Records from this period are far from complete, both at the national and local levels. In August, Jonnett Finlasoun also of Burntisland was acquitted, yet the record of her case suggests that some kind of hunt was underway within this area. The information comes via her complaint to the Privy Council that despite the fact there was no evidence of witchcraft against her, the bailies of Burntisland continued to harass her. Some excerpts from her complaint are enlightening:

73

Map 13 – The parishes in Kirkcaldy Presbytery.

Parish	code	Parish	code
Abbotshall	1	Kinglassie	9
Auchterderran	2	Kirkcaldy	10
Auchtertool	3	Leslie	11
Ballingray	4	Markinch	12
Burntisland	5	Portmoak	13
Dysart	6	Scoonie	14
Kennoway	7	Wemyss	15
Kinghorn	8		

. . . [the bailies] haveing consavit ane haitrent and malis aganis the said complenair without any just caus of offens or injurie done be hir to thame, and thair only purpois and intention being to enriche thamesellfis with the said complenaris guidis and geir, thay have at divers tymes of lait, undir cullour of a commisioun of justiciarie grantit to thame aganis witcheis, takin and apprehendit the said complenair, and putt hir to the knawledge of ane assise for witch-craft.[5]

This harassment continued despite the fact when she had been brought before a panel no evidence could be proven against her. She had been acquitted, yet the bailies 'continewing in thair haitrent and malice aganis hir, intendis still to trouble hir for that cause' and bring her before another assize. The bailies were called to answer before the Privy Council, but as they did not appear, and Jonnet did, the decision to cease all further proceedings against her under the commission that had been granted was made.[6] The ability to travel to Edinburgh to make her case and the existence (and one would assume support) of her spouse, Patrik Murray, were factors in her favour.

While we can only speculate as to what was going on in Burntisland, it is clear that a significant witch-hunt was occurring in the parish of Kirkcaldy. On August 11, 1597 the burgh records note that Margaret Williamsone, Margaret Elder and Issobell Rannaldsone had all been accused of witchcraft. Cautioners (in two cases spouses, in the third case unclear) had come forward to guarantee they would appear at a trial.[7] Six days later, twelve more names were added.[8] The key may lie in the notation relating to Marion Rutherford, spouse to the baxter Alexander Scott. Marion had been declared a witch by 'Marion Kwyne, detector of wichcraft'.[9] The proximity of Kirkcaldy to Abbotshall, the parish from which Margaret Atkin originated, makes this reference all the more fascinating. It is unclear from this record whether any of these individuals were ever brought to trial. The fate of Janet Allen of Burntisland is far clearer. She was executed in 1598, indeed burned alive ('brunt quick'), after being accused and convicted of causing the death of the son of Robert Brown.[10]

Isolated cases: 1603–25

Sketchy references continue through the early decades of the seventeenth century. We have already noted that Janet Small in Largo stated in 1603 that she had done all of her alleged acts of witchcraft under the direction of Agnes Anstruther of Dysart.[11] The next year in Kirkcaldy a vagabond named Dorothy Oliphant was accused of being a sorcerer and of deceiving the people with her claims of being able to 'mend and cure sik paersonis as was bewtchit'. When presented for trial no evidence was found that she was a real witch. She was accused of using witchcraft, but found guilty of 'abusing of the peepil be formis of charms'. Her punishment was public confession at the burgh tron and she was ordered to stand there with a paper on her head which listed her offence, after which she was to be banished from the burgh and from the lands of the Lordship of Dunfermline.[12] In 1613 Agnes Anstruther again found herself in difficulty, this time in the burgh of Kirkcaldy. The dittays against her were to be forwarded to the Archbishop.[13] Apparently nothing further happened, for in 1614 a rebuke is recorded for those who have not forwarded the dittays. In that October, those with any interest in Agnes Anstruther and another witch, Isobell Jhonestoune, were instructed to confer with the Archbishop.[14]

Kirkcaldy witnessed other accused witches in this period, none of whom seems to have been punished severely. In May 1616 Helen Birrell appeared before the session and was ordered to make public repentance for the slander of witchcraft. The session minutes went on to state that the entire congregation needed to be warned that 'all those yat be convict of witchcraft, charmeing, consultation with witches, and such lyk slander, shall mak yair public repentance, and sall be punisit in yair persons be ye civil magistrate'.[15] Three years later, Isobel Hevrie was brought before the session for witchcraft. Hevrie made several appearances before the session before being referred to the presbytery for charming.[16] Two years later in February 1621 Alison Dick was warded in the steeple as a suspected witch. Alison Dick, who appeared again before the Session in 1623 and 1633, will be discussed at length when we consider the witches of Fife in chapter 9.[17] Finally, there is one recorded commission from this period, that issued in 1621 against Marioun Rutherford, a suspected witch who had already been apprehended and imprisoned in the tolbooth as a suspected witch.[18]

Two hunts: 1626–30

After this period of relative calm, a series of serious hunts broke out in 1626–27 and then again in 1630. The 1626–27 hunt involved a total of seventeen accused from the parishes of Wemyss, Dysart and Kirkcaldy. The overall shape of the hunt can be deduced from the commissions granted by the Privy Council: other sources help us to more fully create a picture of what was happening in this area. The first commission was granted on March 13, 1626, against Issobel Mawer of Wemyss who was being warded in the tolbooth.[19] Records from the kirk session of Kirkcaldy state that as of April 4, Janet Pirie, Janet Stark and Helen Birrell were all being warded in the church steeple.[20] On April 13, a commission was granted for one male and three female witches from Wemyss, all of whom were being held in the tolbooth and were said to have confessed. The commissioners were identical to those named in the March 16 commission.[21] Other commissions were granted to apprehend the widow Jonnet Dampstar of Wemyss in June 1626,[22] Elspett Neilsoun (or Wilson) and Annas Munk of Dysart in early September,[23] Helen

Wilsoun of Dysart in November,[24] Margaret Henderson of Wemyss in May 1627,[25] and Katherine Crystie, a widow from Dysart, in November of 1627.[26]

The contents of the commissions, the choice of phrase and those named in the commissions can give us some hints as to what was occurring. In this hunt, the same commissioners appear in many of the commissions, or they appeared in slightly different combinations. It should also be noted that the Archbishop of St. Andrews was involved in all of the commissions issued after June 20, 1626. It is significant that the wording of the commissions changes at this point and for the first time references to the Devil appear. For example, the commission granted against Jonnet Dampstar on June 20 states she had confessed to 'the renunceing of hir baptisme, ressaveing of the devills mark, and geving of hir soule and bodie over to the devillis service'.[27] The two commissions previous to this make no mention of the Devil or anything resembling a demonic pact.[28] Indeed the popular accusations from other sources suggest more common issues. The accusation was made that Janet had fought with a woman of the village, then come and used the woman's spinning wheel (apparently uninvited) and afterwards 'there came a *white ratton* at sundrie times and sat on his cow's back, so that thereafter the cow dwined away'.[29]

The notion that popular beliefs, rather than demonic pacts, were behind this hunt is similarly suggested by the information we have on Helen Birrell, one of the three women accused from Kirkcaldy. We have encountered Helen Birrell before, forced in 1616 to do public penance. Helen had a sharp tongue. William Melvill testified that he heard her chide Cornelius Wilson, saying the 'wiches tak ye and Christ from ye'. Wilson was not innocent in this dispute. He admitted to calling Birrell a 'witch carling' (derogatory, as in 'ugly old witch') and he would get a 'tarr bairill to burn her with'.[30] Other testimony suggests a level of animosity between Birrell and her neighbours. Janet Broune claimed Birrell had stated 'there are three ships set upon the stocks to be bilt, but your guidman will never get ane chappe (berth) upon any of them', a prediction (or curse) which came true. More surprising is the testimony of William Lamb who claimed to have overheard Birrell say 'ane muckle black man come into her house with cloven foote and buckles upon them' and had stayed for supper with her and her family. Helen denied this and the claim that she had said she was this man's 'tenant'. Other accusations were levelled, including the alleged cure of Abraham Thomson, but nothing could be proven. Still, Birrell and the others stayed in ward.[31]

Katherine Chrystie's complaint to the Privy Council about her prosecution also sheds light on these events.[32] She blamed her current situation on 'malicious and invyfull persouns, her unfreinds' which has led to a commission against her and her being warded in the Dysart tolbooth. The claim against her arose from David Clerk, a mariner from Dysart. When the charges were levelled she had him summoned before the presbytery of Kirkcaldy in order to have her name cleared:

> and they after narrow examination found her innocent, and ordained the said David Clerk to acknowledge his offence before the Session.[33]

She claimed this action in her own defence led to greater animosity, not only between her and David Clerk, but with his friends within the burgh 'namely Alexander Simsoun, bailie, his cousin, Mr. William Spitall one of the ministers', who was married to Simsoun's sister, and indeed most of the council. In her continued defence, she stated that not one of those executed at Dysart as witches had named her as either an accomplice or someone who had consulted them seeking aid. She asked to be set free on bond of caution and agreed to appear before a trial whenever called. Her request was granted. She was set free on £1000 caution, with her trial to take place before 'His Majesty's Justice and his deputes in the Tolbooth of Edinburgh'.[34] We do not know if this particular trial ever took place, but Katherine Chrystie had clearly come to be considered by at least some in her community as a witch. Oddly enough it is only as a result of her case that we have evidence that there were executions during this period in Dysart. Executions also seem to have taken place in Wemyss. Again, it is only through another record that we can deduce this. A letter was sent in June 1626 by the Privy Council to various officials in England to seek and return Elizabeth Ross of Wemyss. After being let out on caution, she fled to England. This may have been a wise move, as she had been named by several suspects, 'hir wicked consortis', prior to their execution.[35]

Three years later Dysart again witnessed a witch-hunt. Our first evidence of a hunt comes from a commission granted on March 11, 1630, naming Bessie Guiddale, William Broun, Helen Bissat, Janet Galbraith and Janet Scott as suspected witches.[36] The hunt spread over the parish boundary to Wemyss. Janet Wilkie of Wester Wemyss (the area closest to Dysart) was named in a commission dated March 20: the same commissioners are listed as in the March 11 commission, including the bailies of Dysart.[37] The complaint by Katherine Chrystie in March gives us some indication as to what was behind the hunt, as well as to the reality that others were also being sought. Katherine complained of her illegal imprisonment after two years of living a peaceful life. She maintained that the bailies were her enemies who have, 'at the instigation of their ministers', William Spittell and William Narne, had her placed in ward in the tolbooth. The complainant's son, David Yuile, acted on her behalf and she was set at liberty, on caution of £1000 to appear before the 'Lord High Justice' when charged.[38] In April David Geddie, spouse to the accused witch Janet Beverage, also complained on her behalf to the Privy Council. Although his wife had had a good reputation as 'ane honest woman and was never stained with that nor other suche wicked cryme' she had, based on information supplied to the ministers, been incarcerated in the tolbooth. David Geddie, a baker, appeared before the council as did the ministers and bailies of Dysart. The order was given to finish the trial and examination of Janet Beverage before the Council's next meeting.[39] On the same day the complaint was heard additional commissions were granted naming Alison Neving and Margaret Dawson,[40] and another was granted naming Elspet Watsoun in July.[41]

Scattered cases: 1632–42

The 1630's saw a scattering of cases among the various parishes. In 1632 the minister of Auchterderran, John Chalmer, informed the presbytery of Kirkcaldy of a stranger woman who haunted 'his Pariochin who was suspect of witchcraft'. The advice was to either throw her out of the parish or have her presented for trial.[42] Alison Dick and William Coke were charged with witchcraft in Kirkcaldy in 1633 and executed.[43] In May 1636 a case appeared before the presbytery which skirted that fine, difficult to determine, line between 'curing' and 'witchcraft'. William Hutchen, a braboner (weaver) from Kingorne confessed when 'challengit for cureing one in Kingorne of the fallen sickness be ane charme'. Hutchen declared he did not know this was an evil thing to do.[44] Sentence was passed at a presbytery meeting later in the month. He was

> ordained to acknowledg his fault upon Sunday nixt in Kingorne befoir the pulpett, and crave God and the congregation pardone thairfor with certification that if ever he salbe found to doe the lyk again, he salbe halden guiltie of the cryme of witchcraft and pursued thairfoir as for ane poynt of witchcraft.[45]

In April 1637 another male, John Patowne, was warded in the steeple of Dysart under suspicion of witchcraft and a call was issued from the pulpit for further information.[46]

The next July, 1638, Marion Grig was detained and warded in Dysart for 'certaine appeirances of witchcraft'.[47] Later at the same meeting it was noted that Christian Wilson and her daughters were to appear at the next meeting. When Christian and her eldest daughter Margaret Bannatyne of Kirkcaldy appeared they were confronted with allegations of witchcraft which they denied.[48] Intimation was made in the pulpits of the presbytery that anyone with evidence against Marion Grig should come forward. Her trial before the presbytery took place on August 9, 1638. Marion was accused of various points of *malefice*, in particular the ability to put on and remove various diseases. For example, when William Marshall's wife was pregnant and ill at home, Marion came to the house asking for the 4s 6d owed to her. She demanded it until harsh words were spoken, and Marion cursed Marshall's wife who immediately became 'extreme sick'. Marion was sent for, given the money owed her, and then asked for her forgiveness:

> and she forgave hir and prayed God to forgive her, and thairafter she being delyverit of ane bairne and not being as other women caused send for hir, and the said William went and brought hir, and she causit them to seik hir health for Gods saik, and she said God send hir health thryse, and she mended everie day thairafter.[49]

The story was confirmed by one Janet Reidie, who added that Marion Grig 'mumbled when she ged down the stair'. An extremely similar tale of illness following a refusal to repay money owed to Marion was told by James Rodger and his wife. Again Marion came and removed the illness, this time with the aid of a cloth which when told the pain was in his head and face she took and 'chapit (struck) ay his face'. More remarkable than these complaints was the sentence. The presbytery decided to have Marion placed in the stocks.[50] Still, she continued to be held in the steeple in Dysart in September 1638, but as 'nothing meriting death' could be demonstrated, she was ordered to do public penance and then be dismissed.[51]

The fate of Christian Wilson and her daughter(s) remains less clear. At the August 2, 1638 meeting of the presbytery Margaret Douglas declared she heard Wilson (or 'the woman that was in Cristian Wilsons house') tell another to 'Put in that in your bodies and sew it in and yee sall niver want'. The evidence of the other witnesses was held over to a later meeting.[52] In October 1638 the presbytery decided to ward Wilson and her daughters and seek further information against them.[53] Other women in this area also were charged during this period with various acts of *malefice* and were brought before the presbytery and dealt with as witches.

Janet Durie of Wemyss was accused in late 1638 and brought to trial in early 1639, after James Keddie charged her on his deathbed with bewitching him.[54] Also in 1639, Margaret Douglas of Kirkcaldy was accused of both curing and causing illness in livestock and people.[55] Margaret Lindsay of Kirkcaldy was charged with charming in 1640 for spitting in a child's face in order to cure the 'fallen sickness'.[56] Some individuals 'who ar alledgit to have used some witchcraft' in the parish of Kinglassie, were called to make their repentance in July 1642.[57] Finally, in that same year Margaret Wilson of Dysart was held in the steeple then released on caution when there was not enough evidence.[58] While there were no known executions during this period, a continued interest in the existence of 'witches' was obvious.

The hunt of 1643–44 in Kirkcaldy Presbytery

The year 1643, a year of major witch-hunting in Scotland as well as Fife, saw only a few cases in this part of Fife (See Map 14). In August, Katherine Chrystie of Dysart again found herself warded because of 'syndrie and divers presumptiouns of witchcraft'.[59] In October, Katherine Wallenge and Jonnet Smythe of Kinghorn were warded and examined. Smythe may have been warded but by February 27, 1644 the kirk session believed they had enough evidence against Katherine to have her put to trial. She was tried and executed on March 26, 1644.[60] One final detail which may be of note: Katherine had appeared in church courts ten years previously, accusing several people of slandering her husband as a thief. She was attempting to get the presbytery to force the session of Kinghorn to act on her behalf in this matter.[61] In December, 1643 'ane charmer' named Janet Brown was brought before the session at Markinch. She confessed that she had indeed used the words 'flesh to flesh, blood to blood and bone to bone in our Lord's name' to try to cure a foot. The word 'witch' was not used in this case and her fate remains uncertain.[62]

Early in 1644 more women found themselves suspected as witches, particularly in Dysart. On January 11 the presbytery found there to be enough evidence against Isobell Johnson of Burntisland to have her apprehended and tried.[63] Later in the month, the following was noted:

> The Presbytrie appoynts Mr John Moncrief and Mr Frederk Carmichell ministers and the Laird of Bogie to goe to the baillies of Dysert for dealing with them to hold hand to the watching of thair witches and tryeing of them as also for giving satisfactioun to the sessioun for the moneyes borrowed be them thairfrom.[64]

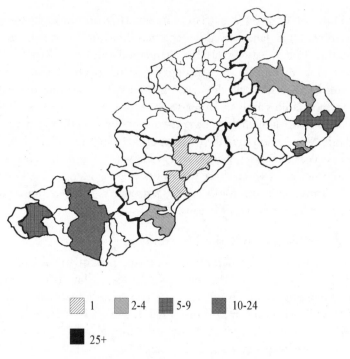

	1		2-4		5-9		10-24

25+

Map 14 – Fife, 1643. Cases by parish

At that same meeting, the presbytery noted the excommunication of Janet Rankyne and Lillias Baxter, accused witches who have fled.[65] Diligence in this matter was promised by the bailies, and on March 27, 1644 enough evidence was considered to have been obtained to seek commissions against three women.[66] The suspected witches, or at least some of them, remained in custody in the tolbooth throughout the summer. In October, William Moresone a merchant burgess in Dysart, appealed to the Privy Council to have his wife, Margaret Young, who had been charged as a 'consulter in witchcraft' and incarcerated for ten weeks set free because she had no previous reputation and had only been accused by 'some malicious persons who wer brunt out of splene and invy'. She was released on caution.[67] What seems clear, however, is that at least some individuals were executed in Dysart during this period.[68] At the same time, the presbytery also had difficulty obtaining commissions for at least some of those who were detained and they were set free on caution to appear again if challenged.[69] These women were set free, but remained under suspicion and remained barred from receiving communion, a serious prohibition at this time.[70] The seriousness of the matter, both from the perspective of the presbytery and the individual barred from the communion table, can be deduced from the fact that Isobel Young was brought before the presbytery in April 1647 for the crime of taking communion in Falkland while she was under the 'slander of witchcraft'. The matter was then referred to the General Assembly with a plea for guidance on what to do with such individuals.[71]

Witch-hunt: 1649–50

The coming to power of a government extremely sympathetic to the more radical Presbyterian faction within the Church of Scotland in January 1649 was followed by an outbreak of witch-hunting in Scotland and in Fife. Most of the cases in Fife focused on the presbytery of Dunfermline, but there was a spillover into the presbytery of Kirkcaldy affecting both Burntisland, which borders the presbytery of Dunfermline, and Dysart. Details, unfortunately, remain somewhat sketchy and must be pieced together from various sources. Commissions were granted for trials in Burntisland and Dalgety (and also Coldingame) in July 1649.[72] In August commissions were issued against Janet Brown, Isobell Gairdner, and Janet Thomson. Brown was accused of meeting the Devil, disguised as a man, while he was in the presence of the other two, with renouncing her baptism and receiving the Devil's mark on her right arm. She was pricked in this arm, the entire pin being thrust in: 'Mr James Wilson, minister of Dysart, in presence of Mr. John Chalmers, minister at Auchterderran, thrust a long pin of wire into the head, and she was insensible to it'. All three were found guilty and executed the same day.[73] This was clearly illegal. Some days later others were brought forward. Isobel Bairdie was accused of drinking a toast to the Devil, and pledging herself to him. Two other unnamed individuals were also convicted, strangled and burned at the stake at the same time.[74] In each of the indictments the prisoners confessed in the presence of 'several ministers, bailies and elders', a situation which led Arnot to comment that he believed 'these inquisitors were produced before the Court, to prove the *extrajudicial confessions*' of the prisoners.[75] Three other individuals were named in commissions issued in September 1649.[76] Burntisland thus witnessed a minimum of six, and possibly nine executions in 1649.[77] A commission was also issued against Elizabeth Simpsone in Dysart on November 6, 1649. Two other cases, possibly related to Kirkcaldy parish, also seem to date from this period.[78]

Records of commissions issued to put suspected witches on trial only tell part of the story for it is clear from the presbytery records that others were accused and held within these parishes during the same period. There was an appeal by friends of those still being warded in Dysart and

Burntisland for their release in March, 1650. The presbytery's response was to have the ministers

> intimate the names of these persons detained in prison in thair severall kirks that if any have anything to declaire aganest them they might come to the Presbytrie and declaire the same.[79]

No information was received, but the presbytery delayed releasing the suspects, then suggested the matter needed to be taken to the synod.[80] In June 1650 there was enough information for the presbytery to seek a commission against Elspett Austein.[81] The tenacity of the presbytery in this period is noteworthy, as was their reluctance to free those so long imprisoned.

Later cases: 1658–90

The 1649–50 hunt marked the highwater mark of witch-hunting in Kirkcaldy Presbytery. Only a handful of cases followed this. Two witches, Margaret Beverage and John Corse, were accused in Dysart in 1658.[82] In 1663 Robert Bruce, the minister of Aberdour, reported to his session that several in his parish had been named by 'dying witches at Aucthertool'.[83] In 1690 Helen Martin was accused of trying to find stolen property using a piece of lace, a bible and a key. The key was placed upon the Bible, while the seventeenth verse of Psalm 50 was read: 'Seeing thou hatest instruction, castet my words behind thee'. (KJV) Then the names of various individuals were spoken. When the key fell off and the Bible turned, one knew that the person named was the thief. For her practice of this charm, Helen Martin was ordered to publicly confess. When she refused and stayed behind locked doors when summoned by the church beadle, the case was referred to the magistrates for her to be incarcerated until she satisfied the church's act of discipline.[84] This incident seems to have been interpreted more as charming than witchcraft.

Summary

The presbytery of Kirkcaldy saw significant witch-hunting in this period from 1590 until 1690. We have looked at considerable depth at the various cases in this presbytery, and in St. Andrews Presbytery (chapter 5) and Cupar Presbytery (chapter 4), in order to gain a better understanding of how the witch-hunt developed, who the accused were, and where the accusations came from. As we have seen in the presbytery of Kirkcaldy, many of those accused as witches were isolated individuals. Some of the complaints focused on the evil done by the suspect, while in other situations it was the presbytery which sought to control the use of charms and cures. In terms of significant hunts, the peak years were 1597 and during the 1640s. Even when there clearly was significant witch-hunting, we have come across no clear reference to torture being used as part of a judicial trial. Rather what we have seen is the church courts operating as vital players in the witch-hunt, even going so far as to execute some individuals they believed were guilty. This role included initial investigations in the more serious cases as well as control of activities which were deemed suspect, but not full blown 'witchcraft'. The church courts also displayed a remarkable tenacity in continually seeking out the same individual suspects who managed to elude them. As we continue to look in detail at the witch-hunt in Dunfermline, the remaining presbytery in Fife, we need to remember these themes and see if the church courts again played a vital role, and if similar suspects found themselves facing accusations as witches.

Notes

1. E.P. Torrie & Russel Coleman, eds., *Historic Kirkcaldy: the archaeological implications of development* (Aberdeen: Historic Scotland, 1995), 14, 15.
2. *Fasti*, vol. 5, 76–77.
3. Case 2308. Spottiswoode, *History of the Church of Scotland* (1655; reprint, Edinburgh, 1851), 66–67. Also Larner, *Enemies of God*, 70–71.
4. Case 2307. Ross, *Aberdour and Inchcolme*, 343–44.
5. Case 877. RPC, vol. 5, 405–06.
6. Ibid.
7. Issobell Rannaldsone (3144); Margaret Elder (3143); Margaret Williamsone (3142). L. MacBean, *The Kirkcaldy Burgh Records* (Kirkcaldy: n.p., 1908), 148.
8. Marion Rutherford (3145). Ibid. After discussing her case the editor notes that 'other entries follow' and lists the accused, and any personal information related to them. They include Janet Bennetie (3148), Margaret Hoicon (3146), William Patersone (3147), Margaret Elder (3156), Isobell Jonstoun (3155) and her husband Thomas Jamieson (3154); Beigis Blakatt (3153); Goillis Hoggone (3152), Bessie Scott (3151); Isobell Jak (3150); and Bessie Osatt (3149). It is interesting to note that there are two males listed. The marital status of six, including William Patersone, is unknown. Goillis Hoggone was the only widow. All of the other eight were married.
9. Ibid., 148–149.
10. Case 2310. Ross, *Aberdour and Inchcolme*, 344. Andrew Young, *History of Burntisland: Scottish Burgh life more particularly in the time of the Stuarts* (Kirkcaldy: Fifeshire advertiser, 1913), 205. Young argues the sentence may not have been carried out, as soon thereafter Allan was accused and sentenced for another death.
11. Anstruther (3103). Smith, *Annotated Edition*, 382. Anstruther did appear before St. Andrews Presbytery at this time, ibid., 383.
12. Case 2319. MacBean, *Kirkcaldy Burgh Records*, 154–55. The banishment was on pain of death. Also in *Extracts from old Minute Books of the Burgh of Kirkcaldy (1582–1792)*, (1862), 18. The latter source suggests it was the thorn (not tron) where she had to stand; the 'hawthorn tree on the west end of the muir, where the head court as often held'. The tron seems a more likely location.

13. Case 3044. SYNFIFE, 61. Also Gilmore, *Witchcraft and the Church of Scotland*, 119.

14. Agnes Anstruther (2339). This is really a duplicate of the previous case (3044). The SBSW mistakenly located Agnes in St. Andrews. SYNFIFE, 61, 71, 75, 79. Isobell Jhonstone (2338), similarly seems more likely to be from Kirkcaldy than St. Andrews, although her locale is less clear. Ibid., 79.

15. Birrell (3157). John Campbell, *The Church and Parish of Kirkcaldy: from the earliest times till 1843*, (Kirkcaldy: Alex Page, 1904), 166.

16. Case 3158. Ibid., 166.

17. Case 3159. Ibid., 166–167. Dick's other appearance in 1633 is also registered as a separate case (2411) as is that involving her husband William Coke (2410).

18. Case 948. RPC, vol. 12, 490.

19. Case 1023. RPC 2nd ser., vol. 1, 246.

20. Pirie (3160); Stark (3161); Birrell (3162). Campbell, *Church and Parish of Kirkcaldy*, 167. This is clearly the same Helen Birrell.

21. Patrik Landrok (1026); Helen Darumpill (1027); Helene Dryburghe (1028); Jonet Pedie (275). RPC, 2nd series, vol. 1, 275.

22. Case 1030. RPC, 2nd ser., vol. 1, 309. The commission was granted to the bailies of Dysart. The deposition bears the signature of the Archbishop of St. Andrews.

23. Neilsoun (1032), Munk (1031). RPC, 2nd ser. vol. 1, 425. There is also a caution dated September 21st, ordering the bailies to execute the commission for these individuals within six weeks. In this commission Neilsoun is spelled 'Wilsoun', ibid., 426.

24. Case 1033. RPC, 2nd ser., vol. 1, 447–48.

25. Case 1064. RPC, 2nd ser., vol. 1, 607.

26. Case 1066. RPC 2nd ser. vol. 2, 122. More information, 12–13.

27. RPC, 2nd Ser. vol 1., 309. The commission notes that 'her deposition marked by John, Archbishop of St. Androis'. Ibid., vol 2, 447 the commission against Helen Wilsoun also includes oblique references to her being at meetings and 'conferences with the devill' and is signed by the Archbishop. Similarly, commission against Margaret Henderson, May 27, 1627. Ibid., vol. 1, 607. The exception is the commission granted in June against Elspett Neilsoun and Annas Munk. The commission bears the Archbishops name, but is in the more traditional form. Ibid., 2nd Ser. vol. 1, 425. The commission for Katherine Chrystie, November 17, 1627 makes no mention of the Devil. It is signed by several people, including the Archbishop. A difference here may have been the fact that Chrystie had yet to be imprisoned. Ibid., vol. 2, 122.

28. There was obviously a certain formula for writing commissions related to witchcraft. Still, the difference is interesting. The first commission issued accused Issobell Mawer 'of the crymes of witchcraft, sorcerie, useing of charmes and inchantmentis, and otheris divilishe practices, offensive to God, skandell to the trew relgioun, and hurt of diverse our goode subjectis'. RPC, 2nd ser. vol. 1, 246. Similar phrasing appears in the commission of April 13, ibid., 275.

29. Case 2373. John Graham Dalyell, *The Darker Superstitions of Scotland illustrated from history and practice* (Edinburgh: Waugh & Innes), 424–425. The original source for the reference is the Dysart kirk session minute of May 5, 1626 as recorded in Muir, *Notices of the Burgh Church . . . of Dysart* (1831). The author could not locate this reference within the Dysart kirk session records; given there are few marginal notes and there was limited time, this should surprise no one. A quick search of the records

for this period showed few cases at the dates when commissions were being granted. The exception was Katherine Chrystie, who appeared before the session on November 6, 1627, and was then ordered to appear before the Presbytery. Dysart KS, CH2\390\1.

30. Kirkcaldy Kirk Session, July 4, 1626. Campbell, *Church and Parish of Kirkcaldy*, 167. The interpretation of the word 'carling' comes from the *Concise Scots Dictionary* (1987), 85.

31. Ibid., 167–168. One would expect, particularly in the records of a church court, to have the black man identified as the Devil. Surprisingly, here and in other cases in Fife, this did not happen. Was this understood? Or was this figure understood as less demonic and more like a mischievous fairy?

32. RPC, 2nd ser. vol. 2, 142–143. The records of the Privy Council contain not only commissions, but counter claims and other information.

33. Ibid., 143.

34. Ibid.

35. Case 1029. RPC, 2nd ser. vol. 1, 297–98.

36. Guiddale (1338); Broun (1336), Bissat (1337); Galbraith (1335); Janet Scott (1334). RPC 2nd ser. vol. 3, 488. The commission is not too enlightening as it is a 'similar commission' to one listed above it, regarding witches being put to a trial in Berwick.

37. Case 1341. RPC, 2nd ser. vol. 3, 496.

38. Katherine Chrystie appears under several different case numbers. This is appropriate in her case, as the proceedings always seem to be new ones! This case is listed as case 1340. RPC 2nd ser. vol. 3, 489–90. The text of this complaint is fascinating.

39. Case 1353. RPC 2nd ser. vol. 3, 532.

40. Neving (1354), Dasoun (1355). RPC 2nd ser. vol. 3, 535. Similar commissions were being granted for other parts of Scotland at this time. This hunt obviously was broader than Fife. What is fascinating is the focus on one locality (12 cases, if one includes Janet Wilkie of Wemyss), with only individual witches being charged in St. Andrews and Torryburn.

41. Case 1381. RPC 2nd ser. vol. 3, 602. The Kirk Session records of Dysart exist for this period. The palaeography is particularly difficult. No mention of the Devil or demonic pacts has been discovered.

42. Case 2400. The SBSW locates this woman in Dysart, the parish where Presbytery met that day. The problem was occurring in Auchterderran. This is the only case known from this parish. Manuscript of the Presbytery of Kirkcaldy CH2\224\1 27. An excellent transcription of this source is William Stevenson, ed., *The Presbyterie Booke of Kirkcaldie: Being the record of the proceedings of that Presbytery from the 15th day of April 1630 to the 14th day of September 1653* (Kirkcaldy: James Burt, 1900), hereafter referred to as the PBK, 35. Like Mark Smith's transcription of the Presbytery records of St. Andrews these are not excerpts, but the complete minutes. Because of ease of availability, the PBK will be used extensively.

43. Coke (2410); Dick (2411). The evidence in this case circulated as a pamphlet entitled 'The Trial of William Coke and Alison Dick for Witchcraft Extracted from the Minutes of the Kirk-Session of Kirkcaldy, A.D. 1636' which can be found in D. Webster, *A Collection of Rare and Curious Tracts on Witchcraft and the second sight; with an original Essay on Witchcraft* (Edinburgh, 1820). The author used the edition found in the Ferguson collection at the University of Glasgow. The completeness of the records makes this a worthy case study, which will be dealt with at length in chapter 9.

44. Case 3134. May 5, 1636. PBK, 92.
45. Ibid., May 26, 1636, 92–93.
46. Case 2419. PBK, 113. Certain 'presumptions' against him were read on May 4. On May 25 the Bishop states he will not come to hear the case, and Patowne is set free, ibid., 114.
47. Case 2422. Presbytery of Kirkcaldy minutes, CH2\224\1 f. 113. PBK, 130.
48. Wilson (2423); Bannatyne (3130). CH2\224\1 f. 113. PBK, 130–131. There is some confusion relating to the daughters of Christian Wilson. Only Bannatyne is named, yet the record from July 12 specifies 'daughters' and on July 26 she is said to have appeared with 'hir two dochters'. CH2\224\1 f. 114. Stevenson, in a rare error, missed the word 'two', 131, which ultimately is of little significance as the focus of attention was clearly on the two women whose names appeared in the Presbytery record.
49. CH2\224\1 f. 116. PBK, 132.
50. Ibid.
51. September 20, 1638. PBK, 134.
52. CH2\224\1 f.114. PBK, 131.
53. RPC, 135.
54. Case 2424. SBSW incorrectly located this case in Kirkcaldy. CH2\224\1 f127–28. PBK, 136, 137, 138, 141. The source of the conflict seems to have been over the treatment of a pig: 'he [James Kedie] having stickit [gored] ane swine to the said Janet Durie befoir for whilk she had professit to causs him rewit.', 141.
55. Case 3131. CH2\224\1 f. 127–128. PBK, 148. The case continued throughout 1639 and into 1640. Douglas never seems to have been warded. Ibid., 148, 162, 173, 174, 178, 179, 184. The eventual verdict was that the charges were not proven.
56. Case 3132. PBK, 187. Lindsay's actions are described as 'practices of witchcraft' at a later meeting of presbytery and she is ordered 'wardit and tryed', 189. How this distinction was made between charming and witchcraft remains a mystery.
57. Case 3135. PBK, 236.
58. Case 3136. PBK, 240. References are made earlier to someone being suspected of witchcraft in Dysart. From the context, it seems that these were earlier references to this case, 236, 237.
59. Case 3163. August 30, 1643. PBK, 256. At the next meeting, September 6, mention is made of the 'woman of Dysert' being tried at the discretion of the minister. This is stated in the context of a discussion of Christian Crystie of Kirkcaldy (a relation?). Christian is essentially accused of uttering a curse: saying to someone the 'devill mak hir als daft as ever,' a charge which she denied. While there is agreement she should be apprehended and put to a trial, exactly when this was to take place was at the discretion of the ministers. Within the same record there is reference to a communication from the presbytery of Dunfermline asking that John Davidson be sent to the Inverkeithing session to state what he knows about Patrick Pearson who has been charged with witchcraft. This gives clear indication of the kind of communication that could move back and forth between presbyteries, making them at the very least aware of cases of suspected witchcraft outside their borders.
60. Jonnet Smythe (2448). Katherine Wallenge appears as three cases in the SBSW: 2449 as Wallace, 2475 in a duplicate record (except for changes in her fate), and as 2476 under the name Wallenge. These records have been consolidated under case 2449 in the SWHDB. Several sources give the same basic information about her, the best

being in anon, *A Selection from the Ancient Minutes of the Kirk-Session of Kinghorn* (Kirkcaldy: John Crawford, 1863), 50. See also, Alan Reid, *Kinghorn: A short history and description of a notable Fifeshire town and parish* (Kirkcaldy: L. MacBean 1906), 23–24 and G.W. Ballingall, *Historical Collection (with notes) regarding the Royal Burgh and Parish of Kinghorn* (Kirkcaldy: Strachan & Livingstone, 1893), 32–33; Gilmore, *Witchcraft and the Church in Scotland*, 266. The process did not come before the presbytery until March 20, 1644, at which time they agreed there was enough evidence for an assize. PBK, 266.

61. PBK, May 16, 1633, 63; August 8, 64; October 10, 68; November 7, 69; April 3, 1634, 73; September 18 and 25, 81.

62. Case 2457. The SBSW gives the source of information as Willis, 31; unfortunately the list of abbreviations gives no further details regarding 'Willis'. The information given here comes from the records of the session of Markinch, CH2\258\1, December 24 and 31, 1643. No further references to Janet could be found.

63. Case 3128. There was no minister at Burntisland at the time. PBK, 264. In August the presbytery again discussed the case, this time determining there was enough evidence to justify a commission, 274.

64. PBK, 265. Given the number of names which appear later in Dysart, this was not entered as a separate 'case' in the SWHDB.

65. Baxter (3137); Rankine (3138). PBK, 265.

66. PBK, 265, 267. Commissions were sought for Agnes Benettie (3139), Margaret Cunningham (3140) and Margaret Halkhead (3141). No commissions are listed in the RPC.

67. Case 1459. RPC 2nd ser. vol 8, 28. PBK, August 7, 1644, 274. In the petition Margaret is described as a young woman. It seems that this case had appeared before, on September 11 at which time the bailies and ministers had been called to appear. One of the ministers, James Wilson, had been present and asked for twenty more days in which to obtain evidence. The request was granted. No further evidence was presented and as neither the bailies or ministers appeared, Margaret Young was set free. One final note in this case: the name Margaret Young appears in 1648 in the PBK in another context. Margaret is seeking permission to marry William Hayes and also to be allowed to take communion. She is given permission for the former, but denied the latter 'till tryell be maid and she is cleired', 319, 324. Either there was another Margaret Young from Dysart delated for witchcraft or the presbytery had a long, and vindictive, memory. The pursuit of Katherine Chrystie in Kirkcaldy suggests the latter.

68. This is a 'true mention' as discussed by Larner. The only other explanation might be that Margaret was named by someone burned elsewhere the same year, however this does not seem likely.

69. Moresone began his challenge before the presbytery on August 7, 1644, PBK, 274. The releasing of others on October 9, 1644, *after* the Privy Council had ruled in Moresone's favour, is suggestive. Ibid., 276.

70. June 11, 1645, witnessed the petition from Alexander Symsoun and William Symesons to have their wives allowed to take communion as nothing had been proven against them. Presbytery passed the matter on to Synod. PBK, 286.

71. Case 3133. Thomson's name appears only here. For the purposes of the SWHDB, she has been placed in Kirkcaldy, although Dysart remains a possibility given the unnamed women accused there in 1644. PBK, 310.

72. Case 1936. *Acts of the Parliament of Scotland*, vol. 6, part 2, 479.

73. The source of this remarkable information is Hugo Arnot, *Celebrated Criminal Trials in Scotland,* 401–403. Arnot claims to be quoting a manuscript which was in the possession of a Major Melville of Murchochcairnie. Gairder (2548); Thomson (2549); Brown (2550). Another minister, Dalgleish, is also said to have been present. In a footnote, Arnot mentions that both Dalgleish and Wilson were turned out of their parishes in 1663 for not accepting 'Prelacy'.

74. Bairdie (2596). The unnamed witches are cases 2585 and 2586. The executions took place sometime in August or early September. Ibid., 402–03.

75. Ibid., 402–403. Italics in the original.

76. The SBSW lists each of these individuals twice, once for the commission issued by the Privy Council, once for the commissions recorded in the Record of The Committee of Estates. Agnes Waterson (1510, 2093); Janet Murray (1512, 2095); and, Elspeth Ronaldsone (1511, 2094). RPC, 2nd ser., vol. 8. 200. NAS, PA 11\8 f. 169r. The dates on both are September 27, 1649. The manuscript states that these three women 'have confest sundrie points of witchcraft attended by the Ministers of Burntisland, and Kinghorne'. A call for information against Janet Murray was issued from the pulpits of the presbytery after the meeting of September 12. She had already been warded by that date. The presbytery also notes that there is enough evidence to proceed with commissions against Murray and Waterson at its meeting on October 3. RPC, 339, 340.

77. Case 2166. NAS PA 11\8\ 187v. She is noted as a 'confessing witch'.

78. Katherine Shaw (3053) and Margaret Reid (3033) are two suspected witches from this area of Fife. No dates exist. The source was Gilmore's thesis, 146. Their names appear in the midst of a discussion on sessions approaching the Privy Council directly for commissions. Gilmore noted that it was 'probably significant that such cases are concentrated in the years 1649–50 when witchcraft being particularly virulent over wide areas of Scotland there was less difficulty than usual in extracting the necessary 'information'. (p. 146). An alternate explanation is that the political situation allowed for direct access from lower church courts to the Privy Council.

79. March 12, 1650. PBK, 350.

80. Ibid., 352–353.

81. Ibid., 361. One may surmise that she was one of those held in custody.

82. Margaret Beverage, case 286. The source cited in the SBSW, Proc. S.R.O. List, was not located. Similarly, John Corse, case 220, JC26\25.

83. Ross, *Aberdour and Inchcolme*, 331–32. Ross notes that no further action seems to have been taken. Case 2683. William Stephenson in *The Kirk and Parish of Auchtertool* (Kirkcaldy: James Burt, 1908), notes that this must have been at the time of Mr. Bells' ministry. He further notes that no 'tradition of their burning remains in the parish, but there is on the Mill farm, not far from Halyears, a brae called the Witches' brae,' 74.

84. Case 3163. Campbell, *Church and Parish of Kirkcaldy*, 172–73. Another version of this same charm uses the 18th verse of the same psalm.

CHAPTER SEVEN

The Witch-Hunt in the Presbytery of Dunfermline

Over the last chapters we have discussed the various accusations made against suspected witches in the presbyteries of Cupar, St. Andrews, and Kirkcaldy. We have discussed the hunts as well as the numerous occasions in which either a single or small number of suspects were questioned. It is now time to turn our attention to Dunfermline, the westernmost presbytery in Fife, which witnessed the fiercest witch-hunt in the shire. Dunfermline Presbytery included in its bounds parishes that were not politically part of Fife. Although geographically in Fife, Culross and Tulliallan were politically part of Perth in this period. The presbytery of Dunfermline included both of these parishes, as well as other parishes from the shire of Kinross. As they are geographically part of Fife, Culross and Tulliallan have been included in this study. Out of the total of twelve parishes in the presbytery, ten will be discussed. The presbytery was established in 1581, but records from the early periods have been lost. The minute books survive from 1647 on. In 1643 Beath and Dalgety were separated from Aberdour and erected as distinct parishes.[1] There were six burghs within the presbytery: Culross, Dunfermline and Inverkeithing which were royal burghs; and, Torryburn, Kinross, and Aberdour which were burghs of barony. This was a relatively populous and economically vibrant area whose main concerns were agriculture but also involved a cloth trade, coal mines and salt works.[2]

Early years

All but a handful of the known cases in Dunfermline Presbytery, the area of Fife that saw the most intense witch-hunting, occurred in the seventeenth century. The exceptions are notable although the details are cryptic. In 1542 there is a reference to payment made to servants transporting witches from Edinburgh and Dunfermline to St. Andrews Castle. The three seem to have been condemned and burned at the castle.[3] The next known case was also a notable one, that of Agnes

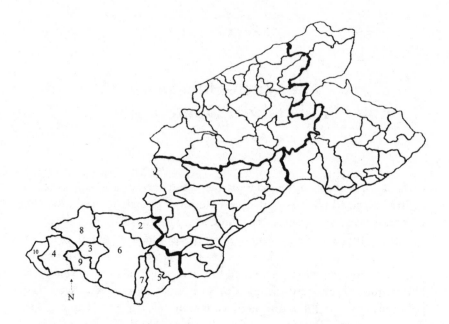

Map 15 – The parishes in Dunfermline Presbytery.

(parishes included in study)

Parish	code	Parish	code
Aberdour	1	Dunfermline	6
Beath	2	Inverkeithing	7
Carnock	3	Saline	8
Culross	4	Torryburn	9
Dalgetty	5	Tulliallan	10

Mullikine, the earliest case in the records of the High Court of Justiciary of Scotland, dating from 1563. Agnes, alias Bessie Boswell, was banished and exiled.[4] Dunfermline also figured indirectly in the infamous North Berwick witch trials. One of the accused Euphame Macalyane (Ewfame Makcalzene in the *Sourcebook*), was said to have consulted with a woman in Dunfermline seeking a love potion for her husband – 'otherwise to be avenged on him' – but there is no clear indication that anyone was sought in this regard.[5] Apart from these brief references our earliest examples of witch-hunting come from the 1620's when several major hunts occurred.

Inverkeithing and environs: 1621–22

In February 1621 the Privy Council issued a commission naming six women in Inverkeithing, all suspected as witches. (There was no wide-scale witch-hunting in Scotland in 1621: Fife, however, saw cases in three different presbyteries, a rare occurrence.) (See Map 16) All of those named had already been imprisoned and investigated by the ministers and magistrates of Inverkeithing. Five had confessed.[6] The commission stated that these women, all of whom admitted to 'thair divilishe practices and geving over of thame selffis saull and body to the divill', were to be tried. The sixth, Marioun Chatto, who had been accused in some of the depositions as the 'principall persone in all thair conventionis and meitingis with the divill and most familiar to him', had not confessed. She was to be put to further examination, which included having the confessed witches confront her.[7] At the end of March, Christiane Couper of Culross was also named as a witch in a commission for her use of charms. Again, she had been apprehended and had confessed. The commission also noted that several 'famous personis as witnessis' had brought testimony against her. She was to be tried on the charges and punished. The 'famous witnesses' comment is intriguing. Could some of these have been those accused in Inverkeithing? Although this remains possible, there is no indication (for example the same names appearing in each of the commissions) apart from timing to suggest a link between these two episodes.[8]

The interest in witches which began in 1621 continued over the next years, affecting other parishes as well as erupting in larger hunts in both Inverkeithing and Culross. In 1622 five women in Aberdour, three of whom were widows, had been arrested and examined on suspicion of witchcraft, in particular for the murder of John Bell. After their arrest by the bailies and the careful examination that followed they had all 'frelie and of thair awne accord' confessed to the murder and to speaking with the Devil, who seemingly had been with them when they committed the murder.[9] The links between these cases and those in Inverkeithing the year previous are clear as three of the commissioners named appear on both commissions: Patrick Stewart of Beath, James Logenee of Coustoune, and John Finne of Quinithill (or, on the commission granted for the Inverkeithing witches, Aberdour). Also, the name William Blaikburne of Inverkeithing appears on the Aberdour commission.[10] Some of these same names appear in commissions issued the next year, 1623, when the largest hunt to this point in Fife broke out in Inverkeithing.

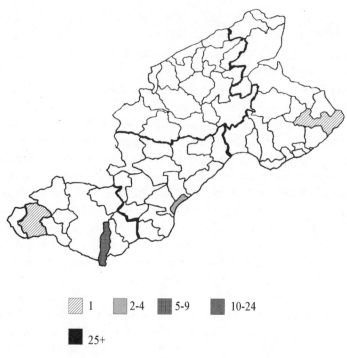

1 ▨ 2-4 ▨ 5-9 ▨ 10-24 ▨

25+ ■

Map 16 – Fife, 1621. Cases by parish.

Inverkeithing: 1623

Fifteen separate individuals from Inverkeithing were named in several commissions issued in 1623. Unfortunately, the commissions are the only source we have for this large hunt. On February 27, 1623 a commission was issued to apprehend Christian Balfour, Margaret Bull, Bessie Logie, Margaret Merschell and Jonnet Robesoun as suspected witches.[11] Another group, numbering four women and one man, were noted as having fled 'thus taking the guilt upon them'. When apprehended they were to be investigated using the testimony of any 'as can gif only light or evidence aganis thame'.[12] The key to what was occurring may be in the next part of the commission where it is stated that three suspects are already in custody and two of them, Bessie Andersone and Marjorie Aitkyne had already confessed to 'sundrie divilishe practizes'. The third, Marioun Henderson, continued to plead her innocence, despite the many charges made against her by Bessie Andersone and Marjorie Aitkyne. Indeed she asked that matters be taken to a trial so that she could clear her name.[13] It is clear that this was a serial witch-hunt which spread from the first suspects who were incarcerated, two of whom confessed and named others. The dynamic which produced these initial confessions – witch-pricking, sleep deprivation, physical torture, or an actual belief on their part that they *were* witches – can only be guessed. What we should note, however, was that it was not 'judicial torture' or torture produced as part of a trial. These women had confessed prior to the commission which put them to such a trial.

Further commissions were issued to deal with the Inverkeithing situation. A commission dated March 18, 1623, noted that seven suspects had been apprehended and subsequently had confessed to 'the cryme of witchcraft, conferring with the devil, and geiving over of thame seffis saule and body to him and his service'. This group included all of those named in the first commission, as well as two new suspects who had neither fled nor been originally named, Jonet Keirie and Beatrix Thomsone.[14] Finally, a commission dated May 14, 1623, named two of those who had fled, Marjorie Gibsoun and Magarett Kinnell, as having been apprehended and having confessed.[15] The final tally lists fifteen different individuals charged as witches in Inverkeithing. Eleven confessed and were taken to further trial. There is a strong possibility that they were executed. One who had originally been incarcerated, Marioun Hendersone, was examined further. We have no record that she ever confessed, nor do we know her fate. Three of those accused, including Johne Young the only male suspect, seem to have been successful in their flight.

Dunfermline presbytery: 1624

Commissions are also our main source for the hunt which occurred the next year in Culross, with one case crossing over into the neighbouring parish of Torryburn. The commission dated February 19, 1624, names Jonnet Umphra, her sister Mayse Umphra, Alexander Clerk, Marjorie Rowand, Marion Stirk, and Jonnet Watt of Culross, as well as Anna Smyth in Torryburn.[16] The charges have a formulaic feel – 'witchcraft, sorcerie, useing of charmes, and consulting with the devill' – as does the fact that the commission states they have all been 'long suspected'. The interesting piece of information is that the accusations seem to have come from Jonnet Umphra, and all of the others were to be brought before her. As all are ordered to be apprehended and warded (including Jonnet) one wonders how or why she came to name the others. What seems clear is that she was at the centre of these accusations.[17] Indeed, another commission dated March 2, 1624, gives permission to put Jonnet, who had by now clearly confessed, to an assize or trial.[18] Later that same month, a commission was issued to put two other confessed witches, Jonnet Tor and Helene Ezatt, both of whom have already been apprehended and examined, to a trial.[19] The fate of the nine incarcerated, three of whom proceeded to a trial, is unknown. Three of the commissioners – Robert Colville the bailie of Culross, Sir John Prestoun of Valyfeild and Robert Bruice of Blairhall – are named in all of the commissions and the first two had also been named in the commission issued against Christiane Couper in 1621.[20] This might mean only that these were the most prominent gentlemen in the vicinity. It is suggestive that there might have been links between the isolated witch arrested in 1621 and the significant hunt which took place three years later. Also of note is the fact another Robert Colvill, the minister of Culross, is named in the February 19, 1624, commission.[21] These hunts represent the first two serial hunts in Fife of which we are aware (the hunt in 1597 seems to follow another pattern) and involved more individuals than any other parishes to this date. It is frustrating that so little is known of the events of these years in the presbytery of Dunfermline.

Scattered cases: 1628–41

The latter part of the 1620's saw only mild interest in witches in this area of Fife. In April 1628 a commission, signed by John Spottiswoode, the Archbishop of St. Andrews, was issued for the trial of Jonnet Reany in Dunfermline.[22] In June the burgh records note the names of three other suspected witches. Effie Herring had named two others, Bessie Stobie and Jonet Thomson, at her execution, leading to the warding of both Bessie and Jonet. Apparently insufficient evidence had been found against them. Bessie and Jonet were released upon the condition that they not leave the town. Flight would be seen as an admission of guilt, with the result that they might 'be brunt but (without) dum (doom) or law'.[23] The next year, 1629, there was a request for information to the Presbyteries of Dunfermline and Muthill for information on a charmer, Alexander Drummond, who was being held prisoner in the Edinburgh tolbooth and was about to be put to trial.[24] A standard commission was issued against a suspected witch in Torryburn in 1630.[25]

Over the next decade the only evidence we have of interest in suspected witches comes from the parish of Culross. The session minutes record four women barred in 1634 from taking communion because they were suspected as witches. Three of the four requested a trial 'only by an assize' and the session agreed to a petition for a commission to hold these trials. Nearly a year later they accepted the trial arrangements and declared they were willing to 'enter into ward' in order to be 'cleansed of that odious imputation or els convicted'.[26] In November of 1635 there is a complaint of being slandered as a witch before the session.[27] The session also heard two complaints of charming in this period, one in 1636 against

Margaret Fields and the latter against William Drysdale in 1641. Both were sentenced to public repentance before the congregation.[28] While these seemingly innocent cases appeared before the session of Culross, it is interesting to note that there is no information on a Katherine Mitchell, apparently executed within the parish in 1641.[29]

Culross, Dunfermline and environs: 1643–44

On January 3, 1643, Margaret Cuthbertsone was brought before the session of Dunfermline and accused as a witch. This was the first case of this year, one which saw extensive witch-hunting throughout Scotland. Six other women were also brought before the session for believing that Margaret was a witch. These women were called upon to make public repentance, and the matter was to be counted as a point of witchcraft against each of them. The confessions were done so that the Devil might not 'take advantage to beguile sillie ignorant bodies therby in making them to believe such idle toys'.[30] Interest in witches shifted to Culross where, by March 5, 1643, so many women had been incarcerated that Catherine Rowan had to be moved from the steeple to the tolbooth to make room for all the accused.[31] April 2 saw the sessions in both Dunfermline and Culross proceeding against those involved in charming. John Waster was fined in Culross for claiming he was a soothsayer.[32] In Dunfermline Robert Shortus was brought before the session and charged with using charms in the curing of his wife and consulting the suspected witch Jonet Insch from Torryburn.[33] Despite three witnesses who claimed he was guilty, Shortus denied the charge and continued to do so until he finally made his public repentance on July 23, 1643.[34]

The notation on April 16, 1643, in the minutes of the session of Dunfermline that Grissel Morris had been found guilty as a witch comes as a startling reminder amidst so many seemingly minor accusations of how seriously these charges were taken. Morris had been warded as a suspect, had confessed, and various witnesses had appeared to speak against her. She was sentenced to be burned on May 17, 1643.[35] Grissel Morris was not to be the last person executed for witchcraft in Dunfermline in this period. In the months of May, July and August five other women were executed.[36] Meanwhile, the hunt for witches continued in Culross. On May 14, 1643, Marion Thomson was accused by Isobel Eizatt as a witch; indeed Marion's reputation as a witch was supposedly well known.[37] Marion and another woman, Elspeth Shearer, were to be tried. Other women also suspected as witches were being 'warded and watched'.[38] On May 28 five witnesses appeared against Marion. Notation was also given that Margaret Hutton was a suspected witch.[39]

The gravity of the situation in both Culross and Dunfermline can be seen not only in the executions but other events which took place. Marion Burgess fled from Culross, supposedly to her mother in Stirling, after being suspected.[40] In June 1643 Jonnet Fentoun of Dunfermline died in prison. Her body was then taken 'to the witch know, being trailed and carted yrto and castin into a hole yt withot a kist (coffin)'.[41] Also in Dunfermline in June, David Crystie and his sister Margaret Crystie were tried for 'ryott misbehaviour and disobedience', namely striking one of the officials in the porch of the church while they had been going to visit her mother, one of the women warded as a suspected witch within the church. Both David and Margaret were found guilty, fined (£6 and £3 respectively), and forced to do public repentance on their knees. At the same time, this incident gives us one fascinating piece of evidence. The record stated that the mother's guilt had been 'sufficientlie provine be certane famous Witnesses'.[42]

The list of names from both Culross and Dunfermline in these years cannot be complete. Still, what is clear is that many women (and men?) were being held as witches in the spring and summer of 1643 in these communities. The scale of the hunt caused difficulties. The kirk session at Culross notes in July that those being held as witches were still under close watch.[43] Dunfermline faced a crisis that same month. A plea went from the magistrates for assistance from those in the 'landward' part of the parish to assist in the warding and watching of the suspects. The burden had so far fallen heavily upon the burgh which could no longer sustain the effort: 'the criminals of that kind being so many and so frequently taine'.[44] Still, the hunt continued. Issobell Mar was accused by her 'neighbour witches in Dunfermline as a witch and was detained in the thieves hole, where she hanged herself'.[45] William Clerk complained to the session of Culross in September that people were calling his daughter a 'witchbird'. That same month witnesses were called to support Andrew Keir's accusation that Jonet Burne was a witch.[46] The hunt continued in both localities, involving both further interest in charming and a commission for an execution.[47] The number of known cases – one in Torryburn, eight in Culross, and eighteen in Dunfermline – underestimates the severity of what seems to have begun as a minor interest in charming.

The same localities continued to be affected by witch-hunting throughout the next year. The main focus of the hunt was in Culross, involving eight cases. One accused person, Marg Donald in Dunfermline, was accused by some 'witches' in Torryburn on March 10, 1644,[48] but apart from this all the cases we know from this year in Dunfermline Presbytery came from Culross, including the apprehension of Beatrix

Bruce as a suspected witch on February 28, 1644.[49] Bruce named three others in Culross as witches, all of whom were apprehended and warded on March 10.[50] Adam Donaldson, known for charming people and livestock, was accused and then brought before the kirk session in June to answer for his activities. Although the charms were described by witnesses the case was not defined as one involving witchcraft.[51] Over the next month those accused by Bessie Bruce as witches, though not yet found guilty, were denied communion.[52]

Insight into what occurred in Culross during this period comes from a petition made by Mary Cunningham, a widow, to the Privy Council complaining about the illegal treatment of her and her daughter Jonet Erskine.[53] This case demonstrated the difficulties women could face when accused and the amount of time that could be absorbed. The first petition was dated August 1644. Mary Cunningham complained that she and her daughter had been illegally imprisoned in the tolbooth of Culross by the bailies of that burgh and had been 'most barbarouslie, cruellie and inhumanelie usit be thame', under the direction of James Kennowie, 'thair clerke'. She stated that they had been illegally arrested at night and without a warrant and taken from their house which was outside the bailies jurisdiction. Their treatment once held in the tolbooth was described:

> when they hade putt us in prisone they causit thair officeris and hangman tirre us mother naked, rype and search our bodies and secreitt memberiss for witchmarkis, and when they could find noen upon us, they patt on sackloath gounes upon us and loakit our leggis in yron gaddis and wald suffer neither meatt nor drink to cum in to us bot by the handis of thair jeavellour, what intercepted the samyne be the way and first satisfied thair owne apietyde thairwith and send in the reversiounes thairof to us, and so throw famyne and cold brought us to great miserie and seikness.[54]

Mary Cunningham and Jonet Erskine had been named as witches by 'tuo infamous person' who had already been incarcerated as witches, and Mary attributes their ill will towards her and her daughter for the reason that she had been accused by these women who were in ward. A commission was obtained, Mary and Jonet were taken to an assize, but when Mary claimed she was able to obtain an advocate to speak on her and her daughter's behalf the trial was swiftly ended.

Mary Cunningham's social class can be deduced not only from the fact that she was able to obtain the services of an advocate, but by her comments about those who would have tried her. After complaining about the 'bitter and malitious speiches' made against her before the trial was adjourned, she comments on the precariousness of her position, having been accused but not allowed to demonstrate her innocence

> and have made us so odius to the ignorant comones, whom they intend to make our assysouris that they wald be content to tear us in peices farr mor to fyle and condemne us upon the most sklender and frivolous meanes that can be alledgit.[55]

She remained imprisoned awaiting trial and continued to appeal for assistance in order to be both set at liberty and have her name cleared.[56] This situation demonstrates that the accusations of imprisoned suspects were taken seriously, and could implicate women of some social stature within their communities, particularly in situations such as the serial hunt which affected this corner of Fife in the years 1643–44. Aftershocks and after-effects from these cases, even perhaps the hunt itself, continued for the next few years.[57]

Continuing cases: 1648

Culross and Dunfermline continued to be centres of witch-hunting over the next few years. Margaret Holden was accused before the kirk session of Culross as a witch in March 1648.[58] On July 16 of that year William Chrictoun, a vagabond who happened to be in Dunfermline parish, was accused of being a warlock. The charges stemmed from an incident when Chrictoun asked for lodging in the home of Manse Huchon in Mylburn. When he was refused, he stated they would 'not rew it ones, bot ever' after which Manse became very ill. Chrictoun was also accused of pissing in the chimney fire of another house: it was not stated what evil was attributed to this action.[59] The records of the July 23, 1649, presbytery meeting contain a brief but important note relating to this case. The presbytery stated that a warlock in Dunfermline who had been watched confessed that he was a witch.[60] This was confirmed at the August 6 meeting of the session where Chrictoun's confession to having made a pact with the Devil twenty-four years ago was received and it was reported that he had been sentenced to be burned a few days after, a sentence which seems to have been carried out by the time of the meeting.[61] This was an illegal execution: no commission to try William Chrictoun was even sought.

The great hunt: 1649–50

A brewer in Dunfermline was accused in January 1649 of using witchcraft (one would assume to make his beer taste better). It is interesting that the year which witnessed the greatest witch-hunting in Fife began with this strange accusation. The brewer successfully took the case to the session and at the next meeting the slanderer was requesting leniency for his comments, and was allowed to repent without having to wear sack-cloth.[62] After such a seemingly comical beginning, events changed dramatically. This was, after all, a turbulent period in Scottish politics and national life, a time of civil war and political strife. The passing of the Act of Classes (January 23, 1649) and the beheading of Charles I in England (January 30, 1649) may have been distant events, but their importance should not be underestimated. In particular it should be remembered that the passing of the Act of Classes, which debarred those who had served in the Engagement, a previous government, from office, represented an achievement by an uneasy alliance of forces dominated by radical Presbyterians.[63]

It not clear when precisely the witch-hunt began in this area of Fife. The first indications that a hunt was underway were vague and unclear. On March 23, 1649, Walter Bruce, the minister of Inverkeithing, was chastised by the presbytery for praying and preaching at the execution of a witch.[64] Furthermore, we know that the Synod of Fife on April 3 heard a petition from the bailies of Inverkeithing requesting assistance in bringing some witches to a confession.[65] The petition was referred to the presbytery, who at their meeting of April 13 ordered the ministers serving Inverkeithing to attempt to bring those 'incarcorat suspct of witchcraft' to confession. The concern regarding this matter can be further seen by the fact that at the same meeting an act was passed against anyone consulting or seeking health from 'witches'.[66] While the details remain obscure several facts are clear: Walter Bruce, the suspended minister from Inverkeithing, had already demonstrated an interest in witches; the synod and presbytery, whatever their feelings about Bruce, offered support in seeking confessions; and, some individuals were being held as suspected witches in Inverkeithing by early April.

The interest that had been shown by the presbytery and synod and in the parish of Inverkeithing spread to neighbouring parishes. On April 22, 1649, at the session meeting at Dalgety, the parish immediately to the east of Inverkeithing, a report was heard concerning Robert Maxwell:

> The Sessione hearing that one Robert Maxwell, put from the communione for ignorance, hes been confessing some things that looks like witchcraft, appoynts him to be examined by the minister and four elders.[67]

Upon further examination Maxwell confessed not only to witchcraft but to a pact with the Devil. This confession was read before the presbytery and a commission was sought to put him to trial.[68] In his confession Maxwell named John Murdoch of Dunfermline as also being a warlock. The response of the session at Dunfermline was to have Murdoch warded and watched.[69] This strategy again proved successful for by May 6 Murdoch had confessed. The session, seeking more information, continued their investigation of Murdoch:

> This day it is reported be the Magistrats that Jon Murdoch the witch was watched as also the Ministers declair'd that he hade come to a confession. It is thot fitt that he be still as yet watched that more confession & tryall may be had out of him.[70]

By May 13 he had named Christian Smythe who was promptly apprehended and warded and by the next meeting a report came back to the session that she was being watched.[71]

While individual names and details give some specifics, in the background other shadowy events were occurring. By May 5, the witch-hunt had reached Aberdour and further confessions were sought from those being held.[72] It seems from the records that at least some of those held were executed by the third of June.[73] The presbytery appointed members on May 23 to try to bring the suspects being held at Inverkeithing to a confession.[74] Interestingly, shortly thereafter two women from Dunfermline parish, Isabell Peacock and Bessie Wilson, were ordered arrested based upon accusations made by witches in Inverkeithing.[75] By June 3, 1649, attention was on three women from Dalgety who had been accused by Robert Maxwell before his execution. Of the three, the main focus of concern was Issobell Kelloch.[76] Standing against Issobell Kelloch was not only Maxwell's accusation but her bad reputation and the fact that she had also been named a witch by those at Aberdour. These accusations, including the claim by Maxwell that she had attended certain meetings with the Devil, were sufficient to cause the session to recommend that Issobell be warded so that she might be brought to confession. By June 17 she had confessed and a commission was being sought.[77] Another woman who had long had an evil reputation, Issobell Bennet, was also being sought. The charges for the commission against Issobell Kelloch were to be 'taken out off the boxe' because Isobell was poor and Lady Callendar, on whose estate she lived, refused to pay the costs. Isobell Kelloch's trial and execution on July 1, 1649, cost the church box a total of £24/4s/4d.[78] Others may also have been charged and possibly executed at Dalgetty in late June.

The two cases we know about for certain are Christian Garlick and Isobell Glenn who were suspected and investigated because they had been named by 'ane dieing witch'.[79]

The initial vague concerns about Robert Maxwell led to several executions and the naming of others in a classic, yet very focused, serial hunt. Of those of whom we have any information the stereotypical characteristics of 'witch' clearly emerge: Maxwell, a vagabond; Kelloch, poor with a reputation; and Isobell Bennet, who also had a reputation. Others were included because they had been named by those accused. Unfortunately we know less about the fate of these individuals – Margaret Orrock, Issobel Scogian, Isobell Glenn and Christian Garlick. Even given the unknowns in Dalgety, it seems the hunt was very focused. It also seems pertinent to note that this was the only year when we know Dalgety to have been involved in witch-hunting.

Meanwhile in the neighbouring parish of Inverkeithing the search was much broader. As already discussed, confessions were being sought by the end of May 1649 from some suspected witches who were being held.[80] The presbytery of Dunfermline took an unusual, and ultimately unsuccessful step, on June 13, 1649, of trying to obtain a general commission which would have allowed them to proceed against any suspects without the necessity of obtaining a commission for each specific individual:

> The Presbytery finding a great and daily discovery of witches within their bounds as lykewayes that comissions for putting of them to an assize cannot be obtained without great charge and attendance have there for resolved to petition the hay and honourable court of parliament for the way of facilitating their commission as their lordships shall think fit.[81]

The presbytery continued to be concerned, meeting in late June in Inverkeithing in order to assist the session with the situation regarding the accused witches, then took the unusual step of suspending those elders who had 'an interest' in some of those being held. The magistrates were to approve four men named by the minister Walter Bruce, whose suspension the presbytery had just lifted, who would have the power to investigate and hold those already incarcerated as well as apprehending any other suspects.[82] In total, nine elders were suspended. The presbytery also passed an act aimed at 'some wicked persons salling with witches' who were advising them that they might 'deny their confessions or ane part thair of'. Anyone found guilty of this would have to make their confession before the congregation.[83] The Inverkeithing council approved those recommended by Bruce in early July. The presbytery continued to ask for the names of those 'delated for witchcraft' by confessing witches from Inverkeithing, Aberdour, Dalgety, Dunfermline, and Kinross.[84]

July saw cases from Inverkeithing appear before the High Court. It is through these documents and the testimony of those accused that we get a sense of how large the hunt was and how many people had become suspects. Nineteen individuals from Inverkeithing were mentioned as witches in confessions presented before the High Court.[85] The confessions also give us some fascinating detail. Robert Bruce, the minister of Inverkeithing, is prominently mentioned as are the burgh officials. Those who appear had confessed, indeed did so 'with tears', being warned that they would answer to God on the great day for any untruth they told. Margaret Mairtine admits to meeting the Devil who appeared in 'the likeness of ane gentle man' in Beatrix Thomsone's house and giving herself over to the Devil's service by placing one hand on her head, the other on the sole of one foot, renouncing her baptism and receiving the Devil's mark. Katharine Grieve also confessed tearfully to meeting the Devil, this time at Margaret Blaikburn's house and giving herself to his service. Katharine also states that the Devil 'had copulation with her'. Startlingly, what is missing from these confessions is any indication of what evil deeds Katharine, Margaret and Beatrix did while they were in the service of Satan. Instead, the concern of the questioners was with how many meetings each attended, who was at these meetings, and who the ring leaders or officers were at these meetings. The ring leader was declared to be Margaret Henderson, Lady Pittathrow. Margaret Blaikburn declared that one of the main reasons Lady Pittathrow called one of the meetings was to 'complaine to the devill' about the minister, Mr. Walter Bruce.[86]

These confessions demonstrate the elite interest in the demonic. Issobell Leitch was directly asked if 'the devill had copulated with hir'.[87] Secret gatherings of women were the opposite of the public gatherings of the church, controlled by the male clergy and elders. Giving oneself over to the Devil from head to toe and receiving his mark, was the opposite of baptism. Yet apart from meeting and, as Katharin Grieve confessed 'dancing and revilling', these witches seem to have done little else. Popular concerns for evil actions or unneighbourly behaviour are not evident. This, the largest witch-hunt in Fife history, had a unique character. The hunt was also opposed, as evidenced by the necessity of purging both session and burgh council of those whose wives had been named. One of those with some status and powerful connections was Margaret Henderson, Lady Pittathrow, who when accused by others who were executed fled from Inverkeithing with assistance of 'all sorts of people from all pairts of the kingdome' and tried to hide in Edinburgh. Eventually, she was caught and warded in the Edinburgh tolbooth while awaiting trial.[88] A petition from the presbytery and Mr Bruce was heard before Parliament on July 31, 1649, which complained that the cases in Inverkeithing had been blocked in the past as some of the wives of magistrates and others who the magistrates would not apprehend had been named, and even after the presbytery's act in appointing those to do its will, 'nevertheles since that tyme the magistrats and toune counsall flights that work and refuises to give them powar in maner foirsaid'. The Estates of Parliament granted the presbytery's petition.[89]

Cases continued in other parts of the presbytery throughout July and into August of 1649. Bessie Mortoun and Marjorie Phillip of Dunfermline were first named before the session on July 15.[90] In Aberdour the wife of Henry Stanehouse was warded as a suspected witch. The wife of Thomas Smith, although under suspicion, was not warded as she was pregnant.[91] In early August commissions were issued for Aberdour and Inverkeithing granted in response to the information received by the ministers and elders of these parishes.[92] Three new suspects, Katherine Smith, Beatrix Douglas, and Marjorie Durie (and possibly a fourth, if Marion Durie was not another name for Marjorie) were accused and warded in Inverkeithing in August.[93] In Aberdour, Margaret Currie was also listed as a suspect in August. The fact that presbytery received a list of those named by 'dying witches' in Aberdour makes it clear that some executions took place around this time within that parish.[94] In Dunfermline, incarcerated witches were being held under continual watch by the magistrates.[95] The kirk session records of September 18 note expenses of £6/16s given to the beadle for maintaining 'some poor witches' (a comment that indicates economic status, not sympathy) and £3/12s paid to the hangman – an indication that executions here were also likely.[96]

Both the hunts and opposition to them continued. In August Robert Brown approached the Committee of Estates concerning his wife Marjorie Durie (as she was known in this record) who was being held in the steeple of Inverkeithing. Robert stated that his wife

> is threatened daylie with brands and his putt[ing] the sark gorm (waxy shirt?) upon her and is lying in that miserable condition upon the ground non of her family having liberty to see her [not] so much as cloathes upon her . . .[97]

After hearing his testimony the Committee of Estates ordered his wife removed from the church steeple and put 'in some other prison house wher she may be safely kept' and ordered that the family have free access to her. The Committee also stated clearly their opposition to 'any manner of torturing or hard usage' of Marion Durie or others held in Inverkeithing. The presbytery was not pleased and sent Walter Bruce and George Belfrage to Edinburgh to try to get this decision overturned:

> The Presbytery finding that the people much wronged, and the worke of god in the descoverie of witchcraft much obstructed.[98]

Both parties appeared before the Committee of Estates in September. The presbytery claimed the Committee had been misled and complained that 'the work of God in punnishing that abominable sin (had been) greatly obstructed' by the orders of the Committee. (Remember, Marion Durie had not been found innocent or set at liberty. The Committee had only ordered that her family have access to her and that she be maintained in a prison other than the church steeple.) The presbytery protested that Marion had previously escaped. Morever, the Devil's mark had been found 'in diverse parts of hir body'. The presbytery asked that she be kept in ward for an indeterminate length of time until she could be made to confess. They also asked that her husband Robert Brown be made to pay the costs.[99]

Presbytery won this appeal to the Committee of Estates. The Committee thanked the presbytery for 'thair time and faithfulness in the discoverie of the said cryme of witchcraft desyring them to continue therein'. At the same time, the Committee ordered the presbytery to 'be sparing in causing torture the persounse dilated for witchcraft'.[100] A similar attempt by John Dunino from Dunfermline to intervene on behalf of Bessie Maghorn, met with the same result.[101] At the next meeting of the presbytery on September 19, 1649, Robert Brown found himself in difficulty, first for 'calmuniating the Presbytery before the estates of Parliament' and second for falsely claiming his wife was in France. He was ordered to repent.[102]

Tensions surrounding the witch-hunt continued. The kin of Margaret Henderson and some members of the Inverkeithing session also found themselves in difficulty. After being warded in Edinburgh, Margaret Henderson (Lady Pittathrow) had apparently committed suicide.[103] Problems emerged in Inverkeithing when she was buried in the church cemetery with the approval of some members of the session.[104] In Dunfermline David Rotsone, the husband of Marjorie Phillip who had been detained since July, appealed for her release because she had been held so long and under such harsh conditions. The session's decision was strange: she was set free upon caution, but banished from the parish of

Dunfermline.[105] Bessie Mortoun continued to be held. In December Mortoun was pricked by John Kincaid, the witch-finder, and subsequently executed.[106] This is the only direct reference to Kincaid's involvement in the hunt in Dunfermline Presbytery in 1649. There are, however, mentions of the Devil's mark being found on Marion Durie. Kincaid's role may have been more to convince the sceptical at this juncture than as the main driving force in a hunt which had begun, however tentatively, at least eight months previously.

In the last months of 1649 the hunt moved into Culross. It must have been difficult with so many parishes in the presbytery caught up in witch-hunting to have been slandered as a witch. Thus in November, Jonet Paterson attempted to defend herself by accusing Isobell Stewart and Bessie Cowsey of slander for 'calling her a witch'. Yet such as strategy was very dangerous. Isobell appeared before the session, claiming that she could prove that Jonet Paterson was a witch. Her evidence must have been convincing for the session noted in early December that there was enough evidence given in against Janet Paterson to put her to a trial.[107] Similarly Janet Anderson came before the session of Aberdour in March, 1650 accusing Isobel Inglis and Marjorie Flooker of calling her a witch. When Isobel Inglis appeared to answer the charge, she suggested that Janet Anderson had used a spell to murder Isobel's child. Again, it was Janet who was imprisoned, although she was eventually released.[108] Robert Cousing's name appeared under different circumstances. He was accused of being a messenger for a witch, and eventually was made to repent before the church for his actions.[109]

In May 1650 Marion Cunningham of Dunfermline was accused by Jonet Hutton and John Colyear as a witch. Again, the case began as one of slander when Jonet allegedly called Marion a witch. Soon, however, the focus shifted to Marion and her saying of a prayer which was not 'lawful' each night as she went to bed. The part which Jonet claimed to remember went

> out throw toothe and out throw tongue out throw liver and out throw longue, and out throw halie harnpan, – I drank of this blood instead of wyne, thou shalt have mutifire all thy days syne, the biter and the baneshaw and manie euil yt no man knowes.[110]

While Marion denied knowing this prayer, other neighbours came forward and stated she indeed did and mentioned a further petition to 'Ladie sweet st marie'. When confronted with this Marion confessed to some things, denied others, and in the end was called a perjured liar by the session and was denied communion.[111] The only other information we have for this year comes from a cryptic reference to a woman in Torryburn who the session warned was 'infamous for theft and witch-craft'.[112]

As has been detailed above, the years 1649 and 1650 witnessed a massive hunt in Dunfermline Presbytery. At this time of political and religious turbulence in Scotland the unique quality of this hunt is especially noteworthy. From rather simple beginnings involving charming and ignorance a serial hunt emerged in which elite notions of witches' gatherings and compacts with the Devil rapidly overshadowed the more traditional concerns with *malefice* and acts of ill will, particularly in the burgh of Inverkeithing. Those who have discussed this hunt have seen Walter Bruce as the key player, suggesting this was one way in which he could divert attention from his troubled ministry.[113] Bruce clearly was a major player in this hunt but he alone cannot be cast as the villain. The fact remains that this large hunt occurred in a burgh which had previously witnessed another dramatic hunt. Inverkeithing was fertile ground for these accusations. The times also encouraged the seeking out of all enemies of God, including witches, as the church sought to finally achieve its goal of building a godly society. The combination of personality, community memory and religious fervour was deadly.

In terms of the dynamics which drove this hunt, there is evidence witch-pricking was involved in the later stages. Torture may also have played a role, although here our evidence is indirect, involving Marion Durie's complaint that she was threatened and how one interprets the Committee of Estates comment to the presbytery to be 'sparing in causing torture'. However, should torture have been used on those held in the church steeple, this would have been illegal, not the 'judicial' torture that was part of a formal legal trial. What did play a role, even the crucial role, was the ability to ward and watch these women, isolate them from the families, and presumably deprive them of sleep.

Scattered cases: 1654–66

The decade of the English occupation saw only a scattering of cases in this part of Fife. In 1654 Margaret Cant asked the session of Aberdour to clear her of certain accusations of witchcraft. They refused until such time as all those who had been accused could be dealt with.[114]

Katherine Smyth of Inverkeithing appeared before the High Court in 1655.[115] The next year an unnamed female from Inverkeithing was executed at the castlehill in Edinburgh.[116] That same year in Culross, Elspeth Craiche was warded in the tolbooth as a confessed witch. The difficulty was what to do with her, as she could not be executed unless murder by witchcraft could be proven against her. The Minister Robert Edmonstoun, who had made enquiries in this regard while in Edinburgh on other business, suggested the council should see if they could obtain a commission. Despite several efforts, no commission could be obtained and Elspeth Craiche had to be set at liberty, in part because of the extreme expense in keeping her.[117]

While the restoration of the monarchy did not cause a major reaction throughout Dunfermline presbytery similar to the one in the presbytery of Cupar, old scores were settled in both Aberdour and Culross. In July of 1661 the session of Aberdour asked that, 'Seeing there are severalls in this toune, that long ago should have been apprehended for witchcraft and never hands yet laid upon them', the bailies arrest Margaret Currie and Catherine Robertson, both of whom had been 'accused by dying witches'.[118] Margaret Currie and Margaret Cant, who had tried unsuccessfully to clear her name in 1654, were soon arrested. After being imprisoned and watched they confessed and named Janet Bell and Susana Alexander as witches.[119] Both of these women were also imprisoned. A witch-finder played a prominent role in the investigation of Janet Bell, a woman whom Lord Morton attempted to set at liberty. The others had confessed before a witch-pricker was brought on the scene.[120] Clearly some long memories were at play, both in the sessions initiating this hunt and in those who were originally examined. Similar memories led to the arrest of Elspeth Craiche in Culross in March 1662. She was imprisoned in the hope of getting her to admit to her former confession and two men were set to watch her, night and day, so that 'she may do no evill to herselfe'.[121]

The next years saw a scattering of cases. Sir George MacKenzie, the famous Scottish legal authority, speaks of some witches who were burned in Culross in 1665, based upon their confessions that they had been transported to public conventions of witches by the Devil.[122] Another curious reference to Culross also refers to a witch's flying. It states that the witch who had to be carried to the execution spot on a chair because she had broken her back when she fell while flying to escape being warded. The date when this incident occurred is not given.[123]

In 1666 commissions were issued against seven witches in Torryburn. All had been imprisoned in the tolbooth. The commission was to put them to an assize and discover whether they 'shall be found guilty upon voluntar confessions of renuncing their baptisme or entering into paction with the divell or that otherwayes malifies be legally and judicially proven against them'.[124] What is interesting to note is that the commission does not state that these individuals have already confessed. This may be as

significant as the phrase 'voluntary confession'. The fate of these individuals is unknown. The concern seems to have spread to the Dunfermline session the next year, although it is unclear whether any
individuals were charged.[125] The interest, however, had not ended. A
decade later in 1677 Andro Currie and his wife accused Isobel Cupar of
slander for calling them a warlock and witch respectively (and also calling
their daughter a thief). Isobel Cupar was found guilty of slander and called
to repent.[126] A similar successful slander charge was raised by Elspeth
Kirkland against Bessie Lamb in Aberdour in 1681, when the latter
named the former a witch.[127] Such accusations of slander seemed easier to
win in this period; it still is fascinating that people would go to the trouble
to make sure their name was cleared.

The Sabbat in the West Kirk, Culross: 1675

In the midst of these accusations of slander, a particularly unique case
occurred in the history of the Fife witch-hunt. In Culross in 1675 four
women, three of whom were widows, were accused before the High
Court of being witches.[128] What makes this case involving Katherin
Sands, Isobell Inglis, Agnes Hendries, and Jonet Hendries, interesting is
that these are the only cases in which certain elements – carnal copulation
with the Devil, and attendance at sabbats held in deserted churches –
often considered the staple fare of Scottish witch-craft cases appear. The
details in this situation are all just too precise, too stereotypical. We have
encountered individuals meeting with the Devil, or giving themselves
over from the top of their head to the souls of their feet, or receiving his
mark, or even in a few rare incidents having sexual intercourse with the
Devil. What is striking in this case is the ordering of the details, the fact
that they are all present, and the sequence: the giving of oneself over to
the Devil's service from head to foot is followed by receiving the Devil's
mark, which is followed by carnal copulation. Even the sexual act follows
a stereotype: his nature (i.e. penis) was cold, and several echoed Janet
Hendrie's comment that he 'used her after the manner of a beast'.[129] The
meetings did not happen out in the field or in their homes (although
some meetings did). The recent gatherings took place in the West Kirk of
Culross, a deserted church which had been abandoned at least since the
time of the Reformation. As much as Katherin Sands, Isobell Inglis, Janet
Hendrie and Agnes Hendrie all made these confessions, and then
admitted to them in court prior to their execution at the gallows between
Leith and Edinburgh on July 29, 1675, we clearly have here the elite
stereotype. That the trial was held before the High Court and the
executions took place outside of the burgh, is of considerable importance.

Whether the other dittays and confessions presented in Edinburgh in order to get commissions to try witches in the individual parishes would have contained the same stereotypical elements is uncertain. Perhaps they did. These, however, were not the kinds of concerns which we have heard time and time again raised in the individual parishes. These complaints centred on suggestions that someone was a charmer or had caused illness or misfortune. The difference is striking.

Indeed it is only when we look beyond the stereotypical elements of the confession that we begin to see the forces that might have been at play. Katherin Sands confessed to being a witch for thirty-four years. She was the daughter of a woman who had already 'suffered for the cryme of witchcraft'. Her economic station is unclear. What is referred to is the fact that she was suspected of poisoning her brother who had wrongfully taken all of the 'goods and gear' of her father, which were supposed to be divided equally among the children. It was this incident which caused her to enter the Devil's service, after which she gave her brother a drink which caused his illness and death. (Although the timing of the drink filled with white powder is unclear, the fact that she was accused of entering the Devil's service thirty-four years previously, suggests the quarrel had been a long one. It also suggests Katherin would have been at the very least middle aged and probably considerably older.) The other three women were widows. Issobel Inglis apparently entered the Devil's service because her fields were not as rich as her neighbours, a condition the Devil promised to rectify: 'he desired her to be of good cheer she would gett it also tymplie doen and with alse good furrows as her neighbours'.[130] Janet Hendrie was aided in a quarrel. Agnes Hendrie was promised, after she complained that 'she had not wherewith to live,' that once she entered the Devil's service 'she should not want'.[131] Although these details are scant, they clearly suggest that these women were at the bottom of the economic scale.[132] They were not chosen at random, even in this confession which most resembles the elite notion of demonic witchcraft and the participation of witches in sabbats.[133] Indeed, the event that brought them notice was assaulting Robert Prymrose while they were returning from one of their meetings at the West Kirk. One final note: there are some details in the confessions which it seems difficult to determine whether these were popular or elite ideas. Notably, Katherin Sands confessed that there were dead people at one of their meetings. Also, she describes a scene of 'the devill dancing and playing and that the devill played to them on a pype and that frequentlie they had a blowe light when it was dark'.[134] Is this an example of elite notions of a sabbat, or popular conceptions of a fairy gathering, or some blending of the two?

The end of the hunt: 1704

The final formal accusations of witchcraft in this part of Fife came in Torryburn in 1704 and blends both traditional accusations with some of the details heard in Culross in 1675. The events began at a special meeting of the session to deal with the story that Jan Bizet had been 'molested by Satan'. Although Bizet is not present at the beginning of the proceedings, others begin the story of how one night while she had been drinking, she began warning that Lillias Adie was a witch. On her walk home that night she was extremely disturbed, crying out, as Agnes Henderson remembered it 'O God, O Christ there is Lily coming to take me and [hir] blue doublets O Mary Wilson keep me she is coming'.[135] At the next meeting of the session a month later, it was discovered that Jean Wilson has also been dreadfully tormented, which led the bailie to incarcerate Lillias Adie nine days previously. At the session meeting Lillias Adie confessed to being a witch, indeed to having had a compact with the Devil 'since the second bury of witches in this place'. She claimed to have given herself over to the Devil, to having had carnal intercourse with him, and then added that his feet were cloven like a cows. She claimed to have been summoned by Grissel Anderson to a meeting one moonlight night where everyone clapped and honoured the Devil as their prince. She claimed to have known no one at the meeting, apart from Elspeth Williamson.[136] At the meeting held two days later on July 31 in the prison, Adie adhered to her confession. When asked if Agnes Currie was a witch, she stated she would flee if charged. Then she was asked if the Devil had a sword. Her reply was that she believed 'he durst not use a sword'. She indicated her anger, for he had promised many things which he had not delivered. She then named Agnes Currie as someone in attendance at the last meeting.[137]

At the next presbytery meeting which was held on August 19, Elspeth Williamson admitted to having attended a meeting of witches by the side of the church-yard and being surprised when there were not any psalms sung. She believed, but was not sure, that Mary Wilson had taken her to this meeting. One final comment of note: she claimed that when the Devil left she could not hear his footsteps on the stubble.[138] And so the accusations came that different individuals had been at various gathering until Janet Whyte, Agnes Currie, Bessie Callander and Mary Carmichael, had been added as suspected witches.[139] Some of the accusations were of long standing, for example the claim that Agnes Currie had bewitched a child who had died after baptism twenty-four years previously.[140] There were few real claims of *malefice*, and those there were centred on Agnes

Currie. For all of the time spent in examining these women and the fact that Lillias confessed and Elspeth Williamson did not deny she was a witch, nothing much came of these events. Lillias Adie died in prison. Events seemed to end in confusion but there are two postscripts. First, five years later Margaret Humble was called in front of the church and forced to repent because she had stated that the minister, Mr. Logan, was daft when he spoke against the witches.[141] Second, many years later, Allan Logan, then the minister of Culross wrote, asking for the records of the 'tryall of the witches in the end of the Queen's reign'.[142]

Summary

Of all the presbyteries in Fife, Dunfermline saw the greatest activity in terms of witch-hunting. It is from this presbytery that we receive our most dramatic references to the Devil, a figure who remains surprisingly absent but for a few cases. It is perhaps no accident that these cases where there are references to meetings or sex with the Devil came either late in the hunt or appear in documents from the highest court in Scotland. Serial hunts occurred with some frequency in this presbytery, spreading the accused beyond the usual stereotypical 'witch' to include those with social status. Still, the driving dynamic was not judicial torture, but was primarily the ability to ward and watch the suspects, thus depriving them of support as well as sleep, and producing the necessary confessions. Resources in communities like Dunfermline were made available to guarantee the success of this procedure. The presbytery fought in 1649 to maintain its control of both the process and the incarcerated suspects, appearing before the Committee of Estates in Edinburgh. Much of the evidence is circumstantial, based upon financial accounts, complaints about treatment, appeals for warders, and even the use of the words 'warded' and 'watched' in session, presbytery and other records yet this method of sleep deprivation seems to have been both commonly used and remarkably successful in creating confessions. This was true not only in Dunfermline, but in the other presbyteries we have discussed.

Over the last four chapters we have seen the kinds of evidence which exists, the sources from which we must build our picture of the witch-hunt in Fife. We have seen how a presbytery shared information and took an active role in the hunting of witches. Given the role it played, the presbytery does seem to be a logical unit to use in order to study the witch-hunt at a regional level. The key role the church played in these events and the role of torture needs to be explored further. Following this we need to turn from our chronological discussion over the last three chapters to an examination of the women who were suspected, arrested,

113

and in some cases executed as witches, as well as the motivations of those who hunted these women as witches.

Notes

1. *Fasti*, vol. 5, 1ff. Benson, *South-West Fife*, 10.
2. Benson, *South-West Fife*, 16, gives a brief introduction to the economy of the area. He estimated that Culross, Dunfermline and Inverkeithing were the most populous parishes, with Torryburn not far behind. Dalgety's population he estimated at about 800, while Carnock and Cleish were among the least populous areas with about 400 people each.
3. The source of this information is Black, *Calendar*, 21. This case is not recorded in the SBSW or the SWHDB as both begin in 1560. The original source of information is Robert Kerr Hannay, editor & translator, *Rentale Sancti Andree: Being the Chamberlain and Granitar Accounts of the Archbishopric in the time of Cardinal Betoun 1538–46.* (Edinburgh: Scottish History Society, 1913), 130, 141.
4. Case 6. Pitcairn, *Ancient Criminal Trials*, vol. 1, 432. Black, *Calendar*, 21. The SBSW lists five other cases in 1563; the only other name given is Nik Neving and he is the only one located in a place, Monaie. The source for these cases is also in Pitcairn, vol 1, 510.
5. Again, this case does not appear in the SBSW or the SWHDB. The source is Ebenezer Henderson, *Annals of Dunfermline* (Glasgow: –, 1879), 241. Henderson notes that a tradition has grown that one of those involved in raising the storm against James was this woman. His source is Dalyell, *Darker Superstitions*, 202.
6. Bessie Harlaw (945); Bessie Chalmers (944); Beatrice Mudie (943); Christiane Hammyltoun (942); Margaret Ent (941). RPC vol. 12, 423.
7. Case 946. Ibid., 423. A report back to the Privy Council was to be made in the case of Marioun Chatto. The fate of all six is unclear.
8. Case 947. RPC vol. 12, 472. The indirect link may have been that the news that there were witches in Inverkeithing may have spurred some in Culross on to pursuing Couper.
9. Janet Robertsone (959), Agnes Quarrier (960), Helen Cummyng (961), Alesone Hutchesone (962) and Agnes Robertsone (958). RPC vol. 13, 49–50.
10. The spellings are irregular in each of the commissions. RPC vol. 12, 423. RPC vol. 13, 42. The role of the church in the Aberdour commission remains obscure, as there is no reference to the minister being present. The commission also states that the accused had been apprehended by the bailies of the Lordship of St. Colme. The Aberdour kirk session records CH2\3\1 contained no information.
11. Balfour (971); Bull, (970); Logie (969); Merschell (968); Robesoun, spelled Robertson in the SWHDB (967). RPC vol. 13, 181.
12. Johne Young (966); Margaret Kynnell (976); Christian Harlow (975); Marjory Gibsoun (977) and Elisabeth Broun (974). RPC vol. 13, 181.
13. Bessie Andersone (972); Marjorie Aitkyne (965); Marioun Hendersone (973). RPC vol. 13, 181. This seems a very brave thing for Hendersone to have done. The idea that it was Andersone and Aitkyne who produced evidence is based upon the interpretation of the following phrase in the commission: 'the depositionis of the utheris personis foirsaidis produceit aganis hir'. Other than the commissioners, the only others named to this point were the confessed witches.

14. The editors of the SBSW assigned new case numbers to those named in this commission. Therefore Christiane Balfour (971) is duplicated as (978); Jonet Robesoun (967), as Jonet Robertsoun (983); Bessie Logie (969) as (981); Margaret Bull (970) as (979); and, Margaret Merschell (968) as (982). The two new names are Beatrix Thomsone (984) and Jonet Keirie (980). An interesting sidelight comes in the marginal notes of the RPC, where these women are accused of 'witchcraft and intercourse with the devil'. The 'intercourse' noted in the commission is not, as many would suspect, sex but 'conferring with'. Even this may have merely been a conventional wording of a commission for witches, not reflecting any specific charges in the case. It is interesting to consider whether this double meaning of the word 'intercourse' may have led to the notion that sexual contact with the Devil was a common feature of all Scottish witchcraft trials. RPC vol. 13, 192–193.

15. Again, these cases are listed as duplicates in the *SBSW*. Marjorie Gibsoun (977) and now (986); Magarett Kynell (976) now as Kinnell (985). The commission notes they confessed 'freelie and of thair awne accord' to the charge of 'conversing with the divell' and giving themselves to him and his service. RPC vol. 13, 230.

16. Jonnet Umphra (996); Mayse Umphra (1000), Alexander Clerk (997); Marjorie Rowland (998); Marjorie Stirk (995); Jonnet Watt (1001); Anna Smyth of Torryburn (999). RPC vol. 13, 439–440.

17. Ibid., 439–440.

18. The SBSW duplicates this case as 994. RPC. vol. 13, 451. The charge again has a feeling of formula to it, specifically the fact that the main charge is that she had meetings and 'conference' with the Devil.

19. Jonnet Tor (1013); Helene Ezatt (1014). RPC vol. 13, 484.

20. RPC vol. 12, 472. RPC vol. 13, 439–440, 451, 484.

21. Ibid., 439–440.

22. Case 1067. RPC 2nd ser. vol. 2, 317. The commission gives few details.

23. Effie Herring (3225); Bessie Stobie (3227); Jonet Thomson (3226). The source is Chris Neale, *The 17th century witch craze in West Fife: A guide to the printed sources* (Dunfermline: Dunfermline District Libraries, 1980), 15. Neale's source is Andrew Shearer, ed., *Extracts from the burgh records of Dunfermline in the 16th and 17th centuries* (Dunfermline, 1951).

24. Case 1159. Alexander's connection to Dunfermline is unclear. The commission allowed for the collection of information about his practices in the locality. The presbyteries were called to 'convene before thame all suche persouns within thair said presbyteries as can give anie light or information concerning the said Alexander his practises of witchecraft and charming'. RPC 2nd ser. vol. 3, 104.

25. Elspet Bladderstouns (1329). RPC 2nd ser. vol. 3, 454.

26. Helen Rowane (3165); Kath Rowane (3166); Grissel Astrin (317); Jonet Dusone (3168). August 30, 1634. October 12, 1634. October 19, 1634. July 5, 1635. Benson, *Southwest Fife*, 266. There is no record of commissions being granted. This case should be explored further.

27. Benson, *South-West Fife*, App. 2, 266. This case was not entered in the SWHDB.

28. These cases have been added to the SWHDB, but only as examples of what charming cases looked like. Margaret Fields (3177) November 20, 1636. William Drysdale (3178) March 7, 1641. Both are listed by Benson, *South-West Fife*, App. 2, 266. The question truly is, why were they accused of charming and not witchcraft? Where was the line?

29. Case 2435. The source is Dalyell, *The Darker Superstitions of Scotland*, 671. Benson, *South-West Fife*, App. 2, 266.

30. Margaret Cuthbertson (3169); Agnes Kinsman (3171); Jonet Tailor (3175); Jonet Moodie (3174); Jonet Horne (3173); Christian Moodie (3172); Jonnet Henrysone (3170). These cases were discovered and the quotation taken from Benson, *South-West Fife*, App. 2, 266. Dunfermline KS records, NAS CH2\592\1 f20–21.

31. Catherine Rowane, (2437). The 'others' are case (3176). The original source is the kirk session minutes of Culross, CH2\77\1, March 5, 1643. Quoted in Benson, *South-West Fife*, App. 2, 266 and David Beveridge, *Culross and Tuliallan or Perthshire on Forth* (Edinburgh: William Blackwood, 1885), vol. 1, 203.

32. Case 3179. Benson, *South-West Fife*, App. 2, 266.

33. Robert Shortus (3180); Jonet Insch (3181). The Dunfermline kirk session record notes that she was from Torryburn and was his wife's fathers sister (an aunt by marriage). CH2\592\1, f 23. Benson, *South-West Fife*, App. 2, 267.

34. Benson, *South-West Fife*, App. 2, 267, notes that Shortus was a surgeon who 'tended wounded after Kilsyth and Dunbar'. His repentance was in sackcloth. KS Dunfermline CH2\592\1 f.25.

35. Case 2458. CH2\592\1 f23: 'that day compeirit Grissel Morrison being accused of sundrie poynts of witchcraft spoken and done by hir'. Benson, *South-West Fife*, App. 2, 267. Also, Ebenezer Henderson, ed., *Extracts from the Kirk-Session Records of Dunfermline (1640–89)* (Edinburgh: Fullarton & MacNab, 1865), 12. Neale, *West Fife*, 15.

36. Margaret Brand (2459); Katherine Elder (2460); Agnes Kirk (2463); Margaret Donaldson (2464); Isobel Millar (2465). All are referred to in Henderson, *Annals of Dunfermline*, 309. Henderson's source for this information was the *Register of Deaths*.

37. Case 3182. Benson, *South-West Fife*, App. 2, 267.

38. Shearer (3183). Benson, *South-West Fife*, App. 2, 267. Jane D. Hogg, *Extracts from the Kirk Session Book of Culross-17th century* (typescript, Dunfermline District Library), 10.

39. Benson, *South-West Fife*, App. 2, 267. Hogg, *Extracts*, 10.

40. Marion Burges (3185) Benson, *South-West Fife*, App. 2, 267. Hogg, *Extracts*, 10. John Kinnaird was accused regarding this in early June (5 or 8), 1643, and efforts were made to have her returned and warded.

41. Case 2443. Source is Henderson, *Annals*, 309. Again, his source on this is the *Register of Deaths*.

42. The 'mother' has not been added to the SWHDB, as she may be someone already known. Neale, *West Fife*, 16. Benson, *South-West Fife*, App. 2, 267.

43. Benson, *South-West Fife*, App. 2, 267.

44. Dunfermline KS Records CH2\592\1 f25. Benson, *South-West Fife*, App. 2, 267.

45. Case 2444. Henderson, *Annals of Dunfermline*, 309–310.

46. Benson, *South-West Fife*, App. 2, 268. Burne is case 3188.

47. A woman named Drummond (3189) was mentioned as a witch in October. It is unclear whether or not she was in custody, as the case was directed against Christian Spears of Dunfermline who had sought her assistance. Dunfermline KS CH2\592\1 f26. Benson, *South-West Fife*, App. 2, 268. Margaret Hutton in Culross, already mentioned as being under suspicion, had commissions issued against her in October for trial and one in November 1643 for her execution. RPC 2nd ser. vol. 8, 12.

48. Marg Donald (3192 and 2523). Dunfermline KS CH2\592\1 f30, reports that the witches of Torryburn (case 3191) have accused her. Nothing more is known of the

latter. Marg Donald's case includes information on watching her. Benson, *South-West Fife*, App. 2, 268, 269. Also, Henderson, *Extracts from the Kirk Session*, 16; Henderson, *Annals of Dunfermline*, 314.

49. Bruce (3190). Benson, *South-West Fife*, App. 2, 268.

50. Cases 3193, 3194, 3195. As with all cases where no name is known, it is possible that some of those whose names appear later were in fact apprehended at this time. It is also possible that Beatrix Bruce may have been the one to name Marg Donald of Dunfermline as a witch. Given the way in the same individual was sometimes referred to as coming from different places (one where they lived, the other where they were warded), this possibility should not be ignored. Still, this is speculation. What remains clear is that this is the continuance of a serial hunt.

51. Case 2490. duplicated as 3196. The accusations began in May but were not presented as a trial before the session until June 30. Benson, *South-West Fife*, App. 2, 268. Hogg, *Extracts*, 10–11. Beveridge, *Culross and Tuliallan*, 208–209. Beveridge includes details of the charms and suggests the penalty was public repentance.

52. The session of Culross raised the issue at the end of July. The minutes note that due to an Act of the General Assembly these women may not take communion. Benson, *South-West Fife*, App. 2, 268.

53. Cunningham (1454). The duplicate record in the SBSW (1456) has been deleted. Jonet Erskine (1455). Source is the RPC 2nd ser. vol. 8, 101–103.

54. RPC 2nd ser. vol. 8, 101.

55. Ibid.

56. Ibid. This information comes from the Committee of Estates, from the same day, recorded on 13. Mary and her daughter are here referred to as a 'gentleweemen'. See also, RPC 2nd ser. vol 5, 103. RPC 2nd ser. vol 8, 37–38, 101–103, 105. Benson, *South-West Fife*, App. 2, 269.

57. Some of the references to cases in the years following, clearly relate back to these years. The *SBSW* had Marg Donald listed in 1645, as case 2523. This comes from the fact that reference to payments made to her date from 1645. There is also a notation giving information on procedures for 'watching the landward witches'! It seems clear, that not only she, but others were still being imprisoned at this time. Benson, *South-West Fife*, App. 2, 269. Henderson, *Extracts from the Kirk Session*, 16.

58. Benson, *South-West Fife*, App. 2, 269.

59. Case 2535. The quote is taken from Henderson, *Extracts from the Kirk Session*, 27. Also see Henderson, *Annals*, 317.

60. Benson, *South-West Fife*, App. 2, 269. Dunfermline Presbytery, CH2\105\1,51.

61. Dunfermline KS CH2\592\1 f76. The session record notes that he was warded for five days before he confessed. A minister and the watchers seem to have been present. It then states, 'some few days thereafter he was brunt'. Benson, *South-West Fife*, App. 2, 270. Henderson, *Extracts*, 27.

62. Brewer (3197). Benson, *South-West Fife*, App. 2, 270.

63. Gordon Donaldson, *James V-James VII*, 338–339.

64. There is no case in the SWHDB related to this rather cryptic reference as it is unclear whether this occurred in early 1649 or had occurred prior to this. Presbytery minutes of Dunfermline, CH2\105\1, 74. Benson, *South-West Fife*, App. 2, 270.

65. Case 3198. SYNFIFE, 208. What is fascinating is the context: surrounding this are all kinds of actions against celebrating Yule, attending holy wells, etc.

66. CH2\105\1, 83. Benson, *South-West Fife*, App. 2, 270.
67. Maxwell (3199). William Ross, *Glimpses of Pastoral Work in the Covenanting Times: A Record of the Labours of Andrew Donaldson, A.M. Minister at Dalgetty, Fifeshire 1644–62* (Edinburgh: Andrew Elliot, 1877), 194. Benson, *South-West Fife*, App. 2, 270.
68. Ibid., 194.
69. Dunfermline kirk session, CH2\592\1 f89. Murdoch is case 2540. He was accused by the 'warlock of Dalgety'. The magistrates were ordered to 'put a watch on him'. See also, Benson, *South-West Fife*, App. 2, 270. Henderson, *Extracts from the Kirk Session*, 31.
70. May 6, 1649. Dunfermline kirk session, CH2\592\1 f96. Benson, *South-West Fife*, App. 2, 270.
71. Smythe (3201) minute of May 13, 1649 & May 20, 1649. CH2\592\1 f90. Benson, *South-West Fife*, App. 2, 270. This page of the kirk session book is variously notated as f90 or f96.
72. Case 3200. Dunfermline Presbytery CH2\105\1, 87. Benson, *South-West Fife*, App. 2, 270.
73. J.C.R. Buckner, *Rambles in and around Aberdour and Burntisland* (Edinburgh: J. Menzies, 1881), 46, mentions that Isobell Kellock had been accused by those executed at Aberdour.
74. Dunfermline Presbytery CH2\105\1, 89. Benson, *South-West Fife*, App. 2, 270.
75. Peacock (2541); Wilson (2542). Dunfermline kirk session minutes CH2\592\1. The notation includes the note that the watch should be from the 'Landwart' area of the parish and that they be incarcerated by the 'landbaillie'. It seems both women were from the rural parts of the parish. See also, Benson, *South-West Fife*, App. 2, 270. Henderson*, Extracts from the Kirk Session*, 31.
76. Kelloch (2543) Also named were Margaret Orrock (3202) of whom not much is known and Issobell Scogian (3224) who confessed to consulting Kelloch in order to have a pain healed. Benson, *South-West Fife*, App. 2, 271.
77. Case 3203. Added by Benson, *South-West Fife*, App. 2, 271. Bennet is noted as being 'this long time under an ill report'.
78. The original source of this information is the session records of Dalgety, which are cited in various sources. The most accessible is J.C.R. Buckner, *Rambles*, 44–46. Ross, *Pastoral Work in Covenanting Times*, 203–204. Benson, *South-West Fife*, App. 2, 270 and Neale, *West Fife*, 13–14.
79. There is a notation in the Acts of Parliament of Scotland dated June 27 that some witches were being sought in certain parishes, including Dalgety and Aberdour. case 1934. APS, vol. 6 p2, 498. Christian Garlick (3205); Isobell Glenn (3206), Benson, *South-West Fife*, App. 2, 272. Further commissions were granted in July, on both the 12 and 21. APS vol. 6, p2, 479 (case 3083) and Ibid. Benson also notes that in mid July the session records of Dalgety record one suspect fleeing, as well as concerns being raised about the cost of the trials.
80. Dunfermline Presbytery CH2\105\1, 89. Benson, *South-West Fife*, App. 2, 270.
81. Transcription as in Benson, *South-West Fife*, App. 2, 271. Dunfermline Presbytery CH2\105\1, 91.
82. Dunfermline Presbytery CH2\105\1, 92, 93. Benson, *South-West Fife*, App. 2, 271.
83. Dunfermline Presbytery CH2\105\1, 93. Benson, *South-West Fife*, App. 2, 271.
84. The phrase is important. In fact, the phrase is 'confessing [dying?] witches'. The word between confessing and witches is unclear. CH2\105\1, 93. Benson, *South-*

West Fife, App. 2, 271. At the next meeting, on July 2, the same request is made. This time the phrase 'confessing witches' is used. CH2\105\1, 94. Benson, App. 2, 271. Presbytery did not meet during the crucial month of July. The next minute is dated August 15, 1649.

85. Issobell Leitch (187); Margaret Aytoune (171); Issobell Guthrie (172); Christine Thomsone (169); Rossina Ossit (170); Barbara Chattow (177); Joannet Grege (180); Hellen Douglas (173); Emie Angus (179); Katharine Smyth (176) Margaret Blaikburne (174); Joannet Smetoune (184); Marjorie Fergie (183) Bessie Wilson (182); Mart Greg (181); Hellane Stanhouse (178); Katharine Grieve (186); Margaret Mairtine (185); Issobell Mitchell (175). The source of these commissions is the Justiciary Records, JC26\13. Names of other accused individuals known from other sources also appear in these confessions.

86. JC 26\13\5. July 10, 1649. The confessions of Margaret Mairtine, Katharin Grieve, and Issobell Leitch.

87. JC 26\13\5

88. Case 2600. *Mr John Lamont's Diary*, 12. Also APS vol, 6, p2, 490. Benson, *South-West Fife*, App. 2, 274. The quote is from Benson. Lamont gives details regrading the suicide.

89. Case 1941. APS vol. 6 p2, 510. Benson, *South-West Fife*, App. 2, 272.

90. Mortoun (3207); Phillip (3208). Dunfermline KS CH2\592\1, f98. Benson, *South-West Fife*, App. 2, 272.

91. Wife of Stanehouse (3213) wife of Smith (3214). The source for this information is Benson, *South-West Fife*, App. 2, 272–273. Little other information is known as the minutes of the Aberdour kirk session records CH2\3\1 are very brief.

92. Case 1944 and 3085. APS vol. 6 p2, 538. Benson, *South-West Fife*, App. 2, 273.

93. Smith (3211); Douglass (3209); Durie (3210). CH2\105\1, 94–95. Benson, *South-West Fife*, App. 2, 273. A commission was issued against a Marion Durie (2063) on August 28. The source is PA 11\8, 135. It is unclear whether these are two individuals, or the same individual. Because of the uncertainty, they are listed as separate cases in the SWHDB.

94. Margaret Currie (3212). Benson, *South-West Fife*, App. 2, 3212. The reference to dying witches comes from the Presbytery record of August 22 CH2\105\1, 95–96. Benson, App. 2, 273.

95. Dunfermline Presbytery CH2\105\1, 97. Another woman, Jonet Matheson (3216), was put to trial on September 19. CH2\105\1, 101. Benson, *South-West Fife*, App. 2, 273.

96. Benson, *South-West Fife*, App. 2, 273.

97. PA 11\8\134v

98. Dunfermline Presbytery CH2\105\1, 98. Benson, *South-West Fife*, App. 2, 273.

99. PA 11\8 157r–157v

100. PA 11\8 157v.

101. Ibid.

102. Benson, *South-West Fife*, App. 2, 273. Dunfermline Presbytery, CH2\105\1, 100.

103. Dunfermline Presbytery CH2\105\1, 107, 108, 109, 122.

104. December 31, 1649; January 7, 1650; January 30, 1650; Benson, *South-West Fife*, App. 2, 240. CH2\105\1 107, 108, 109. The minister of Inverkeithing, Walter Bruce, again found himself in difficulty both in regards to this matter and Robert Brown. May 1, 1650. Benson, App. 2, 241. CH2\105\1, 122.

105. Dunfermline KS November 6, 1649. CH2\592\1, f102. Benson, *South-West Fife*, App. 2, 274.

106. Dunfermline KS December 18, 1649 CH2\592\1, f104. Benson, *South-West Fife*, App. 2, 274.

107. Case 3217. Culross KS CH2\77\2. November 3, 1649, 64. November 6, 66, and December 4, 1649, 69. Benson tells a slightly different story, *South-West Fife*, App. 2, 273–274.

108. Case 2659. Ross tells this story well in *Aberdour and Inchcolme*, 325–28. He also notes that nine years later Janet is asking for a letter of standing, on which the session insisted on noting that she was once accused as a witch. Benson, *South-West Fife*, App. 2, 274–275.

109. Case 2657. Culross KS CH2\77\2, 85–87.

110. Marion Cunningham (2661). Dunfermline KS CH2\592\1, f111. Also, Henderson, *Extracts of the kirk session*, 33.

111. Ibid.

112. Case 3221. Benson, *South-West Fife*, App. 2, 275.

113. Benson, *South-West Fife*, has a good discussion of Bruce's role, 184–190. He argues that ministers of all theological stripes took part in this hunt. At the same time, he sees that Bruce benefited strongly from the crises: 'His prestige and authority were enhanced by the scare'. (189) William Ross, in *Aberdour and Inchcolme*, sees Bruce as an avid witch-hunter, indeed 'the greatest witch-finder of the seventeenth century' within Dunfermline Presbytery (338). What needs to be remembered is that the Inverkeithing hunt happened in the one parish which had already witnessed a massive serial hunt a generation before. However we interpret the role of Walter Bruce, that factor must be part of our consideration.

114. Case 2738. Ross, *Aberdour and Inchcolme*, 329. The SBSW lists several other cases at this period, but this is a misreading of Ross. It seems that the session's wishes were seen to in 1661 when Cant and others were brought to trial.

115. Case 207. The source of this information noted in the SBSW, the Proc. S.R.O. List, could not be located in the Scottish Record Office.

116. Case 2748. J. Nicholl, *A Diary of Public transactions and other occurrences chiefly in Scotland, from January 1650 to June 1667* (Edinburgh, 1836), 175. This is the last known case with any connection to Inverkeithing. Thus the area of Fife which saw the most intense witch-hunting, experienced all of its cases in a 35 year period (1621–56), and almost all of these in two intense hunts.

117. Case 2841. Beveridge, *Culross and Tuliallan* vol. 1, 288–290. Some very interesting details in this case. Even General Monk was sought while in Edinburgh, in an attempt to get the commission. Elspeth was apparently warded for three months before being released in August.

118. Currie (2825); Robertson (2824). Ross, *Aberdour and Inchcolme,* 329. It is not clear which 'dying witches' had named them. The best guess would be that it dated back to the 1649–50 hunt.

119. Minutes of July 1661, 3 August and August 6, 1661. Aberdour KS CH2\3\1 gives some details, especially relating to the concern regarding 'watching' Katherine Robertson and Margaret Cant.

120. Margaret Cant (2826); Janet Bell (2740); Susanna Alexander (2739). Ibid., 329–330. This case will be discussed further in chapter 8.

121. Case 2841, Beveridge, *Culross and Tuliallan* vol. 1, 318.

122. Case 2873. MacKenzie, *The Laws and Customs of Scotland*, 98.

123. The unnamed witch is case 2873. Mackenzie, *Laws and Customs*, 98. Eliot (2939) is referred to in G. Sinclair, *Satan's Invisible World Discovered* (Edinburgh, 1685), 207–208. The information is contained in a letter back to Sinclair approving of the first edition of his book. The author claimed to have seen this execution and the spot where Helen Eliot 'fell'. As the story is told, she became frightened while flying and cried out 'O God,' causing her fall.

124. Elspeth Guild (1841); Margaret Cowie (1848); Agnes Broun (1847) Cristian May (1846); Margret Horne (1845); Grissel Anderson (1844); Margaret Dobie (1843). RPC 3rd ser. vol. 2, 192. The name Grissel Anderson (2981) and that of Euphan Stirt (2983) appear in the SBSW in connection with Torryburn in 1703. The source for this information is the tract 'Minutes and Proceedings of the Session in Torryburn . . . Lillias Adie', Webster, *Rare Tracts*, 138. However, the other records do not list Grissel or Euphan. It seems possible they might have been executed in the period around 1666.

125. The SBSW had case 2875 in Dunfermline in 1667. The source is Henderson, *Annals of Dunfermline*, 338–339 in which Henderson quotes the *Kirk Session Records of the West of Fife*, as noting alarm among the ministers and sessions of the area, especially Dunfermline and Torryburn, about witches and warlocks.

126. Andro Currie (2906); Margaret Douglas (2907). Henderson, *Extracts from the Kirk Session*, 70. Gilmore, *Witchcraft and the Church of Scotland*, 233.

127. Case 2936. Ross, *Aberdour and Inchcolme*, 332.

128. Sands (609) was the only one married. Isobell Ingis (611); Jonet Hendrie (610); Agnes Hendrie (609). These records were duplicated in the SBSW as 2987–2900, the source for this reference being J.E. Simpkins, *Examples of Printed Folklore concerning Fife . . . County Folklore*. Vol. VII. (London: Sidgwick & Jackson, 1914). Justiciary Court Record JC2\14, 346–354.

129. Ibid., 351.

130. Ibid., 350.

131. Ibid., 351.

132. The burgh records note the great expense in prosecuting and executing them and took steps to make sure all of their goods were seized in order to meet these costs. It is unclear how much was involved, or who the claims were against, but the burgh did spend some effort trying to recoup some of its costs. These records are quoted in Beveridge, *Culross and Tuliallan* vol. 1, 350.

133. Historians have assumed that sabbats would be common features of Scottish witchcraft accusations. Larner, *Enemies of God*, 135–136, noted that sabbats were a common feature of confessions. Quaife, *Godly Zeal*, 60. For discussion of the elite notion of witchcraft in Scotland see Cowan, 'Darker Vision'.

134. Ibid., 350.

135. Lillias Adie (2987). Torryburn session, CH2\355\2 meeting of June 30, 1704. Others heard slightly different versions of the call. How much Jean Bizet drank was a matter of some dispute, although it seems those who stated she was drunk were probably close to the truth as the next day Jean was complaining 'of an sore head and in a sweat and she seemed not right'. This information is also excerpted in the witchcraft pamphlet 'Minutes and Proceedings of the Session of Torryburn . . .' in Webster, *Rare Tracts*, 129.

136. Torryburn KS CH2\355\2. meeting of July 29, 1704 'Minutes and Proceedings', 135–136. Elspeth Williamson (2986).

137. Ibid. July 31, 1704.

138. The latter is quoted from 'Minutes and Proceedings', 140. Meeting of August 19. Torryburn KS CH2\355\2. Mary Wilson (2991).

139. Carmichael (3230); Callender (3229); Currie (3228); Whyte (2992).

140. August 29 meeting. Torryburn KS CH2\355\2, 76. 'Minutes and Proceedings', 142. Agnes Currie is listed along with several accused witches from Pittenweem as being released on a bond of caution. JC26\D\245.

141. Torryburn KS CH2\355\2, 102. 'Minutes and Proceedings', 144. Margaret Humble was also accused of calling Margaret Black a bitch.

142. NAS GD124\15\1214.

CHAPTER EIGHT

The Role of 'Torture' in the Witch-Hunt in Fife

On the last day of December 1648 Walter Grieg, the minister of Balmerino, informed the Presbytery of Cupar of some disturbing news. Helen Young, one of the women in his parish, had confessed to being a witch. The presbytery was understandably concerned. Several members of the presbytery were appointed to meet with Helen Young and report back. The report came five days later on January 4, 1649. Helen Young still claimed to be a witch yet when pressed on particular details she seemed either 'to dissemble or els[e] be distracted'. Of greater significance, she stated that two other local women – Helen Small, of the neighbouring parish of Monimail, and Elspeth Seath of Balmerino – were also witches.[1]

What began that last day of December 1648 took over a year and a half to resolve. The story, the legal procedures and investigations of the church courts, becomes somewhat confusing because of the three individuals involved. Besides its startling origin the events raise as many questions as they answer, not only in terms of the details that emerged over the course of the investigation, but in terms of whether or not such cases were in any way representative of the 'normal' accusation of witchcraft in Scotland during this period. We shall return to discuss the fate of these three women later in the chapter.

The particular events from Balmerino as well as our discussions of the witch-hunt in the various presbyteries of Fife raise serious questions about several of the current interpretations of the role torture played in the Scottish witch-hunt. In part, these interpretations seem to arise out of the need to explain why Scotland produced more cases than England. This need to explain the differences between Scottish and English witch-trials dates to the nineteenth century when 'a dreadful and hostile geography' was considered the cause for the greater number of accusations in Scotland.[2] Because of the extent to which this issue has dominated the historiography or writing of the history of the Scottish witch-hunt, it is important to take the time to discuss it thoroughly.

While a 'hostile geography' is no longer considered the key determinant, the 'uniqueness' of England's experience of witch-hunting remains a major feature of English-language historiography. This position was summarized in 1979 by Alan Anderson and Raymond Gordon in their reply to a criticism of their work, in particular their contention of the difference between English and European (including Scottish) witch trials. They reiterated that 'English witch persecution was different quantitatively, legally and conceptually to European'.[3] The authors dismissed their critics, in part, because their English evidence came primarily from Essex, which, citing Keith Thomas, they referred to as 'one, unusually 'Europeanized' English region'.[4] This position was by no means unique. Alan Macfarlane, a major contributor to our understanding of the witch-hunt in England, has suggested that, again apart from Essex in 1645, the English witch-hunt was distinct from that on the continent and in Scotland.[5]

Many authors have argued that it was the different legal systems in England and Scotland which caused this distinction, and have pointed in particular to the role played by judicial torture in the latter. Judicial torture may be defined as the use of physical coercion that is sanctioned by the legal system in order to gain a confession from a suspect who might otherwise remain uncooperative. The use of torture to obtain confessions was accepted in many legal systems, in particular those which had evolved out of Roman law. Elliot Currie differentiates between the inquisitorial system common to Europe and the more 'restrained control' in England.[6] Robert Muchembled extends the argument to Sweden and Denmark, and suggests that few witches were executed in those countries where judicial torture was prohibited.[7] In the summaries of the historical literature this theme is accepted. Brian Levack suggests that, as there was no torture in England, large scale witch-hunts were unlikely to occur, 'and indeed very few did'.[8] Joseph Klaits suggests that England shows us how 'witch trials might have been conducted everywhere had torture not been introduced'. He contrasts this with Scotland, in particular citing the cases which occurred between 1590 and 1597.[9] Geoffrey Quaife gives us a much more gripping image:

> In Scotland, an often insensible victim had his confession mumbled to him by an inarticulate clerk and the sagging of the former's head was taken as an indication that such a confession was now offered freely.[10]

This stereotypical picture lacks only one thing – accuracy. Or to be more precise, which specific instance is the author referring to? Quaife's authority is Russell Robbins article on 'Torture' in his *The Encyclopaedia of Witchcraft and Demonology* (1959), yet nowhere in that article does Robbins describe this scene.[11] The subject of the accuracy of this portrait is one to which we shall turn in a moment.

This distinction between English and European witch persecution has come under serious scrutiny in recent years. In the introduction to the volume of essays which explored the theme of witchcraft in the peripheries of Europe, Bengt Ankarloo and Gustav Henningsen wrote:

> This leads directly to another question: the so called 'peculiarities' of English witchcraft. That it greatly differed from Continental traditions is obvious, but England was not a special case. Most of what has so far been identified as peculiar to English witchcraft should from now on be considered a characteristic for large parts of northern Europe . . . In other words, while studying the case of England, several generations of Anglo-Saxon historians have unwittingly been engaged in a comparison between central and peripheral variants of a phenomenon common to most of Europe.[12]

Later in the same volume Peter Burke argues that the pattern described by Keith Thomas and Alan Macfarlane is not peculiar to England, but in fact is the 'traditional pattern which survived best on other parts of the geographical and legal periphery (defining the legal 'centre' with reference to Roman law)'.[13] In an article which appeared several years prior to this in *History Today* entitled 'Witch Beliefs & Witch-hunting in England and Scotland' Christina Larner argued the same essential position. Pointing to the recent scholarship arising out of the criminal archives in Europe, she suggested the distinction between continental and English (or even British) 'witchcraft control' was artificial. She argued against the use of the word 'unique', and instead commented that English witchcraft was 'merely taken less seriously by the authorities than in some European countries, and more seriously than in some others'.[14]

While there seems to be a movement away from always talking about the European situation in contradistinction to England, the issue of different legal systems, in particular the use of torture, remains one of the differences stressed. Indeed, judicial torture is often used to explain why there are more cases of witchcraft in Scotland than in England.[15] One of the distinctions between the English and Scottish situations which Larner continued to stress was the difference in legal systems, including the possibility of torture.[16] The problem is, as we saw in chapter 2, the pattern of the Scottish the witch-hunt argues against it merely being a series of large serial hunts. If the use of judicial torture was the main cause of the severity of the Scottish witch-hunt, we should expect to see concentrated hunts involving large numbers of witches in only a few specific years. Instead we see a complex mixture of these panics, as well as scattered cases and isolated witches spread out over significant periods of time. The application of torture can certainly be limited to an individual or small group of suspected witches, but this on its own cannot be used to explain why the Scottish witch-hunt was so intense. Were this the case, some other factor or factors would have to have been present. It is important, however, to remember that historians have discussed judicial torture within the context of one accused naming others, leading to a serial witch-hunt. The data does not support this understanding. When we move from the national scene to consider the shape of the hunt in Fife these misgivings multiply. The number of isolated witches and the number of small cases suggests that the kind of scenario usually portrayed, a serial hunt where one accused under torture implicates her neighbours who in turn implicate others, cannot be used to explain all of these cases. There are, as we have seen, some situations where torture may have been a factor. But other than one instance when a laird illegally seized a prisoner, we have encountered no direct evidence of torture. The role of torture, at least as traditionally conceived, needs to be questioned.

Part of the difficulty lies in the imprecise manner in which the term 'torture' has been used to cover everything from brutal treatment to sleep deprivation, from 'swimming' a witch to an inquisitorial procedure in which physical harm was used in order to procure a confession. For example, to return to the article 'Torture', Robbins contrasts Scotland, where witches were tortured, with England where they were not. Yet a few pages later he uses the phrase 'commonest tortures' in reference to England, then modifies it with the interjection – 'perhaps indignities is a better word' – before cataloguing these as pricking, 'walking' (sleep deprivation, more generally referred to as waking) and sitting. This is followed by the comment that sleep deprivation should be considered 'real torture'.[17] Robbins' is a notable, though by no means unique, example of this imprecision. Even a normally careful historian such as Christina Larner succumbs to the confusion. In her discussion she distinguishes between 'direct torture' and sleep deprivation. In the midst of a discussion of direct torture, however, she cites an example of the brutal treatment of Marion Hardie. Yet this treatment was, as Larner noted, an instance of brutality at the hands of a mob intent on inflicting pain, not a judge intent on extracting a confession. That this incident should be preceded by a discussion of the devices used in attempts to extract confession and followed by the particularly famous case of Alison

Balfour, where brutal methods were used to extract a confession, only heightens the confusion.[18]

Precise definitions are crucial. While all of these activities can legitimately be understood as torture, without careful distinction the discussion becomes confused. We therefore need to distinguish between six elements: judicial torture (what Larner called direct torture, that is the application of physical coercion as part of the broadly understood legal process in order to extract a confession); searches for a witch-mark (witch-pricking); sleep deprivation (waking and watching); harsh jail conditions, including cold, poor treatment by guards, and lack of food; mob violence; and finally, the method of execution, however cruel. These distinctions are not intended to in any way downplay what must have been a brutal experience for those involved. Why they must be made is so that a fair comparison can be made between the Scottish witch-hunt and those in other parts of Europe.

An examination of those accused as witches in Fife shows that they did indeed experience harsh conditions, mob actions, and, in many cases, sleep deprivation. There is strong evidence that some were searched by witch-prickers in order to search for the mark the Devil supposedly placed on their bodies. There is, however, no evidence that any of those in Fife accused of witchcraft ever underwent judicial torture. While the pattern and shape of the witch-hunt in Fife clearly suggested that we would not find this in every case, it is still startling given the prominent place that judicial torture has had in explaining the severity of the Scottish witch-hunt to state that there is no evidence of any case where it was used – and this in a shire where the witch-hunt was so intense.

It is tempting to fall back on issues such as the silence of the records and the paucity of sources. And it is true that the records for two of the major panics, the one which afflicted Inverkeithing in 1649 and the one which spread through Cupar Presbytery in 1662 are missing key elements and woefully inadequate. Yet, this should not prevent us from facing the fact that judicial torture was not needed. Other mechanisms, witch-pricking and in particular sleep deprivation, were adequate to drive the witch hunt. (The latter, in particular, was vital within the context of the Scottish witch-hunt. How vital we shall see when we consider more fully the case of Elspeth Seath.) For the moment, though, it needs to be noted: there is no evidence of judicial torture in Fife.

Was Fife unique in this regard? It is tempting to say that it was not, but the simple fact is that we do not know. While the shape of the national hunt suggests that the use of judicial torture was probably not that extensive, within individual shires it may have been a factor. We know this to be true of Haddington where the royal witch-hunt of 1590 originated. Many of the North Berwick witches were brutally tortured in order to extract confessions. Amazingly enough, John Cunningham or Fian held up under this torture.[19] Brian Levack, who has studied the extensive hunt which occurred in 1661 and 1662 in Haddington suggests that torture played a role here. Unfortunately, his otherwise excellent article does not detail or describe any specific instances occurring.[20] When these cases in Haddington are charted the large number of cases in a relatively few years does suggest that serial hunts, driven by either judicial torture or witch-prickers, predominated (see Appendix D). More case studies of the situation in Haddington, in particular the massive hunt in 1649, may shed further light on this subject.

While the extent of judicial torture in Haddington may remain unclear, the main point needs to be reiterated: a lengthy, numerically significant witch-hunt occurred in Fife involving over four hundred cases without judicial torture 'causing' it or even playing a discernable role. The obvious question to then ask is, where and when did judicial torture play a role? Surprisingly few cases are ever cited in the literature dealing with the Scottish witch-hunt and they include the North Berwick witches, Alison Balfour of Orkney, and an alleged incident during the Cromwellian occupation.[21] There is no doubt, as Edward Cowan has suggested, that the use of judicial torture in the trials of the North Berwick witches coupled with the introduction of continental witch theory profoundly affected the witch-hunts which subsequently occurred in Scotland.[22] The 'reality' of witches had been confirmed in the minds of the elite, allowing them to cooperate in or become the driving force behind future hunts. What is surprising is the lack of cases after this date which mention that torture was used to extract confessions. There are no records of a judicial torture similar to that experienced by Alison Balfour and family being repeated in Orkney.[23] Finally, there is the mysterious case involving sixty individuals which occurred in 1652 during the occupation. It is impossible to say more about it, as we do not know where it occurred or the names of any of those supposedly tortured. Until we know more, too much should not be made of this incident.[24] Judicial torture happened in Scotland. What is lacking is any direct evidence of it occurring apart from these and a few other cases. A careful reading of the excerpts provided in George Black's *Calendar of Cases of Witchcraft in Scotland 1510–1727* confirms that torture is rarely mentioned, and sometimes the reference is only to indicate that it was illegal.[25] Perhaps it has taken such a prominent place in the literature on Scottish witch-craft, as Clive Holmes has argued was the case with demonic possessions,[26] not because it was common but because it was the exception. If so few examples are cited, how has the idea of the prominent place of judicial torture developed?

Many of the arguments historians have advanced for the use of judicial torture arise out of Privy Council recommendations on the subject. In October 1591 the Privy Council issued a general commission which included the explicit direction to apply physical torture in order to extract a confession.[27] Larner is correct in speaking of this as a 'licence for an indiscriminate witch-hunt', and given that there are no documents detailing the activities which followed in Larner's words, 'the full extent of the hunt can never be known'.[28] Still, it seems logical to assume that this direction to use torture would also be part of what was rescinded when this general commission was revoked in August of 1597. After 1597, each case required its own commission.[29] Privy Council motions enter the debate again in reference to the 1661 witch-hunt. On April 10, the council ruled that a suspected witch could not be arrested without special warrant, and included a prohibition against pricking, torture or other means to coerce confessions.[30] Given the generic meaning of the word torture, and the inclusion of the concept of pricking, and in the commission cited by Larner of sleep deprivation,[31] we need to be careful not to leap to the conclusion that this proves judicial torture was thus driving the Scottish witch-hunt.

There is one further question that needs to be considered: assuming for a moment the existence of judicial torture in Scotland, when was it applied? As noted, after 1597 a special commission was required in order to try a witch. If torture was to be applied, should we not expect to find this permission granted in the commission? Or, was this done earlier upon the arrest of the suspect, and if so, by whom? Answers to these questions are hard to come by. In the chart 'Processing a witch' Larner has torture occur *before* a commission was granted, at the same time other methods, including sleep deprivation and pricking, might also be used.[32] The difficulty with this model is that the literature on Scots law and criminal cases notes that the use of torture in other instances, for example the trials of the MacGregors, was generally considered a prerogative of the Privy Council.[33] It should have been part of the actual trial or interrogation for the trial once a commission had been granted. If the text of most commissions is to be taken literally, however, it would have been redundant to resort to any form of judicial torture – the standard form granting a commission to put a witch on trial in Fife includes the notation that the individual was a 'confessed witch'. Why then would one need to use judicial torture to bring her to a confession? This issue needs to be addressed. Mechanisms other than judicial torture were far more commonly used. The role of witch-prickers and sleep deprivation needs to be considered. Both of these practices occurred in England.[34]

Searching the body of an accused person for an insensate spot, or 'witch-pricking', has long been accepted as one of the principal means by which individuals were found guilty of the crime in Scotland. Larner has summarized this position by noting that 'the dominance of the witch's mark, which provided an intellectual bridge between popular and educated belief, and the consequent role of the pricker, also appear strongly in Scotland'.[35] W.N. Neill, in an article which appeared in the *Scottish Historical Review* in 1891 argued for the importance of the 'Professional Pricker'.[36] A distinction may need to be made between the searching of a woman, already arrested and suspected as a witch for the Devils mark and the proactive activity of the witch-pricker. The former could occur anytime after her arrest, and at random. In situations where a professional witch-finder was brought on the scene, a hunt could spread to include those normally not considered witches by the community. In these instances one would expect to find a concentration of cases. So, for example, references to John Kincaid appearing in areas of intense persecution in 1649 and an unknown witch-pricker appearing in Cupar Presbytery in 1662 come as no surprise.[37] But, how prevalent was this kind of activity? When did these professional witch-finders operate?

The current evidence from throughout Scotland suggests that such activity was quite limited prior to 1630. Agnes Sampson was pricked for the witch's mark during the 1590–1 hunt.[38] Christina Larner also refers to the case of Margaret Atkin, 'the great witch of Balweary', who, in the period after 1597, acted as a witch-finder. Interestingly enough she did not search with a pin, but instead was noted for finding them by merely looking at them: 'they had a secret mark all of that sort, in their eyes, whereby she could surely tell, how soon she looked upon any, whether they were witches or not'. She was eventually discovered as a fraud, but not before causing the execution of accused witches as far away as Glasgow and was brought back to Fife where she had originally been apprehended.[39] It is interesting to speculate on whether this Margaret Atkin was also known as 'Marion Kwyne, detector of witches' who seems to have been at the heart of a major hunt involving thirteen women and two men in the neighbouring parish of Kirkcaldy.[40] There is no clear indication of any witch finders at work in the other witchcraft cases which took place during this year.

The next indication of a professional witch-finder at work comes in 1632 when the activity of one John Balfour in Corhouse came to the attention of the Privy Council. The Privy Council interpreted his activity as fraudulent, as going about 'the country abusing simple and ignorant people for his private gain'.[41] All of the other cases cited by W. N. Neill took place between this date and 1677, when witch-prickers seem to have been active in Stirling and Haddington, a point after which he argues they began to decline.[42] The most cryptic reference is a quotation attributed to the minister of Gladsmuir, Rev. John Bell:

> I need not insist much in describing this mark, which is sometimes like a blewish spot; and I myself have seen it in the body of a confessing witch, like a little powder-mark of a blea colour, somewhat hard, and withall insensible, so as it did not bleed when I pricked it.[43]

Given the fact that the Gladsmuir-Haddington area witnessed some of the most intense witch-hunts anywhere in Scotland, and given the fact that Bell did not become minister there until 1701, a time when no known cases have been discovered, this is a fascinating, if puzzling, reference indeed.[44] Most of the cases noted by Larner of the activity of witch-prickers, fall within the same period of roughly forty years. The last case she cites occurred in Thurso in 1718.[45]

The research on Fife has uncovered several instances where professional witch-prickers were active, all but Margaret Atkin within this period (1630 to 1670) which spans the greatest years of the hunt. During the intense investigation in 1637 of Alison Dick in Kirkcaldy, there is a reference to someone riding to Preston 'for the man who tries the witches'.[46] In Dunfermline in 1643 we have another curious reference. David Crystie and Margaret Crystie were fined as a result of a disturbance which occurred while Margaret was going into the church to visit her mother, who was being held in the church as a witch. The record speaks of the mother's guilt being 'sufficentilie provine be certane famous Witnesses'.[47] Whether this refers to some individual witch-finder is an open question. What is beyond doubt is the presence of John Kincaid, the famous witch-pricker, in Dunfermline parish in 1649. The session minutes not only note the execution of Bessie Mortoun, one of the nine accused of witchcraft in the parish that year, but include the record of a payment of 20 merks to John Kincaid in Tranent who had come and 'tried the witch mark on Bessie Mortoun'.[48] There is a further notation of a payment to Andrew Thomson for lodging the witch 'triers' (plural).[49] John Kincaid also made another £6 Scots that year for 'brodding' Margaret Dunhome outside of Fife in Burntcastle.[50]

The final evidence of witch-finders active in Fife comes again during a period of major persecution. The cases of Margaret Carvie and Barbara Horniman from Falkland appeared before the Privy Council in January, 1662. At least six weeks previously these two women had been imprisoned on direction of the parish minister and magistrates. During their six week imprisonment they had endured 'a great deal of torture by one who takes upon him the trial of witches by pricking'. Despite their ordeal, Margaret Carvie and Barbara Horniman maintained their innocence and, as there was no evidence against them, the Council ordered them to be set free.[51] It should be noted that these cases appear near the beginning of the significant panic that swept through Cupar Presbytery in 1662. Several months prior to this there is a similar reference in the parish of Aberdour in Dunfermline Presbytery. The minister, Mr. Bruce, informed his session that he had sent for a 'man that tries the witches, for seeking out the devil's mark'. William Ross, a local historian who has studied these records, argues this individual may even have been in the parish, for the agreement is made that the examination will take place the following day.[52] One of the women who seemingly underwent this ordeal was Janet Bell.

While there clearly was a witch-finder present in Aberdour in this period, one should be cautious in attributing to him (or her?) the origin of this outbreak of persecution. In fact, the hunt began sometime earlier with Margaret Currie and Catherine Robertson being arrested and incarcerated in July as suspected witches, as was noted in the minutes of the parish session:

> Seeing that there are severalls, in this toune, that long ago should have been apprehended for witchcraft, and never hands yet laid upon them, wherefore the Session desires the Bailzie to cause apprehend and incarcerate, presently, Margaret Currie and Catharine Robertson, or any of the two if the one be absent.[53]

The long standing nature of this quarrel seems evident based upon the known details. A 'Margaret Currie' had been accused in 1649 as a witch.[54] It is unclear whether or not this was the same individual, yet the records do note that the Margaret Currie and Catharine Robertson arrested in 1661 had been accused by 'dying witches'.[55] The next woman to be arrested, Margaret Cant, had tried to clear her name in 1654, but failed.[56] The evidence clearly suggests some long standing grudges. Also, this witch-hunt was well under way and building momentum before the appearance of the witch-pricker. Indeed Margaret Cant and Margaret Currie had already confessed their guilt, and in their confession implicated another individual, Janet Bell.

Janet Bell had some status within the community. She was ordered imprisoned in one of her homes (she was the owner of several houses in Aberdour). When news of her arrest reached Lord Morton, he ordered her to be released. The session, according to Ross, resisted this order sending the minister to 'inquire on what grounds his Lordship had given this order'.[57] The resolution of the dispute was that Lord Morton was forced to allow Janet Bell to be imprisoned, but made it clear that the session was responsible for the manner in which Bell and the other imprisoned women were treated. It was at this point in the proceedings that the witch-pricker arrived on the scene. Although we know neither the details of the pricking itself nor the fate of these women, there is a further note that Janet Bell had, in her confession, named another woman, Susanna Alexander, as a witch.[58] Given these circumstances, it seems plausible to argue a connection between the social status of Bell and the need to acquire the services of a professional witch-finder. Put simply, because she was of some social standing it was essential that her guilt be confirmed. The witch-finders role was thus not to begin the hunt (which was already underway), but to maintain it at a critical juncture when a crack within the solidarity of the elite began to appear.

We have already discussed another situation where a witch-finder served, not to trigger a witch-hunt, but to sustain one which was already underway. That hunt began in April of 1649 and had spread to five cases before the presence of the witch-finder is noted.[59] Interestingly, the hunt began not with the arrival of a witch-pricker but with the accusations of a confessed warlock in Dalgety. This individual had been warded and watched in order to obtain his confession and receive information about his various accomplices.[60] Thus while we have clear indicators of the presence of professional witch-finders in Fife, it seems evident that they were not the primary driving force behind the hunt itself. The key lies in that apparently subtle form of 'torture' which Larner and others have noted as important – sleep deprivation. To understand how important this method was, it is useful to return in some detail to the case with which we began this chapter, the story of what happened in Balmerino in 1649 and 1650.

To tell the rather complicated account of what occurred following the original accusations it is best to take each of the individual participants in turn. Helen Young, who had confessed she was a witch, died of sickness on January 18th, 1649, only nineteen days after the original incident was brought before the presbytery. Given her sudden end, we need to ask what caused her to confess to being a witch. Was she ill and hallucinating? Was it spite at the end of her life to name two women and call them witches? We can only guess as to her motives. What we do know is, despite the fact she seems not to have accused either Helen Small or Elspeth Seath of anything specific the presbytery conducted in-depth investigations.[61]

This was not surprising for each of these women had a dubious reputation within her own community. Helen Small of Monimail's reputation was particularly striking. She had already appeared before the session of Monimail in 1644 because she was long suspected of various incidents of witchcraft. These stories, told again in 1650, told of a series of conflicts with neighbours which had taken place over the years. For example, once she sent a 'stoupe of barme' (a cup of some kind of broth, or soup) to Thomas Mackassie, to be given to him while he was sick. He later died. In another incident, Helen had a dispute with Alexander Arthur's wife. She became ill. Alexander confronted Helen with this. His cow died, but immediately his wife became better. Another story was told of how when John Skirling had passed Helen on the road, she had cursed him and he had later died.[62] Witnesses came before the presbytery who gave testimony which supported these claims. Other witnesses appeared accusing her of various acts of *malefice* or saying they had heard rumours that she was a witch.

Helen Small herself appeared, on more than one occasion, and denied the charges. Yet, it was clear that she had been aware of the rumours. Indeed, after 'some shifting answeres' under interrogation by the presbytery she admitted to knowing of them. When asked why she had not tried to have these rumours stopped, she answered that she 'could not stope their mouthes, and God would reward them'. She denied all charges. The last we hear of the case is on February 1st, 1650, when the session of Monimail produced its process which was some-what vague in its particulars. It was sent back to the session. Helen was to appear before the presbytery whenever cited. Her subsequent fate remains unclear.[63]

Elspeth Seath's situation was more complicated and thus, because these complications were recorded, fascinating. Like Helen Small, she was brought before the presbytery of Cupar and questioned. On March 15th, Andrew Patrick gave testimony that at the beginning of autumn two years previously as he was coming home between 11:00 and 12:00 at night, he saw seven or eight women dancing 'with a meckle man in the midst of them'. His story became confusing at this point but it seems that they saw him, then took him to the little lake by which they were dancing, and put him into it up to his shoulder blades. The only one of the women he recognised, he informed the presbytery, was Elpeth Seath.

He claimed to have recognised her voice. It was she who told the others to let him go as he was only a 'silly drunken larde'. He ran home wet.[64]

Andrew Patrick did have to try to explain to the presbytery what exactly he was doing out that late at night. He stated that he had gone out to the tailors, and while there, he had sent out for a quart of ale, which he had then consumed. Yet the controversy that raged was not over this, but over who he had in fact claimed to have seen at this loch-side soiree. In his appearances before the presbytery, Andrew Patrick claimed to have only recognised Elspeth. Others heard him state that he also saw Helen Swyn and Isobel Troylus. Great effort was expended to determine who, in fact, Andrew Patrick had claimed to have seen at the loch that night. (Particularly great effort was expended by Helen Swyn and Isobel Troylus, both of whom seemed to have had some status in the community, to make sure their names were not drawn into this matter.) In the end and despite credible testimony that Patrick had indeed mentioned other names, only Elspeth Seath's name was accepted.[65]

In the midst of their investigation into Andrew Patrick's claims the presbytery ran into a major obstacle to their further enquiries. By June 14th the presbytery had received back a response from the Justice in Edinburgh[66] that they did have enough evidence against Elspeth Seath to incarcerate and question her. Further, they were given a warrant. But, the Magistrates in Cupar would not put Elspeth in prison. They were not convinced, despite assurances, that the parish of Balmerino was going to pay the costs. Instead, they offered to incarcerate Elspeth Seath in the thieves hole. This was not acceptable to the presbytery. They wanted her kept in close confinement, with no one able to harm her or see her but the presbytery.[67]

While this dispute dragged on, Elspeth appeared before the presbytery and was accused of being a witch. She was accused of cursing one of Jean Bruice's cows, which would not eat for four days. Jean had then gone, found Elspeth, and had her place her hands on the cows sides. Elspeth had done this and said the words 'lamby, lamby, yee wil be well enough'. The cow recovered. Jean Bruice was also the first person to accuse Elspeth of something else, something very odd: she stated that Elspeth 'used to sitt down in the way when she mett any body'. The next witness, Isobell Oliphant, claimed that one of her cows ate some thatch from Elspeth's house. In the dispute that followed, Elspeth had struck the cow and then cast a spell on it. The cow had died. Isobell claimed she did not say anything about this. Instead, she charged that it was Elspeth herself who had spread the story. The strange comment about Elspeth sitting down at the gate was again repeated.[68]

Several other witnesses were called, each of whom had similar stories to tell. The entire testimony of the last witness, Isobel Black, consisted of the charge that Elspeth used 'ordinarily to hurch down in the gate lyk a hare'. All of these charges Elspeth denied. At this point the case stalled. Testimony had been given. The evidence had been denied.[69] The presbytery continued to try to get the officials in Cupar to incarcerate Elspeth. The presbytery promised that they would appoint some people to watch her at their own expense. Again, they were offered the thieves hole. The presbytery tried to get the central government to force the officials in Cupar to give way, but they failed. On December 6th, Elspeth appears for the last time before the presbytery. Because the town of Cupar 'wold not assist in warding and watching the said Elspet,' she could not be tried. She was told to appear again, if called.[70] As a footnote, the case does not seem to have ended here. In April of the next year, 1650, there is a brief mention of Elspeth in the records of the Synod of Fife. It stated that there would be an appeal from all of the pulpits of the presbytery of Cupar for more evidence against Elspeth Seath. What, if anything, happened next we do not know.[71]

Neither Helen Small nor Elspeth Seath confessed to being a witch and, despite the quantity of evidence of *malefice* and bad reputation that each had, neither was convicted as a witch. Why? The lack of confession seems to have been vital. And it was the inability of the clergy and magistrates in Balmerino, a small parish on the Tay Coast, to force the magistrates in the nearest major centre, Cupar, to incarcerate Elspeth Seath in circumstances acceptable to them, that made the difference. Why did the presbytery continually refuse the offer of the thieves hole? Why was the town of Cupar so concerned about the expenses of incarcerating Elspeth Seath in the manner demanded by the presbytery? It seems what the presbytery was attempting to do was 'ward and watch' Elspeth. For this, as they themselves stated, particular conditions were required, not only in terms of space, but the necessity of keeping her in close confinement: '. . . and put hir in a close prison, wheir none might have accesse to hir, and that they wold appoint some to watch hir upon hir [their?] own expense'.[72] Without this ability to confine Elspeth under these conditions, no confession was possible: no confession, no confirmation that she was a witch.

When careful examination was possible the results were quite different. Janet Robertson, Agnes Quarrier, Helen Cummyng, Alesoune Hutchesone, and Agnes Robertson were all implicated in the 'foull and detestable crymes of witchcraft', in particular the murder by sorcery of Jhone Bell, and after being apprehended by the bailies of Aberdour 'and verie cairfullie truit and examenit be thame upon thair guylteness of the saidis crymes, they frelie and of thair awne accord grantit and confest the said marthour ahd thair conversing with the devill'. A commission was granted to put them to a trial on August 28, 1622.[73] In Crail in 1643 during the hunt that swept the presbytery of St. Andrews, Agnes Wallace confessed to being a witch after being warded.[74] During the same hunt in Pittenweem, the following record appears in the records of that Burgh:

> The quilk day, for the better tryal of the witches presently apprehended, to the effect they may be better watchit and preservit from information of their friends, it is ordainit that ane of the bailies or counsell sall ever be present at the taking off and putting on of the watches, three several times in the 24 hours, and sall injoyn the watches silence; and sall appoint the ablest man of the watch to command the watch until his return. The same day the bailies and clerk, or any twa of them, with concurrence of the minister, are ordainit to try and examine ye witches privately, and to keep their depositions secret, because heretofore, so sonn as ever they did dilait any, presently the partie dilaittit got knowledge thereof, and thereby was presently obdurate, at least armit, for defense.[75]

The baillies in Pittenweem (as in the other centres mentioned) seem to have been far more co-operative than those in Cupar. Why the twenty-four hour watch? Why the careful separation of the suspected witches from any outside contact? The details point to 'waking' of these individuals – sleep deprivation.[76]

The evidence suggests that sleep deprivation was vital to obtaining a confession: a confession was often necessary in order to obtain a commission and a trial which could lead to an execution. We see its effect when sleep deprivation was used, as at Pittenweem and Crail. We also see the effect when it was not used, as at Balmerino. Sleep deprivation was effective against isolated witches. It could also produce large scale hunts, when the names of accomplices were solicited. More than judicial torture or the professional witch-pricker, 'watching and waking' the accused suspects seems to have been the driving force behind of the witch-hunt in Fife. The absence of clear evidence for the use of judicial torture in Fife should lead to a re-evaluation of its role within Scotland as a whole. Judicial torture was used. The question which needs to be addressed is, how extensively? In Fife, there is no evidence of torture ever being used in the judicial process. Explanations which attempt to explain the severity of the Scottish witch-hunt based upon a legal system which allowed for judicial torture need to take this into account. Simple answers will not work. We must look elsewhere to try to understand the reason for the severe nature of Scottish witch-hunting. It is now time to turn our attention again to those who were accused of witchcraft in Fife, and the nature of the charges laid against them.

Notes

1. STACUPR, 129, 130.
2. Christina Larner, 'Witch Beliefs and Witch-hunting in England and Scotland', *History Today,* (February 1981): 32.
3. Alan Anderson & Raymond Gordon, 'The uniqueness of English witchcraft: a matter of numbers?' *British Journal of Sociology*, Vol 30, no. 3., 1979, 361. The article is a reply to J.K. Swales & Hugh V. McLachlan, 'Witchcraft and the status of women: a comment' in the same issue of the above journal, 349.
4. Ibid. The references to Thomas are on p. 523, 528, 536–7, 544.
5. Alan Macfarlane, *Tudor and Stuart England* (1970), 6.
6. Elliot P. Currie, 'The Control of Witchcraft in Renaissance Europe,' in *The social organization of law* ed. Donald Black (London: Seminar Press, 1973), 345, 352.
7. Robert Muchembled, 'Satanic Myths and Cultural Reality', in *EMEW*, 154.
8. Levack, *Witch-hunt in Europe,* 1st edition, 149, 157: 2nd edition, 163. Levack does recognise and state that other factors did allow for witch-hunting in England.
9. Klaits, *Servants of Satan*, 135–137. In his argument Klaits refers to over three hundred cases occurring in Scotland between 1591 and 1597 and cites Larner. This number does not appear in the text of *Enemies of God,* 69–72. One suspects this number originated on the graph on p. 61. More puzzling is Klaits later comment: 'Scotland experienced the simultaneous imposition of Presbyterian Calvinism and Roman-canonical legal procedures', *Servants of Satan,* 146.
10. Quaife, *Godly Zeal*, 138. The distinction between European and English witchcraft is discussed briefly on p. 135–136.
11. Ibid., 138, note 12, refers to Russell Hope Robbins, *The Encyclopaedia of Witchcraft and Demonology*, 1959 ed. (London, Spring Books, 1959), 498–510. Robbins does accept the distinction between England and the rest of Europe, including Scotland, based upon torture.
12. Ankarloo and Henningsen, 'Introduction', EMEW, 1.
13. Peter Burke, 'The Comparative Approach,' EMEW, 440.
14. Larner, 'Witch beliefs & Witch-hunting in England and Scotland', 33. Recent works seem to have accepted this understanding of the English situation as different but nevertheless part of the European experience. Briggs, *Witches and Neighbours*, 12. Sharpe, *Instruments of Darkness*, 32.
15. Klaits, *Servants of Satan*, 135–7; Quaife, *Godly Zeal*, 138. Larner, *Enemies of God*, 27, 70–71, 107–109. The key article that goes against the historiographical grain is R.D. Melville, 'Judicial Torture in England and Scotland', *SHR*, 1905. A good discussion on the subject can be found in Sharpe, *Instruments of Darkness*, 214–215, where he notes the lack of torture within England but then discusses other issues of the legal system. See also: Briggs, *Witches and Neighbours*, 332–333.
16. Larner, 'Witch beliefs', 33, 36. This theme was also articulated in *Enemies of God*, 26. A vital part of the main argument relating to torture (p. 107–109) includes a

discussion of the distinction between the English jurists during the Cromwellian occupation and the hunt which took place at the time of the Restoration.

17. Robbins, 'Torture', 505, 509.
18. Larner, *Enemies of God*, 107, 108, 109. Edward Cowan, in the popular article 'The Royal Witch-Hunt', 406, speaks of method of execution, judicial torture and witch-hunting without making a precise enough distinction between these various activities.
19. Edward J. Cowan, 'The darker vision', 127–129.
20. Levack, 'Great Scottish Witchhunt', 106. It is not clear whether or not Levack includes witch-pricking under the category of torture. In the discussion on 105 it is witch-prickers who are mentioned.
21. Robbins includes individual articles such as 'North Berwick Witches', 'Torture', etc. in his *Encyclopaedia of Witchcraft and Demonology*. Larner, *Enemies of God*, 107–109, 119. Melville, 'Judicial Torture'.
22. Cowan, 'Royal Witchhunt', 406, 409.
23. John D. M. Robertson, ed, *An Orkney Anthology: The Selected Works of Ernest Walker Marwick* (Edinburgh: Scottish Academic Press, 1991), 373.
24. The SBSW lists these cases (709–768) as 'Circuit Court Cases' yet the source is not any government documentation, but a reference to Bulstrode Whitelock, *Memoiralls of the English Affairs*, London, 1682. Sometimes a reference is made to Black, *Calendar*, 63, which quotes the same source and also includes a reference to other individuals brought before the Commissioners in Edinburgh who are described being tortured. These comments are included both in Whitelock and in *Mercurius Politicus*. As to the sixty suspects, it must be recognised that at no other time does such a situation occur where so many people were accused without any other information surviving as to the place, names, or even the month of the year. At the risk of mixing metaphors, these witches are 'phantoms'; there is not enough information about them to explore this case further.
25. Black, *Calendar*. References to torture in the excerpts include John Feane, p. 24, and Alison Balfour, p. 25. Someone was apparently tortured during the Irvine witch-hunt in 1618, 34. The other references, including the one from Crail, all indicate that the torture was illegal, 30, 48, 71, 74, 79.
26. Clive Holmes, 'Women: Witnesses and Witches', *Past and Present* 140 (August 1993): 59.
27. Cited in Larner, *Enemies of God*, 70.
28. Ibid., 70.
29. Ibid., 70–71. This point is not explicitly addressed by Larner. It is suggested by the comment that the Order 'specifically restored to the King powers which he had delegated in 1591 . . .'.
30. Levack, 'Great Scottish Witchhunt,' 105. The confusion between judicial torture, sleep deprivation, and witch-pricking is evident in this discussion. Levack notes that Kincaid and Dick, two prominent witch-prickers, were subsequently arrested. However, the discussion then continues: 'the prohibition of torture, while not absolute, discouraged the use of a judicial tool which was responsible for most of the confessions and implications made during this and other witch hunts,' 105. Judicial torture is implied, yet the direct evidence comes from instances of witch-pricking. If there are cases of judicial torture from this period we need to find them and discuss them. Larner, *Enemies of God*, 76, comments about the changes made by the edict

against torture issued in 1662 by the Privy Council: 'Under previous edicts it was illegal to try an individual without a commission from the Privy Council to named persons, but nothing was laid down as to how the information, preferably including a confession, which was laid before the Privy Council was to be obtained in the first place . . . The objection to torture had been made before during the Protectorate, but this time it was confirmed and made official by the permanent rulers'.

31. Larner, *Enemies of God*, 108, notes the fact that commissions after 1652 frequently gave instructions to avoid torture. The one she cites comes from Dumbarton in 1677 and includes the phrase 'without the use of torture hindering them to sleep or other indirect means'. The meaning one takes from the sentence is very dependent on whether or not one interprets the word torture as standing on its own, or part of the phrase 'torture hindering them to sleep'.

32. Larner, *Enemies of God*, 114.

33. Gordon Hutton, 'Stairs Public Career' in *Stair Tercentennary Studies* (Edinburgh, 1981), 32; J. Irvine Smith, 'Criminal Procedures' in *An Introduction to Scottish Legal History* (Edinburgh, 1938), notes that confessions extracted under torture were 'competent to the Privy Council and the Lord of the Justiciary until restricted', 428–9. As well as writing several articles on Scots legal history and criminal procedures, he edited Volumes II and III of the *Selected Justiciary Cases, 1624–50* (Edinburgh, 1972, 1974). The only cases in Volume II listing torture were not related to witchcraft. For example, 343, has to do with the MacGregors. In a case on adultery (p. 536) permission was specifically given to use torture, including the notation 'and for torturing thame to mak thame confess'. In his article on 'Criminal Law' in the *Introduction*, Smith makes a fascinating reference to witchcraft and torture. Assuming torture to have been used in such cases, he notes that in the records of the period 1624–50 'some trials do not bear' the marks of barbarity in their conduct" but were, in some cases 'dull,' 290. The reference comes from Gillon's introduction to Volume I of Selected Justiciary Cases. R.D. Melville, 'Use and Form of Judicial Torture' cites MacKenzie, *Criminal Law*, to support the contention that torture was a Privy Council and Justiciary court matter, 240–241. It is difficult to move beyond assumptions about torture in the judicial system and to gain specific information. For example, David Walker's article 'Evidence' in the *Introduction to Scottish Legal History*, makes no reference to torture. Neither W. Croft Dickinson's 'The High Court of Justiciary' or C.A. Malcolm's 'The Sheriff Court: Sixteenth Century and Later' are enlightening on this particular topic. Another collection, *An Introductory Survey of the Sources and Literature of Scots Law* (Edinburgh: Stair Society, 1936), has no references to torture in the index nor in the articles 'Roman Law', 'Canon Law', 'Criminal Law' or 'The Influence of the Law of Moses'. Gordon Donaldson's article 'The Church Courts' in *An Introduction to Scottish Legal History* does not discuss torture, but does suggest how church courts served as preliminary hearings in cases such as divorce, then made recommendations to secular courts, 372. A similar pattern was often followed in Fife in terms of witchcraft accusations.

34. Macfarlane, *Tudor and Stuart England*, comments on p. 20 about sleep deprivation being used in Essex in 1645. The role of Matthew Hopkins, a witch-pricker, has also been noted in Macfarlane, 6, and elsewhere. Robbins, 'Torture', comments on both waking and pricking being used in England as well as the practice of 'sitting', 509. In an article dating from the 19th century, Melville argues that despite the law torture was used in England, citing as his source Jardine's *Reading on the Use of Torture in the*

Criminal Law of England (1837). Given the imprecision with which the word torture is used, too much should not be made of this comment.

35. Larner, *Enemies of God*, 205.

36. Neill, 'Professional Pricker'. Levack 'Great Scottish Witch Hunt', 99–100.

37. Dunfermline Kirk Session records, NAS, CH2/592/1 f. 104; Chambers, *Domestic Annals of Scotland,* vol. 2, 279.

38. Larner, *Enemies of God*, 112. Case 42, SBSW.

39. Larner, *Enemies of God*, 70–71; also Spottiswoode, *History of the Church of Scotland*, 66–67, notes she's from Fife. Larner notes Spottiswoode's belief that it was the exposure of this fraud that led to King James VI's recalling 'of the standing commissions against witches'.

40. SWHDB cases 3142–3155. The source is MacBean, *The Kirkcaldy Burgh Records*. No trials are known. The reference to Kwyne comes within the accusation of Marion Rutherford. Balweary is a hamlet in the parish of Abbotshall, immediately to the east of Kirkcaldy.

41. Quoted in Neill, 'Professional Pricker', 206.

42. Ibid., 209.

43. Ibid., 206. Neill's source is Sharpe, *Historical Account*, 208–9.

44. Material on John Bell from the *Fasti Ecclesiae Scoticanae*, Volume 1, 366.

45. Larner, *Enemies of God*, 76, 87, 110–112, 115, 131. Margaret Olsone is referred to on 112.

46. 'The Trial of William Coke and Alison Dick'.

47. Neale, *The 17th Century Witch Craze in West Fife: A guide to the printed sources,* 16.

48. Bessie Mortoun, SWHDB 3207, CH2/592/1 f104; Benson, *South-West Fife*, 274.

49. Dunfermline KS, January 29, 1950. CH2/592/1 f106.

50. SBSW case 2552. Arnot, *Celebrated Criminal Trials*, 433.

51. SBSW cases 2818, 2819. Chambers, *Domestic Annals* vol. 2, 279.

52. Ross, *Aberdour and Inchcolme*, 330.

53. Quoted in Ross, ibid., 329. Margaret Currie (2825), Catherine Robertson (2824) and Janet Bell (2740) are all listed in the SBSW. Please note, however, that major corrections have been made to some of the data listed in the SBSW, based upon a close scrutiny of Ross. The error actually seems to originate in Black's *Calendar*.

54. SWHDB case 3212. Source is Benson, *South-West Fife*, App 2, 273.

55. Ross, *Aberdour and Inchcolme*, 329. There was a serious hunt, involving an unknown number of women, in Aberdour 1649–50. Some executions took place (cases 3215, 3200, 1935). These cases, all of which refer to 'some women' or 'dying witches' may, in fact, be different forms of the same information.

56. Margaret Cant, SBSW, 2738, 2826. She is referred to in Ross, 329 and 330.

57. Ross, 330. This account is dependent upon Ross's work. The analysis is the current author's.

58. Ibid., 330. Ross argues, based upon the fact that they confessed, that they were probably executed. This seems a reasonable assumption. His discussion moves into a discussion of various instruments of torture, after which he makes the telling point: 'It is but fair to say, however, that I have seen nothing to show that any instruments of torture beyond the Brodder's needles were ever used in the cases that occurred in Aberdour,' 331.

59. April 26, 1649, John Machdoch (2540); May 13, Christian Smith (3201); May 29, Isobell Peacock (2541) & Bessie Wilson (2542); July 15, Bessie Mortoun (3207) &

Marjorie Phillip (3208) first mentioned. Data from the SWHDB. However the trial in front of the witch-finder does not seem to have taken place until sometime between November 6 – when Marjorie was still being tried – and the notation of her execution in the Kirk Session records, minute of December 8, 1649. Sources: NAS CH2/592/1; CH2/105/1; Henderson, *Extracts from the Kirk Session*, 31. Benson, *South-West Fife*.

60. Dunfermline KS, April 29, 1649. NAS CH2/592/1 f89, f90.
61. STACUPR, 130.
62. STACUPR, 130
63. STACUPR, 130, 132, 134, 135.
64. STACUPR, 136–137.
65. STACUPR, 137–141, 150.
66. STACUPR, 143, 144.
67. STACUPR, 144, 146, 150.
68. STACUPR, 147–149.
69. STACUPR, 149.
70. STACUPR, 150.
71. SYNFIFE, 168.
72. STACUPR, 150.
73. Cases 958–962. The source is RPC vol. 13, 49–50.
74. Case 2466. Kinloch, *The Diary of Mr John Lamont of Newton, 1649–71*, 6.
75. Cook, *Annals of Pittenweem*, 49. Entry for July 31, 1643.
76. Ibid., 49–50. Those known to have been executed in 1643 include the wife of John Dawson (2450); Margaret Horsburgh (2454); the wife of John Crombie (2455); the wife of Thomas Wanderson (2473); the wife of Archibald Wanderson (2472). Several women were executed as witches in Pittenweem during this hunt. There were an unknown number of others executed in that year, as well as executions in the following year.

CHAPTER NINE

The Witches of Fife

Our information about the witches of Fife is fragmentary, a reality that has become evident in telling the story of how the witch-hunt affected the various parts of the shire. In many cases we have only a name listed in a commission, or a name mentioned in passing. In other situations we do not have even the name but merely a reference that a witch was executed or tried. In other circumstances we have far more detail, although admittedly the details vary in each situation. It is time to see, based upon this variety of information, if we can construct a picture of what a Fife witch looked like. Our discussion will be both quantitative and qualitative, involving both numbers and stories. We will also turn our attention to a few cases where significant information does exist.

Each society defines its 'witches' in a particular way. Scotland in the sixteenth and seventeenth century lived with a particularly harsh under-standing of who a witch was. Traditional distinctions between white and black magic had been obscured, and under the Scottish witchcraft Act of 1563 even consulting with a witch was deemed worthy of the death penalty.[1] The crime of witchcraft was, in theory at least, a crime involving heresy or beliefs at odds with the fundamental religious beliefs of the society. A pact with the Devil was a crucial element in the definition of the crime by both church and state.[2] As Brian Levack has stated:

> The emergence of the belief that witches were not merely magicians but also Devil-worshippers changed the nature of the crime of witchcraft. It made witches not simply felons, similar to murderers and thieves, but heretics and apostates, intrinsically evil individuals who had rejected their Christian faith and had decided instead to serve God's enemy, the Devil.[3]

In our discussion of the witches from the various presbyteries in Fife we have seen this concern that the suspect had rejected her faith and entered into the service of the Devil. Much of this concern, however, was expressed in documents which originated from the central government, in particular the text of commissions to put a particular suspect to a trial.

The accusations which the local populace put forward expressed a different understanding of the crime of witchcraft. Their concerns were with the acts of *malefice* or harmful magic which the suspected witch had used against her neighbours, often over an extensive period of time. These women, and occasionally men, were understood to have remarkable powers to harm and heal.[4] In a society where medical knowledge was limited, the ability to heal humans and livestock was crucial. How, then, did one distinguish between knowledge of folk medicine and casting spells? In the records of the sessions and presbyteries there seems to have been a fine line between what was considered charming and what was considered an act of witchcraft. Both activities were considered immoral by the church and were brought before the particular church court. Consulting with charmers or witches was also considered a crime worthy of censure. It is difficult sometimes to understand how the decisions were made between what punishment the suspect should receive. As we have seen, suspects were tried and executed without there being any explicit reference to a pact with the Devil. The crime of witchcraft thus, seems to have been rather elastic, being defined by public mood and the possible tensions of the time. It is also worth considering that certain qualities of the suspect may have made them more vulnerable to the more serious charge of witchcraft. The categories which need to be considered are those of gender, age and social status or class. The nature of our sources, unfortunately, limits the extent to which we can use specific numbers to address certain questions. What will become clear, however, is that throughout the hunt most of those accused of witchcraft fit a particular stereotype. They were generally older women who lived on the margins of their communities. This chapter will discuss the characteristics of the Fife witch, beginning with two fascinating examples of individuals accused of witchcraft.

The factors of gender and social status were evident in one of the last accusations of witchcraft in Fife, that made against Elizabeth Dick of Anstruther in St. Andrews presbytery, in 1701. Before the session, Elizabeth admitted that she had gone to the mill in order to seek charity (alms). After being refused she left. Those present at the mill (James Osler, the miller Alexander Grub, and Peter Olyphant's wife who had refused to give Elizabeth alms) claimed that after Elizabeth left the grain which was being milled turned from white to red. Elizabeth was sent for and returned. She stated that all she did at this point was to say 'God be in the mill' and sit down and pray 'God have an care of me for my heart is louping' after which everything returned to normal. The witnesses all agreed that after Elizabeth's return the grain turned back to its normal colour. Peter Olyphant's wife added one, perhaps crucial, detail: she stated that she had been the one who had sent for Elizabeth to return, and she had given her a handful of meal before the prayer was uttered.[5] While Elizabeth Dick may not have been typical, clearly the ability to, or even the perceived ability to, curse and remove curses made individuals more likely to respond to an appeal for charity.

This ability to be able to harm or heal was one of the characteristics attributed to witches in Fife. We have seen this in some instances as we have examined the accused from the various presbyteries. We see this with some fascinating details in one of the most complete cases for Fife, that of Alison Dick and her husband William Coke. Alison Dick was first investigated as a witch in 1621, when the session noted her appearance before them on 'sundrie poynts of witchcraft,' which she denied.[6] Two years later, the session noted expenses for warding both Alison Dick and William Coke. It seems likely, given this expense, that their incarceration was recent.[7] The concern was not necessarily with witchcraft, but related to the way in which both Alison and William appeared to treat others in the community. Public intimation from the pulpit was also made declaring that anyone having any information regarding their behaviour should come forward. Insufficient evidence seems to have been forthcoming, for in June they were released upon a bond of caution:

> Comperit William Cok and Alisone Dick his spous, quha of ther own frie will and fredome, actit bund and obleist not to live sic a vitious and licencious lyff, be cursing, swearing, and abusing of the nychtboris of this burgh, in sic sort as they have done heirtofeir. Quhilk, if they doe, they bind and obleis them to be content to be banisht this burgh and liberties, thairof, and iff ever thairafter they be fund to resort within the same, they are content to be scourgit through the towne and banisht. And the said baillies and consaill ordanis them to stand in the jogis on Seterday nixt fra auct horis to twa afternon.[8]

Publicly exposed to the community as troublemakers, their reputations had clearly been established by this point.

A decade later Alison Dick and William Coke again found themselves before the session, this time accused as witches. The first appearance was by Alison Dick on September 17, 1633, when she was accused of some activities 'tending to witchcraft'. She denied the charges, but witnesses came forward who supported the charge. Alexander Savage swore that he heard William Coke say to her 'Thou has put down many ships; it has been gude for the people of Kirkcaldie, that they had knit a stone about thy neck and drowned thee'. Another witness, Andrew Nicol, claimed to have heard an equally sharp retort from Coke to Dick, stating that it would have been better for the women of the burgh if he had been dead, then adding 'I shall cause all the world to wonder upon thee'.[9] More evidence of this rather vitriolic public spat came forward. The female witnesses all agreed, with some variations, to Jean Adamson's claim that Alison Dick had said to Coke:

> Thief! Thief! what is this what I have been doing? keeping thee thretty years from meikle evil doing. Many pretty men hast thou putten down both in ships and boats; thou has gotten the woman's song laid now. Let honest men puddle and work as they like, if they please not thee well, they shall not have meikle to the fore when they die.[10]

Both in content and by the fact that these comments were made so publicly, these harsh speeches were considered the business of session, and seen as 'tending to witchcraft'.

When the session met the following week on September 24, 1633, the focus shifted away from the quarrelling of the couple to the acts that they, particularly Alison, were alleged to have done. Janet Allen, a fisherman's widow, stated that after she had given birth Alison had arrived and asked for some 'sour bakes'. When Janet would not give her any, Alison replied by saying that 'Your bairns shall beg yet' (a prediction that apparently had come true). Janet's husband was drawn into the quarrel, which rapidly escalated from harsh retorts from Alison, to the husband striking Alison. This physical injury to Alison caused her to curse Janet Allen's husband, saying 'she would cause him rue it; and she hopet to see the powarts (tadpoles) bigg in his hair; and within half a year, he was casten away, and his boat, and perished'.[11] Alison and William's quarrelsome nature can be seen from the fact that the next to testify against them was their own daughter-in-law, Janet Saunders. William had interrupted Janet while she was weeping out of fear for the safety of her husband. William scolded her and said that Janet's husband would return 'naked and bare', again a prediction which came true two days later, the ship having been 'casten away'.[12] The next witness, Jean Adamson, told a similar tale of being interrupted, this time by Alison, while crying over her husband who was feared lost at sea. Alison Dick offered comfort, saying that the ship was loading timber in Norway and would soon be home. Again, the prediction proved true. The last witness to appear on this day, Katherin Spens, claimed that Alison had spoken ill of her husband, after which her husband had said to Katherin that 'If I had spoken two words to her the last time she was in the steeple, she would never have gotten out of it'.[13]

The tensions within this family were demonstrated in a record also dated September 24, when Janet Saunders, the daughter-in-law, was accused of slander in calling Janet Brown a witch. Janet Brown was Alison Dick's daughter. Janet Saunders spoke of the incident, in which Alison had come in while she was in despair, wondering how she would feed her children after her husband's death. Janet's testimony was that Alison had stated that Janet Brown had 'done you little kindness' following the sinking. When Alison admitted to this, the charge of slander was seemingly dropped.[14] No new evidence was heard that day, however, the session delegated James Millar to ride to Preston 'for the man who tries the witches'.[15]

This individual was Thomas Robertson the executioner from Culross, who was paid 12 shillings for his efforts. Meanwhile, Alison Dick was held in the steeple.[16] Further evidence was produced against her before the session on October 8, 1633. After being refused the money she asked from Issobel Hay, Alison had stated that Issobel's husband's voyage would suffer great loss. Furthermore Issobel charged that Alison had come into her house, apparently uninvited for Issobel was not there, and taken Issobel's sister by the hands. Since that time the 'maiden had never been in her right wits'. Another quarrel was recounted. Robert Whyt had once struck William Coke. After this, Alison came to Robert, quarrelled with him, and told him he would regret it. Robert replied, 'What sayest thou? I shall give you as much – you witch.' 'Witches take your wit and the grace from you' she responded and according to the witness, indeed that very night, Robert Whyt became 'bereft of his wits'. The matter did not end there. Robert's daughter Janet challenged Alison as the cause of her father's illness. Janet declared the response was

> Let him pay me then, and he will be the better and if he pays me not he will be the worse, for there is none that does me wrong, but I go to my god and complains upon them and within four and twenty hours, I will get amends of them.

Janet's testimony then turned to her own misfortune, a painful thigh and leg, for which she claimed Alison was responsible. A servant swore that Alison Dick had said she had 'gotten a grip' on the thigh, and would soon have the leg.[17]

It was at this juncture that Alison Dick, who had until this point denied all charges, began to make her confession. She first told of another quarrel between a skipper, David Patterson, and her husband William Coke. The quarrel over payment for carrying gear aboard was followed by William cursing David. Inevitably misfortune occurred, including the death of David and all but two or three of his crew. William Coke also fought with his own son. The son failed to give his father his bonnaillie (farewell toast) before leaving on a voyage. William's reply was to say 'The devil be with him if ever he come home again, he shall come home naked and bare', which of course came true. 'Naked and bare' in this context seems to mean impoverished for John Whyt adds testimony that while the ship was lost, he was able to save all of the men from the ship, including William Coke the younger. It was the calm two hours in which they had been able to rescue the men amidst a seven day gale that Whyt noted and the fact that the younger William Coke was the first to come on board. At this juncture, the minister James Simson demanded of Alison 'when, and how she feel in covenant with the devill'. The previous testimony of William's wrongdoings now snapped into focus, for she blamed him:

> she answered, her husband mony times urged her, and she yielded only two or three years since. The manner was thus: he gave her, soul and body, quick and quidder full to the devil and bad her do so. But she in her heart said, god guide me. And then she said to him, I shall do any thing that ye bid me: and so she gave herself to the devil in the foresaid words.

This confession was seen as a dramatic moment in this case. Those present were noted, including James Miller who was acting as clerk in keeping the minutes, as was the time of 'four hours at even' and the fact that the confession was given 'freely without compulsion'. Alison Dick had confessed. The investigation continued.[18]

While Alison painted her husband as the villain, many in the community saw her as equally troublesome and someone not to be crossed. Christian Ronaldson recounted that she had once rented rooms to Alison in the close. On hearing this, her husband declared 'he would not have the devil to dwell above him in the close', and had Alison removed. Alison informed Christian that her husband would soon sail and lose his goods. This occurred when David Whyt's ship was lost, including stock owned by Christian Ronaldon's husband. Marjory Marshall also had a confrontation with Alison prior to the loss of David Whyt's ship. Alison had brought Marjory's husband's clothes from the Castle-haven. When Marjory offered 12d in payment Alison demanded more and a dispute broke out. Marjory claimed there were not that many clothes. Alison retorted 'they shall be fewer the next time'. The ship sank shortly thereafter.[19]

Alison's begging caused a rift between her and Janet Whyt. The incident began when Janet and Katherine Wilson were sitting together at Katherine's house when Alison arrived and begged for silver. Janet would give none and fled into the house. Katherine followed, then came out to Alison and gave her a piece of bread. Janet suggested they also give her a plack (a small coin, worth about 4d), for which she would later reimburse Katherine. When Katherine gave this to Alison, she asked if this was all, then said

> If she had given me ane groat (a more valuable coin), it sent have vantaged her ane thousand punds. This is your doing, evil tidings come upon you.

This curse was followed by action. Alison went into the close and 'pissed at their meal cellar door'. The curse worked with serious results as they were meal-makers but could no longer keep meal in that cellar. The curse was also seen to have affected a horse they bought shortly thereafter, whose death had everyone saying 'that he was witched'.[20]

The final accusations brought against Alison also had to do with disputes, often over money or payment, followed by curses which came true. Euphen Boswell recounted how her husband's ship had been loaded with salt, when Alison came and asked for money. Alison had been one of the labourers who had helped load the ship with salt. When Euphan gave her meat, she asked for money. Euphan's reply was that her husband had already paid her. A curse was uttered, and the next day the ship sank, with the loss of the salt, though not the crew. James Wilson was not so fortunate. A wave swept him away in Caithness, leaving the boy next to him standing safe on the shore. This event was linked to Alison, for she and James had had a violent encounter. Again it began over money. Alison approached James and asked for silver and when he refused she, in the words of the session clerk, 'abused him with language'. His response was to strike her, after which she cursed him saying his hand would 'do him little good' on his next voyage. The hand mysteriously swelled yet nothing could be done about it. Before his next voyage he saw Alison walk between him and the ship, an action which James interpreted as a further act of vengeance. As Thomas Mustard recounted, James said

> Yon same witch thief is going betwixt me and the boat. I must have blood of her; and he went and struck her, and bled her, and she cursed and banned him.

It was on that voyage that James was swept away to sea.[21]

Such was the testimony presented against Alison Dick and William Coke. Throughout the period since October 2, 1633 Alison had been incarcerated within the church steeple. (No mention is given where or if William was being held.) The executioner from Culross, Thomas Robertson, had been sought in late September and had apparently been in Kirkcaldy for references are made to expenses paid to him on October 2nd. The expenses were very minimal, 12s, and the final accounting in the church records notes 'when he went away the first time'. Whether Robertson gave advice or used any kind of force or torture or indulged in 'witch-pricking' is uncertain. If torture was employed, it would have been illegal. Witch-pricking is a possibility although there is no evidence of this. It is possible that Robertson's presence was simply premature. Whatever his advice or purpose, Alison Dick made her confession to the session shortly thereafter on October 8 'freely without compulsion'.[22] The session moved on to the next step in the process. The presbytery was informed of the situation at the meeting of October 17, 1633.[23] Two days prior to this Alison had not only affirmed her confession, but asked forgiveness:

> The which day also Alison Dick having ane great combat with hirself and even at the poynt of confession, she was (therefore?) confessing that she had renounced god and prayed to god to forgive hir all hir witchcrafts.[24]

Despite the confession, she remained in ward and further expenses were incurred in watching her. On October 29, Robert Douglas was appointed to go to the Archbishop with the information that had been gathered.[25] A commission was sought from the Privy Council and issued on November 8, 1633.[26] The presbytery was informed on November 14 that both Coke and Dick were to go to trial.[27] That trial must have taken place shortly thereafter for Alison Dick and William Coke were burned as witches on November 19, 1633.[28] The executioner was paid £8/14s by the town. Other costs included £9/3s for the commission and 24s for coals for the watches. The total costs incurred were £16/18s for the session and £17/1s/4d for the burgh.[29]

So much time has been spent discussing this case, both for the details it offers and the process it demonstrates. All but the trial records themselves (if indeed there were any) have survived. This helps us to better understand other cases where there is only the record of a commission or the accusations made before the session or the presbytery which enables us to place these documents within some kind of context. It also demonstrates how vital the role of the church courts could be in the witch-hunt. The evidence in the case of Alison Dick and William Coke and in many other instances in Fife demonstrates the central role church courts played in hearing and dealing with accusations of witchcraft. Sessions and presbyteries served as a crucial pre-trial body, and were even able with the assistance of the burgh to incarcerate subjects. This warding and watching, as has already been argued, proved vital. In the case just discussed, Alison Dick was warded. Alison Dick eventually confessed. While William Coke was executed, there is no mention of either his confession or of him being held. The completeness of the records allow us to see how the process might work.

This case is also rich in the details, both of burgh life and the kinds of activity that might be labelled as witchcraft. Both Coke and Dick were extremely stormy individuals, fighting with each other, their families, and their neighbours. Alison Dick also seems to have been poor: so many of the accusations had their origin in a dispute over money, either owed or which Alison felt she deserved or was entitled to. Her age may be guessed at as middle-aged, both from the fact of her grown children and that she was suspected as a witch for over ten years. This reputation as a witch stands out dramatically. It seems everyone knew she was a witch, and some clearly feared her and attempted to avoid encounters with her. Janet Whyt fled into a house when Alison came begging, gave her money, then was cursed because she was not more generous. Christian Ronaldson's husband did not want her living nearby. Some of her neighbours not only recognised her as a witch but had strategies to deal with her. James Wilson believed the curse would go away if he physically struck her and drew blood. From the evidence it is clear that Alison to a certain extent revelled in the power that the reputation gave her. As the English historian J.A. Sharpe has suggested, because we do not believe in the reality of witchcraft we tend to see the witch as victim, whereas their contemporaries understood them to be people with power.[30] William Coke and Alison Dick were victims, in the sense that they were executed. At the same time, however, we need to acknowledge the power they wielded, or claimed to wield, in the lives of their neighbours. Curses were frequent, whether because a son had forgot to buy a round of ale before departing or because of some slight, and because enough of the curses seemed (at least in the eyes of the neighbours) to come true, were to be feared. It must not have been pleasant to have had it stated that soon one's husband would be drowned, or that merchant voyages would fail. Sharp tongued and quick to take offence, Alison Dick would have been a troublesome neighbour.[31]

The question of timing remains. Why were Alison Dick and William Coke accused at this particular moment in 1633? Although long suspected and definitely quarrelsome, the exact trigger is unclear. The public spat between Coke and Dick may have been the key. Three witnesses swore to what they heard, and the accusations between husband and wife were clearly that the other was responsible for the deaths and drownings of sailors from the port. Alison Dick, when she first appeared was challenged about this dispute, the content of which was seen as 'tending to Witchcraft'. Kirk sessions cared about many aspects of public life and morality. The trigger may have been this spat. Once Alison Dick had been warded those who had evidence came forward. The frequent mention of tragedy – the loss of ships, the failures of voyages, the drowning of sailors – may also have stimulated interest in having those seen at the heart of these calamities removed from the community. While this theme will be explored more fully in the discussion of witch-hunters, it is worthwhile noting that while the case of Dick and Coke took a great deal of energy from the session, other matters continued to be discussed. These included the usual spate of sexual offences, and as well, an accusation about harsh speech: on November 12, 1633, the session ordered one woman, Christian Kirk, to cease 'troubling' Agnes Young, with her tongue.[32] Rather than victims of a specific hunt for witches, Coke and Dick were brought before the session on account of their public argument and only as events evolved did this move into a full-fledged case of witchcraft.

The maritime nature of the accusations is clearly central. The details of accusations in Scotland have often focused on farming communities and the tensions over cows who gave no milk and animals who died. It has been noted by Robertson in terms of Orkney and by Naess in terms of Norway that among those who made a living by the sea the accusations against witches could be markedly different.[33] Commerce and fishing, ships lost and sailors drowned were the sources of apprehension and concern as the livelihood of the entire village was threatened. The primary accusations against both Dick and Coke dealt with shipping and sailors. It would be interesting to see if other maritime disasters precipitated witch-hunts in other burghs along the coast of Fife, in particular the South coast.

While this case is so rich in detail, we should also note what is not mentioned, or mentioned only in passing. The Devil is not absent from this case, but he has little more than a symbolic part. Even more fascinating, the Devil no sooner appears then he promptly walks off stage. While the margin of the session minutes may note 'Paction' at the time of Alison's confession, no-one explored this dramatic declaration further. There was no (or at least if there was it was not thought worthy to record, something which strains credulity) exploration of when this act of paction happened, what the Devil looked like, when and with whom Alison attended sabbats, let alone references to carnal copulation. Alison Dick had given herself to the Devil, as opposed to God. Once established, the concern for her specific acts of malice against her neighbours continues. The accusation that she was a servant of the Devil met a technical requirement, but Alison Dick was executed for her curses and acts of malice against her neighbours. No attempt seems to have been made to turn this into a hunt by asking for names of other witches. In terms of how Scottish and English witchcraft cases have been depicted in the literature, this case could easily have existed in England. If there was a uniquely Scottish feature to this case it was not judicial torture or the demonic pact but the role played by the church court. Church courts were interested in a far broader range of human activity than the legal understanding that witchcraft involved heresy, or a pact made with the Devil. Sessions and presbyteries were concerned with all human activity which did not meet a narrow definition of being godly.

Shortly after William Coke and Alison Dick were executed in Kirkcaldy, William Hutchen of Kinghorn was found guilty before the session of charming. Hutchen, who stated he was unaware that what he had done was evil, had used a charm to cure someone. The penalty was not harsh. He was made to do public penance before the pulpit, however it was made clear that further incidents would be counted as witchcraft.[34] One incident was charming; but a second made one a witch or warlock? The logic seems difficult to follow, as does the fact that Isobel Hevrie, first brought before the session of Kirkcaldy for witchcraft, was eventually sent on to the presbytery for charming.[35] Around the same time and also in Kirkcaldy presbytery some women were accused of consulting with the 'wyse wyff' Janet Layng. Those who consulted Janet were called to make public penance, but no indication exists that Janet was punished, nor does the word 'witch' appear in the record.[36] Yet David Zeman of St. Andrews, known for his cures and his ability to detect those who had been 'witched', was himself referred to as a warlock.[37] Alexander Drummond, held in Edinburgh as a charmer in 1629, was also referred to as a 'witch'.[38] Yet, several individuals appeared before the presbytery of Dunfermline who were charged with charming but not with the more serious offence of witchcraft. Margaret Fields of Culross confessed in 1636 to charming the servant William Osbourne. Also from Culross, William Drysdale was forced to repent five years later because he 'had robbed God of his glory by seeking his health by suspect means' and in 1646 a husband and wife were brought before the session for using charms on a child.[39]

It is difficult to understand how the line between charming and witchcraft was drawn in the sixteenth and seventeenth centuries.[40] The search for patterns, for a clear answer remains elusive. Cases exist of charming in Fife in the midst of major hunts; isolated cases also exist in years where there was no major concern regarding witchcraft.[41] The vagabond Dorothy Oliphant was the only person accused in Kirkcaldy in 1604, yet within that same presbytery Christian Wilson was warded in 1638 in the midst of a major witch-hunt on the basis of an overheard explanation of a charm.[42] The reason may simply be because the words 'witchcraft', 'witch' and 'warlock' were elastic in the sixteenth and seventeenth centuries. These were umbrella terms which included everything from formalized demonic pacts to evil spells cast against ones neighbours, from cures for illness to the use of charms. Perhaps we cannot find the line because there was no line, only a conviction among the elite that this spectrum of activity was wrong and needed to be suppressed. Those who could heal or offer assistance, sometimes known as white witches or cunningfolk, were as likely to be charged as witches as those with a reputation for malice and cursing. At other times, they were simply referred to as charmers – but nevertheless they were charged, and though the penalties were much less severe, they still represented an attack on what was clearly a common activity. Among those we now consider and catalogue as 'witches' were many whom their communities considered to be healers or helpers. Still, those who could cure an illness certainly were understood to be capable of casting the same on someone with whom they were at enmity. Margaret Douglas of Kirkcaldy was charged with both being able to cure and to cause calamity.[43] The skills and activities attributed to the witch were very broad.

It is also worth considering the charms which were used by those accused as witches. Several have survived from Fife. Isobel's Hevrie claimed to have learned the following charm from a 'wayfairing man':

> Three bitter has the bitten,
> Evil hart, evill eye, and evil Tongue,
> Almost three ply,
> But wyl be Father, Sone and Holy Ghost.[44]

The charm which Janet Brown of Kinghorn used to cure a foot was much simpler: 'flesh to flesh, blood to blood and bone to bone in our Lord's name'.[45] The record never refers to Janet as a witch, nor was Adam Donaldson so named, despite his use of charms and the witnesses who spoke of them. Though people sought him out for their own health, Donaldson's specialty seems to have been curing cows and horses. If a cow gave no milk, Donaldon's cure was to place a piece of rowan under the tail, and recite 'Lord Jesus, send me milk' three times on ones' knees. When buying a horse, Donaldson suggested that when one came to the first south-running water one should dismount while the horse's back legs were still in the water, take some of the sand from the riverbed, and strike the horse three times to drive away any evil spirits.[46] Marion Cunningham of Dunfermline, whose charm or prayer has already been noted, also was accused of using the line 'Ladie sweet st marie' in some of her prayers.[47]

What is striking about all of these 'charms' is their essentially religious nature. There is nothing even remotely demonic about them. Rather, they seem to be expressions of popular or folk Christianity, even survivals from practices which pre-date the Reformation. The reliance on 'three' (a symbol of the Trinity, for which there is no inverse or demonic equivalent), the address to God or Christ, all signify these as prayers. Yet in the eyes of the sessions, such prayers were suspect. In some cases those using these words or a physical charm to aid in curing were punished only mildly, and not even referred to as witches. Yet, in other instances they were seen as involved in more sinister practices. The line was again unclear. Still, one thing we can say with some certainty is that cunning folk, and those who sought them out, as well as scolds and those associated with *malefice*, were all considered to be worthy of discipline by the church authorities in Fife.

We have dealt in detail in this chapter as well as those which told the stories of the witch-hunt in each of the presbyteries, with those who were designated in seventeenth century Fife as witches. A picture, however shadowy, has emerged of the kind of individual most likely to be accused of witchcraft. The Fife witch was as likely to cure as harm, and sometimes the line between those two functions was confused by both the populace and the elite. Equally noteworthy was the characteristic of being a nuisance or scold or troublemaker. William Coke and Alison Dick both had sharp tongues. Elspeth Seath sat down in front of gates. Jonnet Dampstar of Dysart was accused of fighting with a woman in the village, then using her spinning wheel without permission, then causing the death of a cow.[48] Helen Birrell, another witch from Kirkcaldy, was known to have a sharp tongue (she did penance for it in 1616) a decade before being accused as a witch.[49] This characteristic of accused witches is one that has been recognised, both in Scotland and in Europe as a whole.[50] Many of the accused about whom we have information seem to fall into this category.

It is also clear Fife witches were women. Three hundred and fifty-one (351) of the four hundred and twenty (420) known witches from Fife, or eighty-four per cent (84%), were women. Given that in another thirty six instances (8.5 percent of the total) the gender of the accused is unknown, it seems reasonable to assume that some, if not most, of these suspects were also women. To suggest that ninety percent of those suspected as witches in Fife were women does not seem unreasonable. Only in thirty-three situations (7.5 percent) were males named as witches. Witch-hunting in Fife was gender based. Given the discussion in *Enemies of God* and in the literature on the European witch-hunt at large, this comes as no real surprise. Christina Larner's comment that 'witch-hunt is to some degree a synonym for woman-hunting' is apposite.[51] What is more difficult to determine is the significance of this reality or how we interpret it.[52] References to the misogyny found in the *Malleus Malleficarum* seem unhelpful, as there is no known incident of anyone quoting from the *Malleus* in Fife. Even James VI's *Daemonology*, where it was argued that women were more likely to be witches than men, does not seem to have been influential in Fife, at least in terms of the other ideas expressed in the tract.[53]

What little direct evidence we have for misogyny in Fife can be deduced from protests surrounding a sermon preached by Mr. James Symsons of Kirkcaldy in 1650. While not directly related to witchcraft, the sermon was preached while witch-hunting was occurring. Mr Symsons' text was Leviticus chapter 12. The complaint brought before the presbytery of Kirkcaldy was that while preaching on the text

> he did fall in these expressiones giveing a reason wherefoir the tyme and dayes of the uncleannes of women after a maid child is langer than thair separation after a man child and is twyse so long because the superfluitie of issue is twyse so much as after the other so Hippocrates. 2. Wherefoir women were subject to that infirmities and issue of blood, moir than beasts and other creatures: answer – because it is Gods judgement and punishment on them for thair sinne.
>
> When modest heirers wer blushing at this he said Hold up your heads and heir the good word of God it is not the word of Moses nor man.[54]

Symsons' seeming contravention of the rules of 'modesty' in this exposition and a further one dealing with Psalm 8, as well as other alleged shortcomings in his ministry, brought this matter to the presbytery's attention. How representative Symsons was in seeing women as particularly sinful is uncertain. Yet in considering these ideas preached in a sermon, we are discussing educated views and elite, even if local elite, conceptions of women. It is important to remember that the communities themselves seem to have identified women as witches and if the populace were not responsible for initiating the hunts, they clearly had strong ideas as to who the witches in their community were. Those witches were primarily women.

Another way of determining how strong the equation of woman was with witch is to briefly discuss those who were not – the thirty-two male witches of Fife. The charges against some of these individuals, for example Archbishop Sharp, were clearly political in nature. Others were essentially charmers or cunningmen who somehow found themselves facing more serious accusations as a witch or warlock. One, William Coke, was the male equivalent of his troublesome wife, suspected as a purveyor of misfortune and *malefice*. In other cases, we know far less, having only a name. Were males accused as witches more likely to be included in large scale hunts? Or were they solitary figures?

On the whole, men tended to be named during witch-hunts which were already underway. Of the known male witches fifteen were swept up in not only years of hunting, but in the geographic areas where the hunts were taking place. One, Thomas Jamieson of Kirkcaldy, was the husband of one of the women accused that same year (1597) in Kirkcaldy. Unfortunately, the relationships of the other male suspects is uncertain. Many of those accused, both in panic years and in more normal circumstances, were accused as soothsayers or charmers. Of those named in normal years, these include Alexander Drummond who had been incarcerated in Edinburgh, William Hutchen, John Patowne, Patrick Stewart, and William Drysdale. Andro Carmichael's name appears in 1677 when he and his wife charge another person before the session with slandering them with an accusation of witchcraft. Of those caught in the hunts, John Wastwater and Adam Donaldson of Culross, and the unnamed brewer from Dunfermline were all accused as soothsayers or charmers. Only three individuals begin to come close to our stereotypical female witch: William Coke, William Chrictoun and Robert Maxwell. All three were executed. William Chrictoun was a vagabond and in his confession did make mention of being in the Devil's service. Robert Maxwell was originally brought before the session of Dalgety for his ignorance and something which looked suspicious. Maxwell was warded, confessed to being in pact with the Devil, then named another male John Murdoche, as also being the Devil's servant. What is fascinating about these three cases is how unusual they were. Most of these men accused of witchcraft were swept up (as, incidentally, was Maxwell) in panic years. Males could be understood as charmers or cunningmen, could (if they were vagabonds) be summarily dealt with, but only in the panic years when the definition of 'witch' was expanded do they appear in any number and yet even here they remain few. Witches were overwhelmingly perceived to be female, with some confusion in that already discussed grey area between witch and charmer.

Several scholars have pointed out that we are not only dealing with gender in these circumstances, but also with age, marital status and class.[55] The traditional stereotype of a witch as an old, isolated, possibly ugly, and poor female has shown itself to be correct in many of the countries of Europe. For Fife, the data on marital status is inconclusive as the 'unknowns', which number 361, far outweigh the other categories of married (41), single (2), and widows (16).[56]

There is simply not enough evidence of either 'age' or social class to make any quantitative comparisons. Some of the accused clearly were older women. Agnes Wallace of Crail confessed to having been in the Devil's service for forty-three years, while Katherin Sands, arrested in Culross in 1675, was charged with being a witch for over thirty-four years. Interestingly, in other cases there is an indication that the accused was young. Issobell Adam of Pittenweem and Alison Balfour of Byre-hill were both noted as being young. In 1644 William Moresoune appealed his wife Margaret Young's imprisonment noting 'she is ane honest young woman of good reputation without anie scandall or blot'.[57] Whether Margaret Young's youth was considered as a significant proof, as important as her good reputation, that she was not a witch is unclear. Or, the fact that youth is mentioned may be an indication of how unusual it was to have a young woman accused of witchcraft. Many of those accused as witches in Fife were older women, but we do not know how old they were nor can we make any definitive statement about the role age played in accusations.

The evidence for the social class of Fife witches is also sketchy. William Moresoune, the spouse of Margaret Young, was a merchant burgess in Dysart, a man of some stature.[58] Janet Bell of Aberdour owned several houses.[59] We also know that some of the wives of the Inverkeithing bailies were suspects in 1649. Still, both these situations involved an ongoing serial hunt, one that potentially had moved beyond the usual suspects to include others of more status in the community. One of the local histories of Inverkeithing notes the tradition that some wise suspects intentionally named the wives of the bailies and elders, in order to put a stop to the hunt.[60] The hunt continued despite the fact that women of some status were being sought, still the idea that the hunt intentionally moved away from the usual suspects to include those of some wealth and high social status is a fascinating one. Interestingly, one of the women caught up in this hunt who one would assume to have been herself wealthy, Margaret Henderson, Lady Pittathro, was poor and lived on the fringe of the community.[61] Those with some status might be named during the periods of intense hunts, but at other times, the scant information we have suggests that those sought as witches tended to be poor.

Our evidence for the poverty of those accused in Fife is fragmentary and anecdotal. Elspeth Seath's sitting down in front of the gate and blocking people's passage may have been an attempt to extort charity. Whatever the intent, it clearly annoyed the community. Isabell Dairsie was without means. Dorothy Oliphant and William Crichton were both vagabonds. Isobell Kelloch lived on the estate of Lady Callender. When the latter refused to pay the costs of her incarceration, the money was taken from the poor box. There are other references to moneys disbursed to support 'poor' witches who had been held in ward. Of the three executed in Culross in 1675, Katherin Sand's brother had cheated her out of her inheritance, Isobell Inglis's fields were not as profitable as her neighbours, and Agnes Hendrie 'had not wherewith to life'. These misfortunes were seen as the reasons why these women had entered the Devil's service. While not conclusive, the poverty of many of those accused of witchcraft is noteworthy.[62]

An exception may be Marion Grig who was tried before the presbytery of Kirkcaldy in August 1638. Marion Grig was owed money by some in the community. Her difficulties came, as we noted briefly in the chapter six, when she attempted to collect these debts. A tale similar to the one recounted by William Marshall, was told by James Rodger and his spouse:

they being aughtand to hir 4sh 6d she come to thair house and craved them veri harlie for it and stood up aht the fire long, and they bid hir goe away bod thse wold not leave, and that same nyt he took ane sickness and would not lye in the bedd bot becom madd ane the fit took him becours, and he could not byd it, and his speache whent from him and he thought his breathe was goeing away, and he said Yon theife hes done me evil and for Gods saik goe to hir and his wyff went to hir and sought his helth from hir, for Gods saik, thryse, and brought hir with hir, and the paine being aff him he besought hir, for Gods saik to help and ease his paine . . .

After returning and striking him with a cloth, Rodger recovered.[63] The small amounts owing, in each case 4s/6d, and the effort put into trying to have this money repaid is interesting. Had Marion's status declined to the point where she was now poor enough to need this money? The village tensions are evident, as is the belief that the harsh words spoken could lead to an illness, an illness which the individual who had so spoken could remove.

Despite the fact that we have had to construct a picture based upon fragmentary information, it still remains clear that the stereotypical image of the witch was dominant in Fife. The Fife witch was female, old and poor. This stereotype broke down somewhat during the major hunts, but remained remarkably steady. Communities knew who their 'witches' were. The most remarkable thing about the hunt which spread through Cupar Presbytery in 1662 was not how many individuals were involved, but how few. Even in the last witch hunt which occurred in 1704 in Pittenweem, the stereotype held. This also involved the only documented lynching of a witch in Fife.

The events in Pittenweem were in many ways unique. They were known and publicized at the time through a series of pamphlets which took very different interpretations of the events described.[64] These pamphlets, as well as the session records of the time, give us some indication of what occurred in this small burgh on the south-east coast of Fife within the presbytery of St. Andrews. The role of an adolescent accuser, reminiscent of a series of witchcraft allegations made in 1695 in Paisley, sets this case apart. The author of one of the pamphlets, writing under the name a Gentleman from Fife, stated his firm belief that the minister of Pittenweem had actually read the pamphlets concerning the Bargarran case to Patrick Morton, the adolescent affected in Pittenweem. The author of 'True and Full Relation' vehemently denied this charge. The unique nature of what occurred, however, suggests similarities not only with the events in Paisley, but also with the Salem, Massachusetts hunt of 1692 and the massive hunt in Sweden in 1677.[65]

Events began when Patrick Morton, the sixteen year old son of a smith, became convinced that he had been bewitched by Beatrix Laing. He claimed that one day in March while working on some nails he was approached by Beatrix Laing who asked him to make some nails for her. When he refused, Beatrix left 'muttering some threatening expressions'. Soon thereafter Patrick became ill, and when walking by Laing's house he saw a 'small vessel full of Water and therein a Coal of Fire Slockned in the Water' and became convinced that he had been bewitched.[66] As his health continued to decline, he made his suspicions known. Beatrix Laing, and several others were incarcerated. Beatrix soon confessed, and implicated others in the area as witches. Various accounts of what happened in order to bring Beatrix Laing, Isabell Adam, Nicolas Lawson and Janet Cornfoot to confess themselves as being witches are given. The accounts agree that no confessions were made before these individuals were arrested. The author of *An Answer* described drunken guards keeping these women awake 'by pinching and Pricking some of them with Pins and Elsions', the result of which was that they remained without sleep for several days.[67] *A Just Reproof*, a reply to *An Answer* which claimed to set the record straight, admitted there was some ill-usage at the beginning, but this was quickly stopped by the minister and magistrates. Beatrix Laing's own complaint issued a year later to the Privy Council gives her account of what she experienced:

> because she would not confess that she was a witch and in compact with the devill, was tortured by keeping her awake without sleep for fyve days and nights together, and by continually pricking her with instruments in the shoulders, back, and thighs, that the blood gushed out in great abundance, so that her lyfe was a burden to her; and they urging her continuallie to confess, the petitioner expressed several things as they directed her, to be rid of the present torture; and because afterwards avowed and publicly told that what she had said to them of her seeing the divell, &c., was lyes and untruths, they put her in the stocks for several dayes, and then carried her to the thief's hole, and from that they transported her to a dark dungeon, wher she was allowed no maner of light, nor humane converse; and in this condition she lay for fyve months together . . .[68]

Those who confessed named others, so that when the Privy Council was approached for a commission to try these witches on June 1,[69] seven individuals were being held as suspected witches in Pittenweem.

Prior to the appeal for a commission, the kirk session examined Isabell Adam, Beatrix Laing, Nicolas Lawson and Janet Cornfoot. All had by this point confessed 'ther compact with the Devil, renouncing their baptism and being at meetings with the Devil' and others. The decision of session was to take this matter to the presbytery, which dealt with it on June 14, 1704.[70] At this meeting, Janet Horesburgh and Lillias Wallace each denied she was a witch, even though Janet Cornfoot and Nicholas Lawson claimed to have seen them both at one of the meetings. (Presbytery spent time making sure there was no malice between these various women.) Beatrix Laing was also examined. While acknowledging she had been responsible for the charm that Patrick Morton saw, she denied ever seeing the wax picture which allegedly had been made. Beatrix's admission to a 'pact' with the Devil was also qualified by her claim that she had only seen the Devil once upon the moor when he appeared in the shape of a black Dog which she had stroked. Other than this once, she claimed never to have seen him. When asked about the incident on the moor when she saw the Devil in the shape of a Black Dog she stated she knew it was the Devil,

> Because he changed his shape. And she being asked if the Devil had caused her renounce her Baptism? She answered, yes, and that it was upon Coves Moor.[71]

Janet Cornfoot and Isobell Adam admitted not only to entering into a pact but also to being at many meetings.

A Privy Council warrant to hold a trial was issued on June 3, the day before this meeting of the presbytery. The details of the case were outlined in the warrant and permission was given to try the case. In late July, the decision of the Lord Advocate that the trial should be in Edinburgh is recorded.[72] No record of this trial seemingly exists,[73] yet both the author of *An Answer* and Cook claim that the sheriff of Fife, the Earl of Rothes, was not satisfied with the evidence presented and had all of the women released.[74] This result seems to have been unsatisfactory to many in Pittenweem. On January 30, 1705 Janet Cornfoot was returned to the village from which she had apparently escaped. Here she was lynched by a mob. Janet Cornfoot was dragged from a house, taken to the harbour where the mob either tried to swim her or tied her to a rope stretched between a ship and the shore and pelted her with rocks (accounts and interpretations of these events vary), then dragged her back into the street where she was pressed under a door on which heavy stones were laid until she died.[75]

The blame for these events was a topic of discussion at the time. The author of *An Answer* clearly blamed both ministers and magistrates, while the author of *A Just Reproof* not only argued the minister was uninvolved, but claimed that those responsible were not locals. On February 15, 1705 the Privy Council heard from a committee of enquiry into this murder. Those involved were named, including four held in prison, as well as some who had fled. A process was ordered into the failure of the magistrates to keep the peace in the burgh.[76] Yet no one was ever taken to trial for this lynching. Furthermore, the bailies of the town refused to take out a bond of peace in order to protect Beatrix Laing.[77] The session remained firm in its conviction that these women should have been brought to trial.[78] The only admission that there were problems related to these events in 1704 and 1705 came in October 28, 1710 when William Bell, one of the former bailies, stated 'I am convinced of the rashness, illegality and unwarrantableness of our proceedings, having proceeded on idle stories' and that Morton 'was then labouring under a melancholy distemper'. The statement was made as a result of an action brought by Janet Horseburgh for her wrongful imprisonment.[79]

As the last major outbreak of witch-hunting in Fife, the events of Pittenweem in 1704–05 demonstrated how strong the stereotype of 'witch' remained, even as some members of the elite moved away from the very concept that there might be witches. Witches were women. More than that, witches were older and generally outcast women. These women may have lived on the fringes of their village or town as a result of their poverty, their sharp-tongue, or some other idiosyncratic behaviour, but their communities knew them, sometimes even feared them, as witches. The definition of the crime of witchcraft was elastic, and generally far more concerned with acts of magic (good or evil) than with pacts with the Devil. Even those involved in acts of healing or charming ran the risk of being accused as witches. Consulting with charmers and witches was also considered an activity worthy of the kirk's interest and discipline. It was generally only during those occasions when serial hunts occurred that the stereotype of the witch broadened to include women who did not fit the stereotype and men. Witch-hunting was, as Larner suggested, woman hunting. Debate will continue to rage as to what is the precise meaning of this reality. The society of sixteenth and seventeenth century Scotland was patriarchal. Keith Brown's recent article 'The Laird, his Daughter, her Husband and the Minister' explored how a ballad interpreted the events surrounding the murder by a wife of her husband. The husband, an older man, was known to have beaten Jean Livingson. Yet in the ballad Jean was portrayed as sharp-tongued, and to an extent deserving of the ill-treatment she suffered at the hands of her husband:

> But Waristoun spake a word in jest:
> Her answer was not good;
> And he has thrown a plate at her,
> Made her mouth gush with bluid.[80]

Jean's attempt to escape her predicament by plotting and then helping to put into effect her husband's murder met with no sympathy from the elite. Rather, as Brown states, it was necessary for the elite to bring her to a confession, for they needed 'a subservient and apologetic victim'.[81] It is not difficult to imagine under these circumstances how women might be particularly vulnerable to being targeted as evil or as witches. Indeed, if we take into account the efforts of sessions and presbyteries to reshape the mores and values of the population and to criminalize acts of superstition such as charms and healing prayers, it is no wonder that women who played a prominent role in child birth, child-rearing and were practitioners of folk medicine found their actions suddenly dangerous and open to legal action. Those who survived by claiming control over the power to curse found themselves particularly vulnerable to such charges. It was this ability to define what was acceptable behaviour, to shape the very image of 'witch' which was crucial to the development of witch-hunting. It was the witch-hunters who constructed this image of woman as witch, and it is to them which we now must turn.

Notes

1. Larner, *Enemies of God*, 9.
2. Ibid., 10–11, 95–96, 200–201.
3. Levack, *Witch-hunt*, 2nd ed., 8.
4. Ibid., 4–9. Larner, *Enemies of God*, 7–8, 10–11, 106–107.
5. Elisabeth Dick (2976). Anstruther Easter KS CH2\625\2. The session decided to turn this matter over to the presbytery. There is no indication as to the outcome.
6. Kirkcaldy KS February 13, 1621. Campbell, *The Church and Parish of Kirkcaldy*, 166–167.
7. Kirkcaldy KS, April 22, 1623; May 20, 1623; and, May 27, 1623. The amount in each case was 36s. Campbell, ibid., 167.
8. Quoted in MacBean, *The Kirkcaldy Burgh Records*, 157–158. MacBean also includes the text of the kirk session record of May 22 1623 on p. 344. Unfortunately, he doesn't note that the next reference – to September 24 – relates to documents from 1633, not 1623.
9. The transcription is that found in the pamphlet 'The Trial of William Coke and Alison Dick . . .' in Webster, *Rare Tracts*. Kirk Session of Kirkcaldy, minutes of September 17, 1633. For the information in this case see also Campbell, ibid., 168–172. Also excerpts were included in John Sinclair ed., *The Statistical Account of Scotland 1791–99,* vol. X, Fife, (Edinburgh: EP Publishing, 1978 edition), 807–816. Despite the evidence being fairly broadly published, this case has not had a prominent place in the literature. Future notes will refer only to the source being directly quoted.
10. Ibid., 114. Kirkcaldy KS.
11. *Statistical Account for Scotland*, 808. Kirkcaldy KS records September 24, 1633.
12. 'Trial', 115–116.
13. *Statistical Account*, 810. Kirkcaldy KS.
14. Kirkcaldy KS. This incident is not recorded in either the Statistical Account or the Pamphlet. Who said what about whom does become confusing. Tensions within the family are evident. This may have also been an attempt to discredit Janet Saunders as a witness against William Coke.
15. Kirkcaldy KS. *Statistical Account*, 810. The session and town agreed to pay the expenses.
16. Kirkcaldy KS, October 2 1633. 5s were spent for 'coals to warme in Alison Dick' in the steeple. There is no reference to William Coke being held.
17. Kirkcaldy KS. The translation differs slightly from that given in the Statistical account, 810–811, and 'Trial', 117. The former seems to depend upon the latter. The gist is correct in these published accounts. Some words are changed or left out.

18. Kirkcaldy KS. October 8, 1633. William Coke the younger's actions are confusing. At one point it states he 'was perished; and he saved all the men in the ship'. 'Perished' suggests this was the fate about to befall the crew. William Coke the younger's presence was clearly seen as a factor, but whether it was understood to be at his own instigation or not that they were saved, seems unclear. Was this perceived as a battle between two 'sorcerers', the one trying to sink, the other to save? *Statistical Account*, 811–812. One important change is made in the long quotation. The printed source has it as 'God', where in the Manuscript it is 'god' with no upper-case.

19. Ibid., 813.

20. Kirkcaldy KS. *Statistical Account*, 813–814. The exact wording relating to the incident at the cellar in the Statistical Account is: 'And she went down the close, and pissed at their meal-cellar door; and after that, they had never meal in that cellar, (they being meal-makers).'

21. Kirkcaldy KS. *Statistical Account*, 814.

22. The excerpted records leave out much of the information relating to expenditures and process. Kirkcaldy KS, October 2, 1633. The confession on October 8 is recorded.

23. PBK, 68.

24. Kirkcaldy KS, October 15, 1633.

25. *Statistical Account*, 814.

26. National Library of Scotland, Adv. Ms. 31.310, f64v. Michael Wasser discovered this commission while doing research on these records. These commissions were not included in the printed versions of the Records of the Privy Council.

27. PBK, 69.

28. Kirkcaldy KS, November 19, 1633. *Statistical Account*, 815.

29. The expenses relating to this execution have been published in several places. MacBean, *Kirkcaldy Burgh Records*, 344–345; *Statistical Account*, 815–816; 'Trial', 123.

30. J.A. Sharpe, 'Witchcraft and women', 185.

31. John Campbell, in *The Church and Parish of Kirkcaldy*, also spends time on this case. While not believing Coke or Dick were witches, he suggested that they were 'simply ignorant, coarse, violent people, pretending to a mysterious power over their enemies, and trading upon men's fears.', 171.

32. Kirkcaldy KS. The references to other offences usually came at the beginning of the meeting and included fornication, drinking at home while the sermon was being preached, as well as non-attendance at church.

33. John Robertson, *An Orkney Anthology*, 352, 368. Hans Eyvind Naess, 'Norway: The Criminological Context,' in EMEW, 373.

34. Case 3134. PBK, 92.

35. Case 3158. Campbell, *The Church and Parish of Kirkcaldy*, 166. Kirkcaldy KS.

36. PBK, 114.

37. Smith, *Annotated edition*, 221.

38. RPC 2nd ser. vol. 3, 104. In the commission reference is made to Alexander's practice of both witchcraft and charming.

39. The source for all of these cases is Benson, *South-West Fife*, App. 2, 266 and 269. None of those mentioned here were entered into the SWHDB.

40. Godbeer, *The Devil's Dominion*, 67 has a good discussion of both popular and elite attitudes. 'Even healers who used neither charms nor occult rituals were vulnerable to accusations of witchcraft, so hazy was the boundary between magical and non-magical treatment.' That haze existed in Scotland, as well as New England.

41. Many cases involving suggestions of charming have already been discussed in the chapters on the various presbyteries.

42. Oliphant was found innocent of witchcraft, but guilty of charming. MacBean, *Kirkcaldy Burgh Records*, 154–155. Christian Wilson, Ch2\224\1, f114. It is difficult, in part, to see the relationship between these two activities because in listing 'witchcraft' cases in Black, the *Sourcebook*, and the SWHDB, it is sometimes impossible to determine what is witchcraft and what is 'charming'. Generally speaking, cases of simple charming, where the word 'witch' appears, were not included in the *Sourcebook* nor in the SWHDB – but there are some exceptions. Yet, without a comprehensive listing of all of the cases of charming, it is difficult to see if they were more or less prevalent during major hunts. In some instances we know from the Presbytery of Dunfermline, a concern for witchcraft and witch-hunting did seem to cast a wide enough net to include those who used charms.

43. CH2\224\1, f127–128.

44. Campbell, *The Church and Parish of Kirkcaldy*, 166.

45. Case 2457. Markinch KS CH2\258\1 December 24, and 31, 1641.

46. Beveridge, *Culross and Tuliallan*, 208–209.

47. Dunfermline KS CH2\592\1, f111. Henderson, *Extracts of the kirk session*, 33.

48. Case 2373. Dalyell, *Darker Superstition*, 424–425.

49. Case 3162. Campbell, *Church and Parish*, 167.

50. Larner, *Enemies of God*, 97–98. Levack, *Witch-Hunt* 1st ed., 152. Quaife, *Godly Zeal*, 171.

51. Larner, *Enemies of God*, 3.

52. Historians continue to struggle with this subject. Larner's comments, ibid., p. 3 are worth noting. Clarke Garrett, 'Women and Witches: Patterns of Analysis,' *Signs* 3 (1977): 461–470, and Carolyn Matalene, 'Women as Witches' (1978) in *Articles on Witchcraft, Magic and Demonology*, edited by Brian P. Levack. Vol 10, *Witchcraft, Women and Society* (New York: Garland, 1992.), 51–66, offer summaries of the interpretations of the question to that point in time. One article by a non-historian, biblical scholar Rosemary Ruether, 'The Persecution of Witches: A case of Sexism and Agism?' (1974), also reprinted in Levack, vol. 10, makes the case strongly for the witch-hunt being driven by male hatred of women. On why so many accused women were older, Ruether concluded: 'Thus the fury and hatred of woman as sexual being is logically directed not against the young girl but against the idea of the older woman as a secretly lusty creature.' (p. 253–254). While theoretically stimulating, no evidence has since been produced which would support the thesis. In his text Klaits argues strongly for misogyny as a key force in driving the witch-hunt (*Servants of Satan*, in particular p. 72, 84) while Geoff Quaife devoted two chapters to the discussion (*Godly Zeal*, chapters 6 & 7, esp p. 90). Quaife is even able to weave Staislav Andreski's argument regarding the introduction of syphilis into Europe into the argument on misogyny. Brian Levack offers a balanced discussion of the issues, *Witch-hunt in Early Modern Europe*, 2nd edition, 133–141. See Clive Holmes, 'Women: Witnesses and Witches', *Past and Present* (1993) and Susanna Burghatz, 'The Equation of Women and Witches' (1988) for two recent discussions of this issue. Holmes explores women, not only as victims, but as accusers, yet still concludes we cannot yet remove either gender or misogyny as 'key category for any discussion of witchcraft beliefs and prosecutions,' 72. Burghatz makes the fascinating point that even before the publication of the *Malleus*, 91% of victims were women (p. 63). The movement away from seeing the entire issue as if every cleric

accepted the ideas of the *Malleus* unquestioningly (let alone was aware of them), has led to a growing sophistication in terms of the debate. J.A. Sharpe's 'Witchcraft and Women in seventeenth-century England: some Northern evidence' (1991), not only questions the role of the *Malleus*, but also poses significant questions about why older, poorer women were more likely to be considered as witches. Specifically on Scotland, J.K. Swales & Hugh McLachlan 'Witchcraft and the status of women: a comment' (1979) used Scottish evidence to challenge the arguments of Alan Anderson And Raymond Gordon.

53. King James VI, *Daemonology*. G.B. Harrison, ed., *Daemonology* (1597) and *Newes from Scotland: Declaring the damnable Life and death of Doctor Fian, a notable Sorcerer who was burned at Edenborough in January last* (1591) (New York: Barnes & Noble, 1966). The question of why women are more likely to be witches than men is posed. The suggested ratio is 20 women to 1 man (!) and the reason given is that women are weaker than men 'so it is easier to be intrapped in these grosse snares of the Deuill'. The example of Eve is then cited, 42–44. It is always difficult to trace the influence of a book, unless it is directly cited. All that can be said of *Daemonology* is that some of the key themes of the book (the witch's sabbath, meetings in churches) have little influence in Fife, and the one unique contribution of the book – the notion of a witch's transport being only in spirit and not the physical body – was argued against in a late tract which used extensive evidence from Fife. See G. Sinclair, *Satan's Invisitble World Discovered*; also Stuart Clark, 'King James's *Daemonologie*'. One of the few sermons known to have been preached at a witch-craft trial which has survived, failed to make the argument that women were more likely to be witches, and blamed Adam as well as Eve for the fall. George Neilson, ed. 'A Sermon on Witchcraft in 1697,' in *Articles on Witchcraft, Magic and Demonology,* ed. Brian P. Levack. Vol 7, *Witchcraft in Scotland* (New York: Garland, 1992), 394–395. That men, as well as women, were named in this case (the Bargarran case) should be noted.

54. PBK, 353.
55. J.A. Sharpe, 'Witchcraft and Women', 182. Levack, *Witch-hunt*, 1st ed., 141–156.
56. Data is from the SWHDB.
57. Margaret Young (1459). RPC 2nd ser. vol. 8, 28.
58. Ibid., 28.
59. Ross, *Aberdour and Inchcolme*, 330.
60. Ibid., 342.
61. Bensen, *South-West Fife*, 187.
62. Elspeth Seath, STACUPR, 147–150. Isabell Dairsie, STACUPR, 15. Isobell Kellock, Buchner, *Rambles*, 44–46. Dorothy Oliphant, L. MacBean, *Kirkcaldy Burgh Records*, 154–155. William Crichton, Henderson, *Extracts from the Kirk Session*, 27. Poor witches who couldn't pay are noted in Benson, *South-west Fife*, 273. Culross witches, JC2\14 350–351.
63. PBK, 132.
64. The pamphlets include *A True and Full Relation of the Witches at Pittenweem to which is added . . .* Edinburgh (1704) and *A Just Reproof to the False Reports and Unjust Calumnies in the Foregoing Letters* (1705) both written by the same individual, sometimes known as a 'Lover of Truth'. The opposition is staked out by 'a Gentleman in Fife' whose tract *An Answer of a Letter from a Gentleman in Fife to a Nobleman* (1705) contains two separate letters. All of these pamphlets can be found in Webster, *Rare Tracts*, in the Ferguson collection in the University of Glasgow Library.

For more detailed information on the tracts see John Ferguson, 'Bibliographical Notes', 71–73.

65. *An Answer*, 3. *A Just Reproof*, 89. The massive literature on Salem has already been briefly discussed. All of these hunts involved adolescents as the primary accusers. There are other elements which set them apart. See Ankarloo, 'Sweden: The Mass Burnings', 295–303. The possible connections between these hunts needs to be explored further.

66. These details come from *True and Full Relation*, 7, 8.

67. *An Answer*, 2. *True and Full Relation* notes it was only after the individuals were arrested that confessions came, 8–9.

68. Beatrix Laing's petition to the Privy Council, May 1, 1705. In Cook, *Annals of Pittenweem*, 124–125.

69. Cook, *Annals of Pittenweem*, 109.

70. Pittenweem KS CH2\833\3 May 29, 1704.

71. June 14, 1704 meeting of St. Andrews Presbytery, St. Andrews Presbytery Records, volume 4, St. Andrews University Library Muniments. There is a particular moor around Pittenweem to which Beatrix Laing kept referring which is rendered here as 'Coves'.

72. Recorded in Cook, *Annals*, 109–116, including lengthy notes and comments.

73. Cook makes no reference to it in amongst all of the other documents he mentions. The SBSW lists the source of information on these cases as the tracts collected and published by Webster. One assumes the compilers of the SBSW were not able to locate the trial records within the central records.

74. *An Answer*, 3. Cook, *Annals*, 116–118. Cook records that five of the women had been released on bail in early August. He also includes the text of the warrant setting one of the accused, Isobell Adam, at liberty for lack of evidence. Seeing that Isobell had already confessed (she was also the only one to admit to having had carnal relation with the Devil) and had been implicated in the supposed murder of a fisherman, these traditionally serious charges were not being taken at face value by the judiciary.

75. *Just Reproof; An Answer;* Cook, *Annals of Pittenweem*, 122. Cook argues that the report in *An Answer* is too sensational. He agrees with Charles Mackay, *Memoirs of Extraordinary Popular Delusions* vol. 2 (London: Office of the National Illustrated Library, 1852 edition.), 156, that the mob was trying to swim her. If so, this would be one of the rare examples of this happening. The pressing is also unique. One can't help but wonder if this idea was carried to Pittenweem by accounts of what had occurred in Salem, where pressing was used against a suspect who would not confess.

76. Cook, *Annals*, 119–124. Two of those who fled were supposedly English. Cook leaves the names of those implicated who were from the village blank.

77. Minute from the town council, May 11, 1705. Quoted in Cook, *Annals*, 127.

78. Pittenweem KS CH2\833\3. June 4, 1705.

79. Quoted in Cook, *Annals*, 128–129.

80. Keith Brown, 'The Laird, his Daughter, her Husband and the Minister: Unravelling a Popular Ballad' in *People and Power: essays in honour of T.C. Smout*, ed. Roger Mason and Norman Macdougall (Edinburgh: John Donald, 1992), 112.

81. Brown, 'The Laird', 114.

CHAPTER TEN

Creating a Godly Society: The Witch-Hunters of Fife

While those accused of witchcraft tended toward a certain stereotype, the decision to pursue and prosecute them was at all times in the hands of the elite. The elite was comprised of all those with political, economic or religious power in society such as the clergy, the burgesses, the local lairds, and the nobility. As Christina Larner has suggested it was the elite who controlled both the supply and demand for witches,[1] a reality we have witnessed in the telling of the story of the witch-hunt in the various presbyteries. But which group among the elite, the lairds or the clergy? What purpose, if any, did the witch-hunt serve for this group? What was the interaction between the populace at large and those controlling the mechanisms of power, between popular ideas and elite notions? And, what caused the witch-hunting in Fife to cease?

The question of which group among the elite was most interested in witch-hunting has received two distinct answers: the clergy or the lairds. Seeing the clergy as avid witch-hunters was fairly common among works published in the nineteenth century and early twentieth century.[2] For example, the editors of the *Records of the Privy Council* noted that it was the clergy, 'whether individually in their parishes or collectively in their presbyteries, that were zealous for the detection and prosecution' of the crime of witchcraft.[3] Specific ministers, such as Alan Logan of Torryburn and Walter Bruce of Inverkeithing, were also seen as major witch-hunters.[4] Gilmore in his thesis on the church and witchcraft saw the clergy playing a key role and as slower to abandon their belief in the reality of witchcraft than were others within Scotland.[5] While some local studies have continued to see the clergy as central,[6] the role played by the lesser nobility in the witch-hunt has come to be seen as more significant. Isabel Adam argued that the main witch-hunter in the Paisley cases was the laird of Bargarran.[7] Christina Larner suggested that it was the lesser nobility who were active in witch-hunting, a fact which Brian Levack stressed in his discussion of the great witch-hunt of 1661–62.[8]

In some ways the question is artificial. Clergy on their own certainly could not have produced the kinds of witch-hunting which Scotland witnessed. Brian Levack's statement that as 'long as witch-craft remained a statutory crime triable in the secular courts, it was difficult for the clergy to take a leading role in its prosecution' is certainly true.[9] Larner noted that it was the 'landowners rather than the ministers who requested most of the commissions, and they who conducted most of the trials from which the clergy were normally excluded except as witnesses'.[10] When it came to the point when commissions were needed to move the process to an assize or trial, the support of the local authorities, be it magistrates, nobility or burgesses, was crucial. In this sense the church could rarely act independently, a fact which was made evident when the local or judicial authorities would not cooperate. The church needed lay support. Commissions were given to the lairds and burgesses. But, that should not lead us to conclude that the role of the church was insignificant, or that the clergy did not take a leading role. We need to consider where most of the interest originated. Who gathered most of the evidence which was needed before a commission to take a witch to trial would even be granted?

The answer, as we have seen, is sometimes less than clear. Where cases originated and who heard the first accusation is in many situations an unanswerable question. Still, the prominent role of the church as the place where we have at least our first information recorded about charmers, consulters and suspected witches is apparent. Katherine Key was charged in 1653 in Newburgh before the session, and the case remained before the session for over two years.[11] When John Chalmers, minister of Auchterderran, approached the presbytery of Kirkcaldy in 1632 with his concern about a vagrant woman who seemed to be practising witchcraft, the response demonstrated remarkable confidence: expel her from the parish or have her put to trial. The presbytery did not speak of having to consult with the local nobility or officials, but assumed that Chalmers could and should deal with the situation. That confidence was not misplaced. While in 1616 the session of Kirkcaldy had stated that those accused of charming, consulting with witches or witchcraft itself should be punished by the civil magistrate, this did not mean that the original accusations like those against Isobel Hevrie in 1619, Alison Dick in 1621, or Janet Pirie, Janet Stark and Helen Birrell in 1626 were not heard before the session.[12] These cases were investigated by session, and in the case of Alison Dick continued to be pursued in that court. The use of the church steeple in Kirkcaldy as a prison for suspected witches is interesting: Kirkcaldy had a tolbooth which could also (and at times did) serve this purpose.[13] The presbytery of Dunfermline not only tried William Chrictoun in 1648 but had him executed.[14] The number of cases which had their origins before the church courts is noteworthy. The session and the presbytery played a key role in the initial investigations, investigations which might end with more minor punishments such as repentance within the church or might move on to a full trial which required a confession.

Commissions are an imperfect way of assessing who was behind a witch-hunt. While the names of local officials and lairds were prominent, so was the notation that the individuals suspected had already confessed. To have 'confessed' would have meant that someone had already started the process, indeed had already conducted a preliminary hearing or investigation, and even had the suspect incarcerated and examined. The commissions issued for suspects in Cupar Presbytery in 1662, for those in Kirkcaldy Presbytery in 1621, and for those in Inverkeithing in 1623 all noted that the suspects had confessed. The question remains, who began the process? There are a few occasions when a commission stated that the person named had not confessed. These commissions tend to come later in the seventeenth century in the period after the great witch-hunt at the time of the restoration. The change can be noted within St. Andrews presbytery. While commissions were issued to St. Andrews presbytery in 1662 to put two confessed witches, Elizabeth Clow and Jonnet Annand, to a trial two years later the commission granted in the case of Margaret Guthrie clearly stated she had not yet confessed.[15] The commission issued against Issobell Key in 1666 also noted she had not confessed, as did the commission issued for seven witches in Torryburn (Dunfermline presbytery) that same year.[16] Still, even these women who had not yet confessed were being detained in the local jails. Some group or body must have met and decided to incarcerate these women. As important a source of information as commissions are, they cannot be used to identify who had initiated the witch-hunt. Instead, they give us a snap shot at the mid-point of the process.

The fact that commissions are an imperfect source for determining who initiated a witch-hunt can be seen from the one case for which we have a virtually complete record, that of Alison Dick and William Coke in 1633. There is nothing in the commission which would signal to us that suspicions had been expressed twelve years previously before a church court. There is nothing in the commission which makes it clear that it was the session of Kirkcaldy which heard the complaint, ordered Alison Dick to be warded, gathered evidence, and eventually obtained a confession. The commission names Coke and Dick as confessing witches and orders them put to an assize with various prominent individuals given the responsibility of seeing that justice was administered. The one fact which might indicate church involvement was the fact that this process had been seen and approved by the Archbishop of St. Andrews.[17]

The evidence from Fife would tend to argue against Christina Larner and Brian Levack's identification of the lesser nobility as the driving force within the elite when it came to hunting witches. This is not to say that there were not times when local members of the nobility or the magistrates were dominant. James VI's role during the hunt in the Lothians in 1590 is clear. Similarly, Brian Levack has demonstrated that the role played by some of the nobility in Haddington during the hunt which followed the restoration was vital. The elite controlled witch-hunting, but at different times different factions could drive that process. For Fife, we can divide the cases we know into three general categories. In the first, we simply are not sure which group among the elite took the lead. This was true of the hunt in Cupar Presbytery in 1661 and 1662. Given the prominence of some of the lairds, in particular Sir John Aitoun, this might have been a royalist reaction, a demonstration of power and support for the monarchy. It might be true that on this occasion 'the royalist professions of hatred for revolution and rebellion created a public mood, at least in some communities, conducive to witch hunting'.[18] Unfortunately, our sources of information about this hunt are sparse. The session records of Newburgh and Falkland make no reference to these events, yet this hunt which spanned the presbytery could have been coordinated by the presbytery whose minutes, unfortunately, have been lost. This is one instance where we have no idea which group among the elite drove the hunt and the evidence we have could be used to argue either group were the initiators.[19] Similarly, it is unclear in St. Andrews Presbytery in 1643 who began the hunt. What is evident, is that the presbytery soon became heavily involved.[20]

The second category are those situations in which burgh officials or the laity took initiative. The bailies of Burntisland were accused by Jonnet Finlason of harassing her and continually putting her to trial, despite the lack of evidence.[21] It is from the burgh records of Kirkcaldy from the same period that we learn of the massive hunt there.[22] Other complaints from individuals of rough treatment while being held as suspected witches, also mention the bailies. Mary Cunningham complained in 1644 of her harsh treatment at the hands of the bailies of Culross. Still, that complaint needs to be heard in the context of the major ongoing witch-hunt, in which the session of Culross and presbytery of Dunfermline were active.[23] Both the ministers and bailies of Dysart were identified by Katherine Chrystie as responsible for her being warded in the tolbooth.[24] Finally, there is the unusual incident in 1598 when the laird of Lathocker brutally tortured Geillis Gray. Notably, this occurred in the midst of an ongoing concern for witches by the church, including the presbytery of St. Andrews' attempts to gain more evidence against her. Indeed, Geillis had been in the custody of Andrew Duncan, the minister of Crail when the laird of Lathocker took her into his own custody.[25] What is noticeable is not how many cases there were in which the laity took a leading role, but how few.

Most cases in Fife fall into the third category, where it was the church courts which initiated actions against various individuals. It was church courts in Kirkcaldy, in Pittenweem, in Inverkeithing, in Dysart and many other communities that began the process of investigating charming, consulting and witchcraft itself. It was church courts that continued to pursue Alison Dick, Katherine Chrystie, Katherine Key and others. And it was to church courts that individuals generally turned in order to have their names cleared when community rumour slandered them as witches. The power of church courts in this process can be seen from the fact that some people did not want to appear before a church court at all. In Culross three women who had been banned from taking communion because they were suspected as witches petitioned to have their names cleared by an assize or secular trial, not the session.[26] Apparently these women considered it wiser to appear before a secular court. Robert Brown in 1649 continually tried to have his wife warded in the burgh prison house, not the church steeple of Inverkeithing, arrangements which the presbytery vehemently opposed.[27] Church courts were the main place where accusations of witchcraft were initiated and they played a vital role in maintaining those initiatives, long after interest had waned. It was the minister of Crail and the presbytery of St. Andrews which attempted in 1675 to obtain a commission against Geilles Robertson, despite the fact that there were no magistrates in the burgh and the seeming lack of interest among other members of the laity.[28]

The prominent role of church courts in the processing of suspected witches in Fife is clear. Yet this role which church courts played was not given a prominent place in *Enemies of God*, particularly on the chart, 'Processing a Witch'. In that chart the session was seen as having a minor role as one of several bodies involved in the initial stages in collecting evidence, after which other bodies were responsible for arrest, examination (including sleep deprivation, pricking or torture which might take place), and the investigation which took place before a commission was sought. The evidence we have seen from Fife stresses that all of these activities occurred within the session or presbytery; indeed the church courts were often the driving force in having the suspect incarcerated, demanded to be present when the suspect was examined, collected evidence, tried to obtain confessions by having the individual warded and watched, and even pushed, when others were unenthusiastic, to obtain commissions. In other parts of Scotland other bodies may have played similar roles, but in Fife the church courts were at the centre of the witch-hunt.

Given this concern on the part of church courts and the clergy for witch-hunting, was one particular theological faction within the clergy more likely to be involved in witch-hunting than others? The difficulties in even beginning to investigate such a question are real. Given how little we know about many of them, how would we differentiate the theology of the various clergy? What meaningful categories would we use? One of the most obvious would be whether or not a particular minister accepted the restoration of episcopacy and bishops after the restoration of the monarchy. In one sense, this might separate the more radical 'presbyterians' who refused to adapt to any other system from those who were more moderate and willing to compromise. Yet, this approach seems wrongheaded. For one thing it fails to recognise the complexity of theological factions, how those who could disagree bitterly on some issues could find common ground on others. David Mullan has noted that while there were divisions among clergy which centred around 'politics and ceremonies', there was also much common ground on other issues.[29] None of the theological factions argued over the need for church discipline, therefore it seems unlikely that they would be divided on the need to eradicate superstition or witchcraft. William Ross, exploring this question over a century ago, commented that the differences could not be used to explain who was and who was not involved in witch-hunting. He noted that Robert Bruce of Aberdour was involved in hunting witches, both 'when he was a Presbyterian, but also at a later period when he conformed to Episcopacy'.[30] Walter Bruce of Inverkeithing did accept bishops. Andrew Donaldson, minister at Dalgety, did not conform yet during his tenure as minister of the parish witch-hunting had taken place in 1649.[31] Obviously, such simplistic categories do not work. Rather than personalities, witch-hunting had its roots in common beliefs among the elites, and a common systemic desire. That desire was for order and for the creation of a godly kingdom. The church courts were the means to that end.

In the pursuit of this godly society, the nobility and others among the elites cooperated. Keith Brown has argued that in the early seventeenth century the elites gradually came to publicly support the church's official views on sexual morality.[32] (The only qualification which should be added is that they supported these views when they were not the ones being hauled in front of church courts for these 'moral offences', a state of affairs which held true for most of the seventeenth century.) Indeed, church courts overlapped with other judicial bodies. Magistrates often sat on the session, easily allowing the church court to begin to tap into the power of the civil magistrate.[33] In our exploration of the witch-hunt in Fife, the overlap is obvious, for ministers and bailies were able to work closely together. The local lairds served on the commissions. Even late in our period in Pittenweem in 1704, the bailies and session stood together both in their attempts to have the suspected witches taken to trial and in the aftermath of the lynching. The difficulty here was that it was another crucial player among the elite, in this case the judiciary, which broke ranks. We shall return later to the subject of how disunity among the elite affected the outcome of witch-hunting, both throughout and at the close of the seventeenth century.

Throughout most of our discussion we have focused on the role which the elite played. In part, this is natural: the elite controlled the records which have survived. Popular attitudes are more difficult to deduce. It is far more difficult to determine why, for example, the community decided to testify against Alison Dick in 1633, let alone in 1621. Sometimes the complaints went back over years and demonstrated how long grudges were held within these communities. But how willing were neighbours to testify? Did they ask the session to arrest the community witch because they had had enough? Or, was it only once the process began they were willing to testify?

The process began with the elite's concern, with the decision at the session or presbytery level to investigate a certain woman as a suspected charmer or witch. The populace did not initiate witch-hunts. This conclusion (stated so boldly for something we can only surmise) can be supported only from circumstantial evidence, yet the evidence when taken together is solid. We have seen no instance when an individual has presented him or herself before the session and charged someone as a witch. It was the church court which began the investigation, then called for witnesses from the community. The contrast becomes all the more obvious when we look at those situations where someone did appear before the session and made the charge that someone was slandering them and calling them a witch. For example, in Culross in 1649 Jonet Paterson appeared before the session to accuse Isobell Stewart and Bessie Cowsey of 'calling her a witch'. It was only when thus challenged, that Isobell Stewart appeared and stated that Paterson was indeed a witch, and she could prove this.[34] Again in Aberdour in 1650, Isobel Inglis only appeared to accuse Janet Anderson of murder by witchcraft, after Janet charged Isobel with slandering her as a witch.[35] Even the deathbed accusation made by James Keddie against Janet Durie seems to have found its way to the ears of the presbytery of Kirkcaldy, not because of a direct accusation made by a member of Keddie's family on the floor of the court,[36] but because of community rumour. Indeed the very idea of having to clear one's name before the church court when someone 'called' you a witch, indicates that these rumours were taken seriously and could lead later to one being brought before the session or presbytery. Initiative was shown in trying to clear one's name: there is no evidence of initiative in formally accusing others before the session. Only in one instance, Helen Young in Balmerino, did an individual come forward and confess that she was a witch.

Another indirect factor which suggests that the populace did not initiate charges against the local witches comes from the number of instances when individuals were charged with consulting witches. The community knew who the local witch might be. They also knew who in the community might provide a charm, or proof that they had indeed been bewitched. David Zeman continued to be consulted by various members of the community even though he had been placed in ward by the presbytery of St. Andrews. They seem to have perceived him in a positive light, as a healer and someone who could name those who were responsible for their misfortune. David Zeman had been able to assure Thomas Watson that it was Beatrix Adie who had taken the milk from his cow. He also had a cure: go to Beatrix and ask her to restore the milk again in God's name. This, according to Thomas Watson, solved the problem.[37] The populace seemed glad to have someone with Zeman's skill among them. Even the bailies saw nothing wrong with allowing him to go with Walter Gourlay to see if Gourlay's son had been bewitched (Gourlay had someone in mind, Margaret Smith, a suspicion Zeman confirmed). The continual concern by sessions and presbyteries to stop people consulting healers, charmers and witches suggests that the populace were not bringing these individuals before the church courts to have them disciplined.

Even in those cases which involved sharp tongues, irritable personalities and direct suspicions of acts of *malefice*, there is no indication that the community took the initiative in prosecution. William Coke and Alison Dick's very public spat would naturally have come to the attention of the session. There is no indication in the original notation that anyone had formally charged either. Indeed the first witnesses merely recounted what had been said in a public place.[38] Equally relevant is the fact that when Alison Dick had been charged more than a decade previously, little information came forward despite a call from the pulpit.[39] Similarly, the session in Newburgh called in 1653 for more information about Katherine Key. Initial charges had been made, but no more were added in 1655.[40] One explanation for this lack of further complaints might be that all the acts of ill will had been discovered. Equally plausible is the notion that the community feared its witches, and was reluctant to testify unless it was clear that the result would be the removal of the source of their problems. The populace might testify; the evidence suggests that they did not initiate witch-hunts. This makes the response of communities to national trends more understandable, and also suggests why communities were able to name suspects when called upon to do so.

As well as giving evidence against individual suspects, the populace also chose under different circumstances to oppose the hunting of witches. This opposition came mostly from family members especially during those times when the hunt spread beyond the usual suspects. Grissel Gairdner's husband had successfully intervened to prevent her execution during the hunt which took place around 1597. At the time of her second trial in 1610 she was a widow.[41] Others, for example George Hedderick of Pittenweem and some 'wicked persons' in Inverkeithing during the 1649 hunt were accused of giving suspects advice on how they might escape being convicted.[42] During the hunt which swept St. Andrews presbytery in 1645 Andro Strang fought to have his wife Christian Roch set free 'using all means for obtaining heirof'.[43] Others appealed to the Privy Council or Committee of Estates, as did David Geddie and David Yuile in 1633, and Robert Brown in 1649.[44] The need to remove members of session and bailies from office in Inverkeithing is perhaps the most clear indication of opposition. The need to have forty to fifty of the strongest young men of Pittenweem in arms for the executions in 1643, is a more subtle indication that opposition was feared.[45] It is not surprising to find this evidence of opposition coming at times when hunts of some magnitude were underway. Isolated witches or those who had alienated their community might not have much support; but for those caught when named by dying witches or suspected in serial witch-hunts, popular support, if only from family, was possible.

The general populace thus had a mixed relationship to the witch-hunts which occurred in their various communities. At times people were willing to give evidence, in particular against an especially troublesome neighbour or someone suspected of various acts of ill will. At other times, the community took a more passive role, either out of fear or a desire to have people in their communities who could offer to them cures and information about who else might be casting spells against them. Direct opposition arose during times of significant witch-hunting, in particular when those accused suddenly were people who heretofore had no previous reputation within the community.

The events in Pittenweem in 1704 and 1705 were distinct. Here the populace took direct action when the authorities failed to deal with Janet Cornfoot. But even this incident should not be seen as the result of an ignorant, superstitious rabble. It was, after all, the church courts which began to seek witches in Pittenweem. The ministers and bailies, if they did not take part in the actual lynching, seem to have taken no action to prevent it nor did the elite seek to deter further actions against those most strongly considered to be witches. There was a strange interrelationship between elite and populace, even at this late date. The true split which had emerged was within the elite itself.

This interrelationship between elite and the general population was vital. The elite controlled the timing of the hunts, the when and where. The populace had a different attitude to the 'witch' within the community. That individual was often sought out for her ability to cure or offer charms. Yet, such power could be dangerous and frightening. The curses of Alison Dick must have been difficult to live with. To those in her community she was a witch. When called upon to do so, and one assumes when there is some hope that the complaints will be taken seriously, a local witch could be identified. They were, however, rarely identified by the populace unless this individual was already suspected by a church court. Then, evidence could be and was presented but the populace did not take the initiative and name someone as a witch unless they were asked. This interaction also affected the very notion of what or who a 'witch' was. Christina Larner suggested that in the writing of the history of European witchcraft it was evident that elite values eventually altered how the populace conceived of the witch.[46] The demonic pact and the witches' sabbat are often conceived as one of the central features of the Scottish witch-hunt. The Scottish legal theorist William Forbes expressed in 1730 the traditional belief that witchcraft was 'wrought by Covenant or Compact with the Devil, express or Tacite'.[47] In discussing the difference between English and European witchcraft, Larner noted that the English Witchcraft Acts

> knew nothing of the notion common to Roman Law countries such as Scotland that the crime was that of being a witch, that the primary act of witchcraft was the Demonic Pact, and that all witches were part of a Satanic conspiracy.[48]

Geoff Quaife distinguished between the beliefs of the Scots peasantry and those of the French peasantry:

> On the other hand the Scots populace generally accepted the reality of the Devil but played down his sovereignty. They readily accept the concept of the pact, sexual intercourse between Devil and his followers and the link between ill-fame and diabolic alliance – concepts resisted by the peasantry in other parts of Europe. Yet even the Scottish lower orders did not incorporate adoration of Satan into their image.[49]

Larner's comments reflect what the elite believed. But did this belief move easily to the peasantry, as Quaife suggests?

As both Larner and Quaife have also noted, elite notions of demonic theory, sabbats, the presence of the Devil, and the demonic pact, are most clearly evident in records which originated from the central government.[50] In discussing a witch-hunt which occurred in South-west Scotland in 1671, Larner noted that the concern with the demonic pact which was found in the records of the Circuit Court had not existed in the initial accusations made at the local level.[51] The evidence from Fife supports this idea that traditional concerns were the primary interest of the local community, as distinct from the elite concerns with demonology. The demonic pact, and other elements of elite theory seem to have had little impact on initial accusations. Indeed it is possible to argue that they were not even central to the local clergy or local officials. These individuals were willing to prosecute cases of witchcraft and even execute people with little thought to the finer points of pact or sabbat. To further test this theory it is necessary to note again where and when concepts such as the pact or meetings with the Devil occurred, and how prevalent these were among the elite, before seeing if such ideas influenced the populace.

In Fife, the Devil was almost exclusively a concern of Dunfermline presbytery and even here his name is generally confined to those records which originated from or pertained to the central government. During the hunt in Inverkeithing in 1621 the commissions issued by the Privy Council noted that the suspects had met with the Devil and entered his service.[52] Two documents before the High Court, those involving suspects from Inverkeithing in 1649 and the accused from Culross in 1675, included the notion of entering into the Devil's service and in some cases having sealed that bargain with the act of sexual intercourse.[53] This most explicit feature of elite demonic theory – sex with the Devil – occurred only one other time, in the case of Lillias Adie before the kirk session of Torryburn in 1704.[54] Indeed, the other references to the

Devil's presence are very ambiguous. Grissel Gairdner from Cupar Presbytery, who also appeared before the High Court, was accused of having consulted with the Devil.[55] During the hunt in Kirkcaldy Presbytery in 1649, it was claimed that some of the accused had met with the Devil, while others had drunk his health.[56] We have also noted the role the Devil played in the case of Alison Dick. The Devil does appear in Fife witchcraft cases. What is interesting is that his appearances seem to be primarily in those documents which originated from the central government, and while the Devil's presence may have increased somewhat over time it was still not universal nor often that crucial. Sabbats and sex were not a main feature of local concern or belief.

The notion of some kind of demonic pact appears far more frequently. Yet even here the source for this information tended to be commissions issued by the Privy Council and not every commission made reference to this pact. The text of the commissions issued on January 23, 1662, simply state that the accused have 'acknowledge themselves to be guiltie of witchcraft'.[57] Because they tended to follow certain formulaic ways of establishing the charges, the text of commissions are not always the most reliable of sources. Still, it is noteworthy that even here and even as late as 1662 it was not always considered essential to include the notion of the demonic pact. Still, it is within commissions which we do find the most frequent references to the pact. Robert Maxwell's confession, before the presbytery of Dunfermline, to having entered into a pact with the Devil was unusual. He made this confession after being warded and before a commission was sought.[58]

If the presence of the Devil and the notion of the demonic pact are relatively rare in Fife, the virtual absence of the witches' sabbat is even more surprising. The clearest articulation of the idea of sabbat was that describing the meeting in the abandoned West Kirk in Culross in 1675. Apart from this one incident, what we find is an occasional reference to the Devil sitting drinking in people's houses, or vague references to gatherings at which uncertain numbers of individuals were present. Yet, details are scarce. Most remarkably, when confronted with clear elements of what could have been interpreted as a sabbat, the clergy seemed unaware of what they were witnessing. The meeting by the lake of the unruly women where Andrew Patrick claimed to have seen Elspet Seath, should have been transformed by the members of the presbytery of Cupar into a sabbat. We should expect to see them more concerned about what these women were doing and to aks more questions about the man who stood amidst their dancing, yet we do not. Why? The obvious, if surprising, answer is that these elite notions of the sabbat had not strongly taken hold, not only among the populace but even among the clergy.

If European elite notions of demonic witchcraft had been dramatically unsuccessful in shaping the picture of the Fife witch, why was there the concern for the demonic pact? If we look closely at the concern for these pacts or bargains in the few cases where they exist in the local records, as opposed to commissions, it is clear that not all of the elite elements (in particular as we have noted the sealing of the bargain through the act of sexual intercourse) were generally present. Instead what we see is a concern with giving oneself over, from the crown of the head to the souls of the feet, into the Devil's service. This act was sometimes followed by the marking of the body by the Devil. Larner has written that 'witch-beliefs represent an inversion of the positive values of the society concerned'.[59] Note how this mild form of pact is a complete inversion of baptism. In a sermon preached in 1697 at the time of the Paisley trials, James Hutchisone discussed the demonic pact:

> It requires that there be a reall compact between Satan & that person either personally drawn up & made, or Mediately by parents immediat or mediat having power of the person: adding yr unto his mark. The Ground of my assertion is this, there is no Less requisite to the constituting a person a visible professor of christ, then a personal compact and the external sign of Baptism supper-added, or a reall compact made . . . No Less doth Satan require of them that will follow in his way then either personal covenanting with him, and recei-ving his mark upon yr flesh, or that the parent give their children to him, and they receive his mark . . .[60]

There is no comparable evidence from Fife. Still, such a conception of a pact as the opposite of baptism, particularly among individuals who only seem to have been able to think in terms of such absolutes, one served God or the Devil, and could not be neutral, seems plausible. This even explains to some degree the concern for others who were present, for if some were opposed to God, there might be others.

Clearly, elite notions and beliefs did not deeply permeate Fife society. Instead we have a mixture of elite and folk beliefs in which elite notions while sometimes evident were not dominant. Indeed the popular conception of the witch remained remarkably resilient. Beliefs about fairies were as likely to be woven into this picture as were beliefs about the demonic. The early case involving Alison Piersoun clearly showed explicit references to fairies. Yet those references continued, even though they were mostly implicit. The meeting by the lochside which Elspeth Seath attended fits the description of a fairy revel equally well, if not better than, a sabbat. Note that the women did mischief to Patrick by dragging him into the lake. Jean Bizet in Torryburn was tormented on her late night walk home after a few drinks. The session believed she had been tormented by Satan. Yet fairies also traditionally tormented people when discovered alone at night. Once warded, Lillias Adie confessed to being a witch, even to having had sex with the Devil. But there are other parts of her testimony which stand out as being contrary to elite notions. When asked if the Devil had a sword, she said he 'durst not use a sword'. Nothing in elite belief explains this: however, the fact that fairies could not touch metal does. Similarly, her statement that the Devil's feet could not be heard when leaving fits more comfortably with a description of a fairy than a description of Satan.[61] The resilience of the belief in fairies and its being woven into the concept of witchcraft in Fife needs to be further explored. Still, it is clear that elite conceptions did not simply sweep away popular notions of what constituted a witch.[62]

If elite conceptions of the witch such as the sabbat and demonic pact were not central to the 'success' of witch-hunting, elite solidarity was. While the clergy were the dominant force behind the hunts, they needed the assistance of the other members of the elite. When this solidarity was intact witch-hunting flourished. When it crumbled, no amount of pressure from the clergy seemed capable of altering this reality. The session at Pittenweem continued to believe in 1705 in both the existence of witches in their community and the necessity of putting them to a proper trial:

> The Session thought moot here to narrate that after the presbytery cited the woman arraign'd for witch-craft before them, these processes were never return'd back to the session; their confessions are particularly mention'd in the Presbytery-book; and tho' application was made by the Presbytery, Session & Magistrates to those who were impowered by Law to give a commission for the judging of these witches, yet they could never obtain it; and so they escap'd punishment.[63]

Yet it was not always the central government or the judiciary which put the brakes on a witch-hunt. The refusal of the bailies of Cupar to incarcerate Elspeth Seath in 1648 prevented a conviction in that case. In Crail, no one would seek a commission against Geillies Robertson. By the end of the hunts, these splits had become dominant. In many ways the change had little to do with a disbelief in the reality of witchcraft, but a change in the certainty with which people were convinced they could determine that a particular individual was a witch. The cautions and restriction on warding after 1662 may have been a significant contributing factor. Yet individuals were still being warded into the early eighteenth century. The difficulties of obtaining commissions to put the confessed witch to a trial was the key factor in the decline of witch-hunting in Fife, for without being able to move to a trial the entire costly process seemed a waste of time. The lack of success would also make the populace less likely to testify. Splits among the elite were thus central to the decline of witch-hunting in Fife. Therefore, the answer to that very puzzling question, 'what caused the witch-hunt in Scotland to end?', seems to lie in the breakdown in the solidarity of the elite towards witch-hunting. Belief in witches remained. What had changed was a distrust of the ways of identifying a particular individual as a witch. Witch-finders and witch-prickers had been discredited. Certain kinds of witnesses who had previously been believed now faced scepticism. This scepticism did not have to be widespread. For witch-hunting to result in prosecutions all of the various groups within the elite had to stand together. Once they ceased to, convictions were unlikely. The failure to successfully convict witches also meant that the populace was less likely to produce names when asked. The end of the witch-hunting was thus, as we've seen, not dramatic but gradual.

Belief continued in witches long after formal processes and trials ceased. Yet the question still remains, why were the clergy and church so interested in hunting witches? Simplistic notions that they were merely following a text from the Bible or the spirit of the times are inadequate. What we need to do is see this aspect of church interest and concern within the context of the church's larger interest in discipline and the creation of a godly society.[64] Church courts prosecuted many offences other than witchcraft. For example, the kinds of cases which came before the presbytery of Kirkcaldy in the five year period from 1645 to 1649 can be seen in table 2.

Table 2 – Kirkcaldy Presbytery, discipline cases, 1645–49
(Source – *Presbyterie Booke of Kirkcaldie*)[65]

Offences	1645	1646	1647	1648	1649
Fornication	6	2	11	5	3
Adultery	9	2	7	3	1
Other Sexual	1	2		3	2
Witchcraft	2		1	1	3
Sabbath breach	1	2	1		1
Misc.	6	9	11	2	7

The abundant concern for sexual behaviour is clearly evident. For example William Smith was brought before the session in January of

1646 'trelapse' (third time) for fornication.[66] The parade of those found 'guilty' of this offense in 1647 was noticeable. Sometimes as in the case of William Orrock and Elspeth Arnott, it was clearly spelled out who the various partners were,[67] but the majority of those who appeared in this and other years were women. Obviously pregnancy was a major way in which the session discovered that a young woman had been sexually active. It also would have been one of the ways in which adultery was discovered. Yet, the ability of members of session to be aware of whatever scandalous behaviour was seemingly going on was truly remarkable. Even those who were members of the elite found themselves before the session on the grounds of sexual offences. In March 1646 the Laird of Balmuto was ordered to satisfy the discipline of the session of Auchterderran for fornication between he and Katherin Symson. The Laird resisted, but was forced to comply with the presbytery's orders by late May. It should be remembered that these are the cases that made it to the presbytery: many such offences would have been dealt with simply at the level of the kirk session.

The category 'Other Sexual' covers a variety of concerns on the part of the session. Infanticide was suspected in 1645 and 1649. William Bolton's wife was suspected of giving Isobell Arnott a concoction of herbs to drink in order to induce an abortion in April of 1645.[68] That same year the dead child of Marion Henrison was baptised, but Marion was forced to 'find caution that if it sallbe proven heirafter to have been otherway in that caise she sall satisfie accordinglie'.[69] In September 1649 the presbytery noted that Jean Weyms was thought to have murdered the child she bore and was a fugitive from the session of Wemyss in Holland. The presbytery approved of the diligence of the session in trying to have her brought back, and appealed for assistance from two of the local lairds.[70] Janet Jolie was forced to do penance on the stool in Leslie for her 'whorrishe behaviour' while Helen Millar was forced to appear not once but twice for her scandalous behaviour with a soldier in 1648. In the last incident she was found naked in her bed, and as she had 'relapse[d] in fornicatioun befoir' she was ordered to do a six months of penance on the stool of repentance, the last three weeks in sackcloth.[71] Even sexual behaviour that was suspected, yet not proven, was prosecuted. Alexander Wilson and Catherine Thomson were charged with 'slanderous behaviour of adulterie'. They admitted to the 'slander' but denied any action.[72]

Such attempts to regulate sexual behaviour are difficult for twentieth century people to imagine, yet the power which church courts were able to wield in this period was truly remarkable. The presbytery of Kirkcaldy not only prosecuted what might be deemed as 'moral offences' but moved far beyond this to regulate peoples lives. This control extended down to the right to marriage. The minute of September 17, 1645:

> The Presbyterie grants [William Kay's] desyre [for marriage] upon conditioun that after his mariage he shall return to his service[in Balcarres troopers] whilk he promeises to doe. Anent Helen Wood whose husband was killed at Tippermore the Presbyterie thinks that she may have the benefit of mariage.[73]

Controlling whether or when a widow may remarry is powerful control, even more powerful when it is remembered that any sexual activity outside of marriage was likely to be prosecuted. Even a marriage breakdown was considered the presbytery's responsibility. Andro Birrell and his wife Grissell Page were living apart in July 1647. Andro was willing to reconcile but Grissell did not wish to 'goe home to him or byde with him'. The presbytery ordered her 'to goe home and remain with hir husband betwixt this and the first meiting of the Presbyterie, or else they will proceid aganest hir with the censures of the kirk'.[74] For failing to live together after three separate warnings they each were declared 'contumacious' or defiant.[75]

The control church courts attempted to exercise extended beyond sexuality to a wide range of human behaviour and belief. The church was particularly adamant that Sunday remain a time in which no work or pleasurable activity was enjoyed. Henry Christie was charged with refusing to come to communion, while Margaret Bennet was accused of not coming to communion for two years because she was not reconciled to her neighbour.[76] Robert Durie faced similar charges. His refusal to be reconciled had its origins in a lawsuit and he requested extra time to solve the problem.[77] John Paterson was ordered to abstain from selling alcohol on Sundays.[78] James Dick was ordered to do public repentance for being drunk on the communion sabbath.[79] The most serious complaint was against those who worked in the salt industry who were known to work on Sundays, and thus raised the ire of the church. On October 14, 1646 the presbytery stated that as the salters so frequently worked on the sabbath even after having done public repentance, the punishments would be doubled and they would be suspended from communion until proof was given of their 'reall reformatiuon'. The presbytery believed this was necessary 'for the terror and shame of such impudent and obstinate offenders'.[80]

The presbytery's understanding of how the sabbath should be marked was made clear in a statement made in January of 1647 which is worth quoting at length:

The Presbyterie considering the great profanatioun of the Lords day notwithstanding the former acts maid aganest the profancer thairof doe thairfoir judge it necessarie to mak particular enumeratioun of such profanatiouns as were most cowmon within the bounds of the said Presbyterie, and not expressed in former acts such as goeing about any civill business, abroad in other congregatiouns or at home in thair owne upon the Lords day, the setting of horses for hyre or travelling homewards with these horses that have been sett the goeing to taverns or alehouses betwixt or after the sermons with the towns or places of people ordinarie residence, and for all others the drinking of that which is beyond necessairie refreshment or mis-pending time lairglie sitting and tippling beyond the time necessarie for the refreshment and this to strik aganest the sellers of the drink as weill as the buyers thairof in manner foirsaid, the vaiging abroad, sitting or walking idle upon the streets and fields whereby the sanctifying of the Sabbath in families is uttelie neglectit and the occassioun of idle and worldlie conference fostered.[81]

Penalties were then outlined for breaking any of these conditions. The third offence brought suspension from communion.

Beyond breaking the sabbath in all and sundry ways, offenders were charged with a multitude of offences. Fighting with the minister or elders, cursing one's son, and misbehaviour on the stool of repentance by answering back were all dealt with.[82] Margaret Adamson of Kirkcaldy was ordered to make repentance for the 'mocking pietie under the new name of Puritanisme'.[83] Political speech was also prosecuted. Henrie Vertie was ordered in 1645 to carry some ammunition from Burntisland to Falkland. He refused. He was called to appear before the presbytery for stating, after it had been told to him that this was God's cause, that it 'is the Devills caus'.[84] Henrie Vertie was someone who attempted to defy the presbytery, refusing to come when called to appear, but eventually he did appear before that body.[85] The victory over Montrose at Philliphaugh was celebrated as a day of thanksgiving.[86] In 1649 the salter William Graham was forced to do penance for his 'blasphemous speeches'. He had stated that 'he knew not whidder the sojours wer fighting for God and the King, or for the Devill and the Ministers'.[87] Such opinions were prosecuted. Graham had to do public penance.

The strong support for the Covenanting army and cause which is clear in the presbytery minutes throughout this period, came to a head after the fall of the Engagement. Numerous members of the laity were called before the presbytery to answer for their support of the Engagement.

(These 'offences' were not listed in Table 8.1. Indeed the presbytery's concern for this matter may explain why there were fewer sexual offences brought forward in 1649.) On January 17 Robert Kirkcaldie of Grange was allowed to submit to the covenant and receive communion as nothing had been proven against him.[88] On March 7, several officers in the former army appeared, asking 'to be reconciled to the kirk and be admitted to the covenant and communion'. They were accepted.[89] Not everyone was treated so leniently. Sir John Mackenzie also asked in March to be allowed to subscribe to the covenant. He admitted that he had raised a regiment for what the presbytery referred to as 'the lait unlawfull engagement,' an action which he now regretted. His case was forwarded to the General Assembly.[90] Other engagers were accepted in August and the remainder of the year, many after having confessed their wrongdoing in supporting the previous regime: 'Compeired George Low in Kirkcaldie declared his sorrow for his accessione to the laite unlawfull engagement'.[91] The adjective 'sinful' was often used to describe this government.

It is within this context in which everything from political thought to sexual behaviour was under scrutiny and control, that allegations of witchcraft were heard. This context is vital. All forms of behaviour were considered the business of the church courts, and attempts were consciously made to transform behaviour. As well as the allegations of witchcraft from this presbytery already discussed in chapter 6, major concern was expressed for an incident of charming in 1646. On March 11 a sailor named David Wood appeared and confessed that he had 'turned the key' in Kirkcaldy. The charm was outlined: one placed a key in a Bible and read the eighteenth verse of Psalm 50 – 'When thou savest a thief, then thou consentedst with him, and has partaken with adulterers' (KJV) – then named all those who sailed in the ship. When the name of the individual suspected (apparently as a thief) was read, if that person was guilty the key would turn. David Wood taught the charm, however, as something that was done whenever one of the ships company was 'wanting something'. The incident came to the presbytery's attention because Andro Allan had apparently wanted some money and had sought out people who could help him obtain it. David Wood admitted to teaching the charm, but not taking part in the exercise in the house of Margaret Law.[92] He eventually confessed to both teaching and practising the charm. Janet Dick was also found guilty of turning the key in order to get gold from James Kininmonth.[93] While the line between such attempts at folk magic and witchcraft was often vague, both were prosecuted before the church courts and were a significant element in the church's attempt to enforce discipline, both of action and thought.

The concern for 'discipline' displayed by Kirkcaldy Presbytery in this period was not unique or atypical. On April 30, 1645 Thomas Bonar was brought before St. Andrews Presbytery for singing a song and drinking to the health of 'Bobo Finla' (a mysterious figure, but possibly King Charles). Bonar admitted to singing the song which he learned (he would not say where he had learned it) in Edinburgh, but denied knowing who 'Bobo Finla' was. The presbytery decided to refer the matter to the General Assembly, but in the meantime to have him incarcerated by the magistrates of St. Andrews or have them arrange sufficient cautioun (bail) so that Bonar would appear when called again.[94] Johne Moreis was brought before the presbytery in 1643 for 'takeing upon him to heale the Cruelles (scrofula) by touching them, as the seventh sonne of a woman'.[95]

In the midst of their concern in the case of Elspeth Seath and Helen Small, the presbytery of Cupar dealt with the issue of those who had supported the Engagement.[96] The years 1649 and 1650 saw some of the greatest interest in discipline, with the Synod of Fife ordering all presbyteries to seek out those who celebrated 'the Yuile day', or went to 'wellis denominat from Saintis', or took secret oathes or used 'the Meason word',[97] but this was merely an intensification of concerns expressed throughout the entire period. The presbytery of Dunfermline had an act against all people feasting and celebrating Yule (Christmas) read from their pulpits in 1640.[98] At the end of our period while concerns for witchcraft were ongoing, the session of Pittenweem continued to hear traditional discipline cases. Someone must have been counting months, for it was decided that Sophia Powtso's child had been conceived before she and her husband had been married. After some initial denials, the husband confessed to 'uncleanness before marriage' and both were sentenced to be publicly rebuked.[99] Cases of attempted rape and possible infanticide also appeared before the session in the early eighteenth century.[100]

The prosecution of witchcraft has to be understood within this context of a broader attempt to shape the values and beliefs, the attitudes and behaviour of a society. The attempt was to create a 'godly' society, godly defined by the clergy and church courts. In this sense Larner is correct, witches were 'enemies of God'; yet, only one of many enemies. And it was not only demonic theory or supposed alliance with Satan which made the witch the enemy. Cures and charms, the ability to heal, and all of these folk practices were deemed inappropriate, evil, and were to be eradicated. The intensity of the concern for witches might change over time, but its eradication was always part of a broader attempt to fundamentally change popular culture. John Di Folco has defended the role which church courts played in their exercise of discipline:

> Too much attention has been directed towards a singling out of the alleged censorious aspects of the Session's work, and this it is claimed here, is often badly defined by the writers, frequently non-existent, and, if present, fully justified on sound social as well as religious grounds. It has not been possible to find evidence to substantiate the extravagant, isolated claims that discipline had a pernicious effect on the people or engendered systems of clerical espionage and we see on the other hand, proof that a spirit of reciprocal co-operation and participation was sought through various strata of society both in given parishes and further afield and that it was achieved, however modified, with minimal coercion, can only redound to the Session's credit. One is justified, I believe, on the basis of the evidence in taking a more generous view in assessing the Sessions and their divulged social picture. Of the three courts it had the immediacy of contact and proximity that translated so much into practical reality for those it served.[101]

The evidence does not support such a 'generous view'. In terms of witchcraft, Di Folco's statement that church courts acted only 'as an advisory and investigatory authority' with no powers to punish is not only false, but misrepresents the significant role played by church courts.[102] He also seems to misunderstand key factors in one of the few cases of witchcraft he discovered in this area, that of Elspeth Seath, Helen Small, and Helen Young. The suggestion that the presbytery's action in enquiring of the central government if there were enough evidence for a civil trial of these suspects was 'an effort to restrain the case'[103] is to completely miss the assertive role presbytery took in trying to obtain a conviction. Church courts aggressively enforced discipline in their attempt to build a society they deemed 'godly'.

Such an attempt was not restricted to Fife. Stephen Davie's study of the role of the various courts within the Scottish legal system, using Stirling as an example, confirms the importance of church courts in cases of witchcraft and other 'moral offences'. His research also discovered concern, not only with sexual offences and sabbath breach, but with a range of folk belief and customs, including 'the use of 'holy wells' and the practice of resorting to 'cunning' men and women.' He also notes how in some instances a case which began as simple charming, developed into 'a fully-fledged witchcraft case'.[104] In Orkney as well, sessions took an active role in cases of witchcraft and charming: 'minister and kirk sessions frequently acted as their own court of inquiry, interviewing witnesses, receiving confessions, and formulating the charges'.[105] The historian of crime J.A. Sharpe has noted the role which church courts, with the support of the government, played in attempting to create a godly society in England. There as in Scotland church courts dealt with cases of sexual behaviour, alcohol abuse, failure to attend church, even scolding, charming and formal cursing (a close cousin to witchcraft).[106] Conversely, one of the distinctive differences between the Netherlands and Scotland, was that church councils in the former 'performed nothing like the police function' which courts in Scotland did.[107] Michael Graham's recent study, *The Uses of Reform: 'Godly Discipline' and Popular Behaviour in Scotland and Beyond, 1560–1610*, shows the centrality of church courts in the imposition of 'discipline' upon the local Scottish communities after the reformation.[108]

In seventeenth century Fife, the witch was one obstacle in the way of the creation of a godly society. Homosexuals were another, as were those who committed 'incest', or adultery, or had sex before they were married, or in any other ways broke the moral code outlined by the church.[109] The church enjoyed the support of other elements of society in this goal throughout much of the late sixteenth and seventeenth centuries. Yet as splits developed in the elite, not only over the practical issues of how a witch might be identified but also between the various factions of the church itself leading to the various disruptive purges of the late seventeenth century, the solidarity required for witch-hunting to be effective was lost. These factors, rather than any change in beliefs, were responsible for the collapse of witch-hunting in Fife. The elites controlled the timing and supply of witches. When they could no longer agree, the hunts collapsed.

Notes

1. Larner, *Enemies of God*, 22, 1, 60.
2. Campbell, *Church and Parish of Kirkcaldy* (1904), 164. Andrew Young, *History of Burntisland* (1913), 207, states the ministers of Kinghorn and Burntisland were authorities at finding witches. James Wilke, *The History of Fife* (1924), 391, 394, 396. Eunice Murray, *Scottish Women in Bygone Days* (Glasgow: Gowans & Gray, 1930), 144.
3. RPC 2nd ser. vol. 1, c. Also, 1st ser. vol. 14, lxxxviii; 2nd ser. vol. 2, xlii notes the clergy using the alms money to pay the costs (presumably of warding and watching witches); 3rd ser. vol. 3, xliii states the 'clergy were as convinced as ever'.
4. Allan Logan is portrayed as particularly zealous in John P. Hunter, 'Witches of

Torryburn: The 'Inquisition' of a Fifeshire Minister' in *Scots Magazine* (1936), 306. Walter Bruce's role in Inverkeithing is noted by Benson, *South-west Fife*, and William Stephen, *History of Inverkeithing and Rosyth* (1921), 439–445.

5. Gilmore, *Witchcraft and the Church of Scotland* (1948), ii, 320.
6. Harry Watson, *Kilrenny and Cellardyke* (1986), 37, 38.
7. Isabel Adam, *Witch Hunt* (1978). Adam not only sees the laird of Bargarran as key, but defends the actions of the ministers, 234.
8. Larner, *Enemies of God,* 84. Levack, 'Great Scottish Witch Hunt', 95, 96.
9. Ibid., 96.
10. Larner, *Enemies of God*, 85.
11. Laing, *Lindores Abbey*, 223–227. A commission was sought to try her eight years later at the time of the restoration. RPC 3rd ser. vol. 1, 90. The commission notes that she had already confessed. The role played by the session in 1662 is unclear.
12. Campbell, *Church and Parish of Kirkcaldy*, 166–167.
13. Dennison & Coleman, *Historic Kirkcaldy* (1995), 30. The vault under the tolbooth had served as the town jail since 1566. Apparently, up to five individuals could be held at one time and repair work on this facility continued throughout the seventeenth century.
14. Henderson, *Extracts from the Kirk Session*, 27. Dunfermline KS CH2\592\1, f76.
15. RPC 3rd ser. vol. 1, 208. RPC 3rd ser. vol. 2, 165.
16. RPC 3rd ser. vol. 2, 246, 192.
17. Commission against Coke and Dick, Adv.ms.31.3.10 f. 64v.
18. Levack, 'Great Scottish Witch Hunt', 107.
19. One piece of circumstantial evidence supporting the involvement of the church is the fact that Katherine Key, who had been pursued so diligently during the English occupation by the session of Newburgh, was among the first to be acted against.
20. This hunt apparently began in Anstruther in 1643. The presbyteries own records are unclear as to who was responsible. First the presbytery appealed to the bailies to delay the execution so they can speak to the condemned (and ask who else was a witch). The court then complained to ministers that they should inform the presbytery that any witches 'with them' exist before they were executed. While the minister and burgh officials both were involved, it is not clear whether the accusations were first heard before the burgh court or session. STACUPR, 13.
21. RPC vol. 5, 405–406.
22. MacBean, *Kirkcaldy Burgh Records*, 108. The surviving kirk session records of Kirkcaldy begin in 1614.
23. The complaint is found RPC 2nd ser. vol. 8, 101. The session had been warding people has accused witches earlier in the year. Benson, *South-West Fife*, App. 2, 268.
24. RPC 2nd ser. vol. 2, 142–143.
25. Smith, *Annotated Edition*, 290.
26. Benson, *South-west Fife*, App. 2, 266.
27. Records of the Committee of Estates PA 11\8, 134v, 157r–157v.
28. STACUPR, 90–91.
29. David Mullan, 'Theology in the Church of Scotland 1618c-1640: A Calvinist Consensus?,' *Sixteenth Century Journal*, xxvi/3 (Fall 1995): 617.
30. Ross, *Pastoral Work in Covenanting Times,* 197–198.
31. Ibid., 225. For Bruce conforming, *Fasti*, vol. 5, 43.
32. Keith Brown, 'The Nobility of Jacobean Scotland 1567–1625,' in *Scotland Revisited*,

ed. Jenny Wormald (London: Collins and Brown, 1991), 68. Jane Dawson's recent research on St. Andrews supports the idea of elite solidarity on discipline, ''The Face of Ane Perfyt Reformed Kyrk': St. Andrews and the Early Scottish Reformation', 427.

33. A. Ian Dunlop, 'The Polity of the Scottish Church 1600–37,' 176. 'Superstitioun, Sabbath breaking, absence from church, adultery, etc. etc. all provided matters to be dealt with. The presence of a magistrate or magistrates on the Session meant that warding and fining could summarily be inflicted.'

34. Culross KS, CH2\77\2, 64.

35. Ross, *Aberdour and Inchcolme*, 325–328.

36. PBK, 141.

37. Smith, *Annotated Edition*, 222–224.

38. 'The Trial of William Coke and Alison Dick' in Webster, *Rare Tracts*, 113–114.

39. Campbell, *The Church and Parish of Kirkcaldy*, 166–167.

40. Laing, *Lindores Abbey*, 223–227.

41. Laing, *Lindores Abbey*, 219–222.

42. Hedderick was actually charged. Cook, *Annals of Pittenweem*, 49. A warning was issued, complete with the fact that those found guilty would have to do penance, during the Inverkeithing hunt. Dunfermline Presbytery CH2\105\1, 271.

43. STACUPR, 23.

44. RPC 2nd ser. vol. 3, 489–490, 532. PA 11\9\134v.

45. Cook, *Annals of Pittenweem*, 49.

46. Larner, *Enemies of God*, 15.

47. William Forbes, *The Institutes of the Law of Scotland*, Edinburgh (1730), vol. II, 33. Forbes seems to have been stating his understanding of the Scottish legal tradition. In the Appendix to the chapter in which he discussed witchcraft, he was far more cautious, refusing to venture an opinion on issues such as the Devil's pact or carnal copulation, only noting that these were presented 'as Matters of Fact' previously in courts, 373.

48. Larner, *Enemies of God*, 200.

49. Quaife, *Godly Zeal*, 59.

50. The confusion on this topic is apparent in the literature. Clearly the demonic pact was one element of Scottish witch theory, indeed of elite belief. The key questions are: how extensive was belief in the demonic pact? Did this elite notion successfully influence the general populace? The answers to these questions are less that clear. Quaife, who as we have noted in the text argued that Scottish peasants accepted such demonic beliefs fairly readily, had noted earlier that the evidence presented before kirk sessions 'differed considerably from that which Commissioners considered relevant for formal prosecution'. He noted the 'layers of belief' which existed, 41. See also Klaits, *Servants of Satan*, 58.

51. Larner, *Enemies of God*, 120.

52. RPC vol. 12, 423.

53. Justiciary Court Records JC26\13\5. July 10, 1649. JC2\14, 346–354.

54. Torryburn KS CH2\335\2, 135–136.

55. Pitcairn, *Criminal Trials*, vol. 3, 95–98.

56. Arnot, *Celebrated Criminal Trials*, 401–403. The original source of this document cited was from the Kirkcaldy area, not the central government.

57. RPC 3rd ser. vol. 1, 141.

58. Ross, *Glimpses of Pastoral Work*, 199.
59. Larner, *Enemies of God*, 9.
60. Neilson, 'A Sermon on Witchcraft in 1697,' 393.
61. Torryburn KS CH2\355\2.
62. The importance of fairy belief was stated in 1921 by J.A MacCulloch 'The Mingling of Fairy & Witch Beliefs in Sixteenth and Seventeenth Century Scotland,' 229. Carlo Ginzburg has commented on the subject in *Ecstasies*, 97, 108. Interestingly, much of the literature about Scottish witches include notions about fairies as well. MacKay, includes a verse from Fife which states 'Witches in the Watergate, Fairies in the Mill.' A.J.G. MacKay, *A Century of Scottish Proverbs and Sayings: in prose and rhyme current in Fife and Chiefly of Fife Origin* (Cupar, no date), 50. David Arnott's play *The Witches of Keil's Glen, a dramatic fragment* (Cupar, 1825) has both witches and fairies present.
63. June 4, 1705. Pittenweem KS, CH2\833\3.
64. Larner suggested that witchcraft needed to be understood within the context of crime in her lecture on 'Natural and Unnatural methods of Witchcraft Control' in *Witchcraft and Religion*, 127–128. Given the prominence of church courts in Fife in prosecuting the 'crime' of witchcraft, it seems logical to examine which other 'offences' were part of these courts concerns. On church discipline see Leah Leneman, ''Prophaning' The Lord's Day: Sabbath Breach in Early Modern Scotland,' *History* 74 (1989): 217–231; Leah Leneman and Rosalind Mitchison, 'Acquiescence in and defiance of church discipline in early-modern Scotland,' *Scottish Church History Society Records* xxv/1 (1993):19–39; and, Rosalind Mitchison and Leah Leneman, *Sexuality and Social Control: Scotland, 1660–1780* (Oxford: Basil Blackwell, 1989). This chapter had been written before the publication of Michael Graham, *The Uses of Reform*, which follows a similar approach. The more examples we have, the better our knowledge of the functioning of church courts in this period.
65. PBK, 279–347. In terms of fornication and adultery, the number represents each incident recorded not each individual who appeared. This was particularly confusing in the cases of adultery, where the parties were often forced to appear and do penance more than once.
66. PBK, 292.
67. PBK, 310. Interestingly, Orrock admitted adultery but denied the child was his.
68. PBK, 284.
69. PBK, 281. This incident appears in the chart as miscellaneous.
70. PBK, 339.
71. PBK, 294, 321–322.
72. PBK, 333.
73. PBK, 289.
74. PBK, 313–314.
75. PBK, 316, 321.
76. PBK, 284, 338.
77. PBK, 343, 346.
78. PBK, 302.
79. PBK, 316.
80. PBK, 304. It is unclear from the text whether this was a mass suspension to take place immediately, or would apply only to those who subsequently offended. The

former is not impossible. Salters also found themselves in difficulties in Dunfermline Presbytery. At times they were able to escape punishment because of the support of the lairds and their employers.

81. PBK, 306.
82. PBK, 294, 297, 301, 295, 312.
83. PBK, 311.
84. PBK, 280.
85. PBK, 280–281. Apart from the wife who refused to live with her husband, there is no evidence of anyone defying the presbytery successfully in this five year period.
86. PBK, 289.
87. PBK, 343.
88. PBK, 331.
89. PBK, 332.
90. PBK, 332–333.
91. PBK, 340, 338, 339, 341–2, 346.
92. PBK, 293–294.
93. PBK, 295.
94. STACUPR, 24.
95. STACUPR, 15.
96. STACUPR, 133.
97. SYNFIFE, 165–166.
98. Henderson, *Extracts from the Kirk-Session Records of Dunfermline*, 8.
99. Pittenweem KS, CH2\833\3, 242–243. It is cases like this which make clear the weakness in the arguments of apologists for church discipline such as John Di Folco, *Aspects of Seventeenth Century Social Life in Central and North Fife* (B. Phil diss., University of St. Andrews, 1975), iv, 87, 194–195. Sessions disciplined those who were married if the child was deemed to have been conceived prior to the ceremony.
100. Pittenweem KS CH2\833\3, 242 for the attempted rape. The instance of infanticide can be found in the next volume of the Pittenweem KS records, CH2\833\4, 26–27.
101. Di Folco, *Aspects of Seventeenth Century Social Life,* 87.
102. Ibid., 131–132.
103. Ibid., 135.
104. Davies, 'Scottish Legal System', 127.
105. John Robertson, *An Orkney Anthology*, 347. The author discovered no indication of a Privy Council commission for Orkney.
106. J.A. Sharpe, *Crime in Early Modern England 1550–1750* (London: Longman, 1984), 50, 85, 87, 88, 151.
107. Marijke Gijswijt-Hofstra, 'Witchcraft in the Northern Netherlands,' 84.
108. Graham, *Uses of Reform*. Both the research in this book and in Michael Graham's work have arrived independently at similar conclusions.
109. John R. Hardy, *The Attitude of the Church and State in Scotland to Sex and Marriage: 1560–1707* (M. Phil. diss., University of Edinburgh, 1978) includes an appendix listing prosecutions for sodomy and bestiality which begins on page 586. Hardy also discusses incest and other sexual attitudes, 103, 317–337.

CHAPTER ELEVEN

Conclusion

Over the last chapters we have explored the witch-hunt in Fife. The story is both fascinating and complex. It is also a very frustrating story. Key questions cannot be answered because the data is missing. Still with the records available to us we have been able to test many of the assumptions with which we began. We can also comment on the challenges that are raised to the general stereotype of the Scottish witch-hunt.

We have seen that although the local nobility and burgh officials played a key role in the witch-hunt, the most significant group among the elite was the clergy. The church courts, in particular the kirk sessions and the presbyteries, were the major local bodies which investigated, pursued, interrogated, and on rare occasions even executed, suspected witches. Church courts encouraged the nobility to cooperate, including providing facilities within the burghs to hold the suspects. The dynamic which drove the hunt fit well into the participation of the church courts. Whereas physical torture used in a trial would have to have been applied in a secular court, it was possible for the kirk to ward and watch the suspects, and through sleep deprivation gain the necessary confessions. There were several occasions when witch-finders or witch-prickers appeared in Fife, but in several of these instances the hunts were already well underway before these individuals arrived. Sleep deprivation, not judicial torture for which there is no direct evidence, was the force that drove the persecution in this shire. Presbyteries and kirk sessions were able with the assistance of the local officials able to hold, interrogate and 'wake' the women suspected of witchcraft.

If the church played a key role in the Fife witch-hunt, the same cannot be said to be true of the Devil. As has been noted, there are some scattered references to the Devil, and more frequently to some form of giving oneself over to demonic service, but these certainly do not appear in all cases. The most common complaints of the neighbours of the suspects are of *malefice* or harmful magic. References to the Devil are more common in documents which came from the central government than they are in the minutes of sessions or presbyteries. The European elite notion of the

195

demonic nature of witch-craft does not seem to have been particularly successful in filtering down to the level of the local clergy, let alone the common people. This is an important consideration. Two recent studies, Stuart Clark's *Thinking with Demons* and Ian Bostridge's *Witchcraft and Its Transformation*, have added greatly to our understanding of the intellectual idea of the 'witch' and its place within western intellectual thought.[1] While these ideas may have affected the intellectual elites, we need to be cautious not to assume that every individual was reading or aware of these ideas. In Fife, we have seen little evidence of demonic theory being used. When Satan does appear it is relatively late in the witch-hunt and he is most commonly described in language which derives from beliefs about elves and fairies, not elite concepts of the demonic. These folk beliefs proved remarkably resilient. Nor were the sessions and the presbyteries particularly sophisticated in their use of diabolic theory. Whether in-dividual members of the clergy were aware of this literature is beyond the scope of this study. What has been obvious is that certain instances which could have been interpreted as sabbats were not.

In part this may have been because the clergy were not particularly interested in whether witchcraft was or was not a heresy. Their concerns were with the practical application of magic, white or black, and with the imposition of church discipline on the parishes. Discipline, not diabolism, was the concern. Michael Graham has recently defined church discipline as the attempt 'to convert reformed doctrine into practice, and to move the religious changes which were taking place from the realm of theology and worship into the realm of everyday life'.[2] This 'early example of an attempt at social engineering on a societal scale'[3] was not concerned with fine distinctions between cures and curses, between magic used in healing and magic used to harm. All forms of magic, including consulting in order to be healed, were condemned. This concern to eradicate charms and witchcraft was one aspect of a broader attempt to create a godly society. Witches were not only the enemies of God, but of a godly community.

Consensus was needed in order to build this godly society. Other members of the elite, the lairds, burgh officials, nobility and judiciary, were willing – for whatever reasons – to assist in this endeavour, as long (as usually was the case) as they were not brought under the discipline of the kirk.[4] When that consensus was broken, witch-hunting was no longer possible. The judiciary played a vital role in quelling the Pitten-weem hunt of 1704–05. Yet their scepticism was not shared by either the clergy or the local population. The lynching which resulted, as well as the inability to effectively prosecute any of those who had taken part, demonstrates that even as the possibility of witch-hunting declined, belief in witchcraft continued. That belief continued in rural and port communities for many years.[5] While the repression of witches and magic ceased to be an effective part of the program, the attempt to build a godly society also continued into the eighteenth century.

The role of the elites in witch-hunting is significant. In contrast, Robin Briggs in his new survey *Witches and Neighbours* has stressed the role played by the neighbours of the suspects. Healers, according to Briggs, were only a minority of those accused of witchcraft and got into trouble only as a result of disputes with their neighbours.[6] He argues that witch-hunts were not managed from above. He summarizes this position as a vision in which 'it is readily portrayed as an oppressive technique, serving selfish ends, exploited by bigoted and cynical ruling groups'.[7] A few pages later he suggests that 'the supply of victims was largely regulated by the population at large'.[8] This was not the experience in Fife. While the local population knew who the witches were in their community, they took little initiative to deal with them. That initiative came primarily from the church courts, from sessions and presbyteries. Once a suspect was being held the populace might (or might not) come forward with accounts of all the evil which that particular individual had done. Larner's contention that it was the elites who 'controlled and manipulated the demand and supply for witchcraft suspects' is a more accurate description of what we have witnessed in Fife.[9] Those deemed witches lived on the fringe of society. Many did dabble in curses and cures. Some were difficult and quarrelsome and ungrateful even when given charity. That they incurred the anger of their neighbours is understandable. But it was the attempt to impose a new morality, a godly society, both in terms of sexual behaviour and other attitudes which created the climate in which these women found themselves in danger.

The establishment of a godly State was a revolutionary idea. It was radical in its particulars. Michael Graham has spoken of the idea of using discipline to 'encourage a revolution' in the populace's attitudes to 'illness and misfortune'.[10] The broader agenda of a godly society where actions and political beliefs could be scrutinized and punished was even more ambitious. Church discipline was not cynical. It had a goal in mind, a goal which was quite worthy. The unfortunate problem was that too many people stood in the way.

Creating a godly society meant eradicating evil in all its forms, both of thought and practice. Witchcraft was one of those forms. While other sectors of the elite may have had other reasons and beliefs which led them to persecute witches, the church was driven by its vision of what society could be. We tend not to think of persecution being the result of an attempt to achieve something 'good' or 'noble'. Yet be the goal a godly society or a social paradise defined by the political right or political left, those who are perceived to be obstacles to the attainment of that goal are often brutally dealt with by those trying to create this idyllic society. The Khmer Rouge executed anyone wearing glasses, because it was feared that they might be educated and that education would corrupt the new society which was being constructed from year zero. During the cultural revolution in China those whose thoughts were seen as too bourgeois were sent to be 're-educated' in the countryside. Improper thought was established as a crime, just as support of the Engagement was in Fife in the period 1649–50. Nazis wanted to build a Reich which would last a thousand years, and so built extermination camps in order to eliminate those deemed racially impure and a danger to that society. We demonize these regimes, and so miss that from the perspective of the true believer those who stand in the way of the achievement of their goal are obstacles, barriers to progress which must be overcome at any or all costs. This is what we should understand – and fear. In seventeenth century Fife, witches were seen by the godly as a threat to the building of a godly society.

Notes

1. Clark, *Thinking with Demons* (1997). Ian Bostridge, *Witchcraft and Its Transformation c1650–c1750*. (Oxford: Clarendon, 1997). Bostridge includes a discussion of the role in which witchcraft theory played in Scotland, in particular the relationship between the Calvinist covenant and the demonic covenant. The political role of witchcraft belief is a theme worth further exploration.
2. Graham, *The Uses of Reform*, 1.
3. Ibid., 2.
4. Ibid. Graham argues that social problems such as bastardy, poverty and unrest among the poor led even the more secular nobility to offer support to the establishment of church discipline, 345–346. He places significant stress on the problem of bastardy and the strain that overpopulation placed on scarce resources. While not agreeing with this particular interpretation, the question is one that needs further exploration. Why were the secular officials willing to support the church?
5. Sharpe, *Instruments of Darkness*, 277, gives only one of many examples of continued belief.
6. Briggs, *Witches and Neighbours*, 5–6.
7. Ibid., 398.
8. Ibid., 401.
9. Larner, 'Crimen Exceptum?', 63.
10. Graham, *The Uses of Reform*, 308.

Bibliography

Secondary Sources: General

Adler, Margot. *Drawing Down the Moon: Witches, Druids, Goddess-Worshippers, and other Pagans in America Today*, Revised and expanded ed. Boston: Beacon Press, 1986.

Ankarloo, Bengt, and Gustav Henningsen. *Early Modern European Witchcraft: Centres and Peripheries*. Oxford: Clarendon, 1990.

Ankarloo, Bengt. 'Sweden: The Mass Burnings (1668–76).' In *Early Modern European Witchcraft: Centres and Peripheries*, ed. Bengt Ankarloo and Gustav Henningsen, 285–317. Oxford: Clarendon, 1990.

Anderson, Alan & Raymond Gordon. 'The uniqueness of English witchcraft: a matter of numbers?' *British Journal of Sociology* 30, 3 (1979): 359–361.

Baroja, Julio Caro. *The World of the Witches* (1961). Translated by O.N.V. Glendinning. Chicago: University of Chicago Press, 1964.

Barstow, Anne Llewellyn. *Witchcraze: A New History of the European Witch Hunts*. New York: Pandora, 1994.

Beik, William. 'The Dilemma of Popular History.' *Past and Present* 141 (November 1993): 207–219.

Ben-Yahuda, Nachman. 'The European witch craze of the fourteenth to seventeenth centuries: a sociologists perspective.' *American Journal of Sociology* 86 (1980): 1–31.

Ben-Yahuda, Nachman. 'Problems inherent in socio-historical approaches to the European witch craze.' *Journal for the Scientific Study of Religion* 20 (1981): 326–338.

Bethencourt, Francisco. 'Portugal: A Scrupulous Inquisition.' In *Early Modern European Witchcraft: Centres and Peripheries*, ed. Bengt Ankarloo and Gustav Henningsen, 403–422. Oxford: Clarendon, 1990.

Bostridge, Ian. *Witchcraft and Its Transformations c. 1650–c.1750*. Oxford: Clarendon, 1997.

Boyer, Paul and Stephn Nissenbaum. *Salem Possessed: The Social Origins of Witchcraft*. Cambridge, Mass.: Harvard University Press, 1974.

Briggs, Katharine Mary. *The Fairies in tradition and Literature*. London: Routledge and Kegan Paul, 1967.

Briggs, Katharine Mary. *The Personnel of Fairyland: A Short Account of the Fairy People of Great Britain for Those who tell stories to children*. Oxford: Alden Press, 1953. Reprint, Detroit: Singing Tree Press, 1971.

Briggs, Robin. *Witches and Neighbors: The Social and Cultural Context of European Witchcraft*. New York: HarperCollins, 1996; New York, Viking, 1996.

Bullough, Vern L. 'Postscript: Heresy, Witchcraft and Sexuality.' In *Sexual Practices and the Medieval Church*. eds. Vern L. Bullough and James Brundage, 206–217. Buffalo: Prometheus Books, 1982.

Burghatz, Susanna. 'The Equation of Women and Witches: A Case Study of Witchcraft Trials in Lucerene and Lausanne in the Fifteenth and Sixteenth Centuries.' In *The German Underworld: Deviants and Outcasts in German History*, ed. Richard J. Evans, 108–140. London: Routledge, 1988.

Burke, Peter. 'Witchcraft and Magic in Renaissance Italy: Gianfrancesco Pico and His Strix.' In *The Damned Art: Essays in the Literature of Witchcraft*, ed. Sydney Anglo, 32–52. London: Routledge and Kegan Paul, 1977.

Burke, Peter. 'The Comparative Approach to European Witchcraft.' In *Early Modern European Witchcraft: Centres and Peripheries*, ed. Bengt Ankarloo and Gustav Henningsen, 435–441. Oxford: Clarendon, 1990.

Burke, Peter. *Popular Culture in Early Modern Europe*. New York: Harper and Row, 1978.

Bynum, Caroline Walker. 'Religious Women in the Later Middle Ages.' In *Christian Spirituality: High Middle Ages and Reformation*, ed. Jill Raitt, 121–139. New York: Crossroads, 1988.

Clark, Stuart. 'The Scientific Status of Demonology.' In *A Lycanthropy Reader: Werewolves in Western Culture*, ed. Charlotte F. Otten, 168–194. Syracuse: Syracuse University Press, 1986.

Clark, Stuart. *Thinking with Demons: The Idea of Witchcraft in Early Modern Europe*. Oxford: Clarendon, 1997.

Cohn, Norman. 'The Myth of Satan and his Human Servants.' In *Witchcraft Confessions and Allegations*, ed. Mary Douglas, 3–16. London: Tavistock, 1972.

Cohn, Norman. *Europe's Inner Demons*. Sussex: Sussex University Press, 1975; Granada, 1976.

Crawford, J.R. *Witchcraft and Sorcery in Rhodesia*. London: Oxford University Press, 1967.

Currie, Elliot P. 'The Control of Witchcraft in Renaissance Europe.' In *The Social Organization of Law*, ed. Donald J. Black, 344–367. New York: Seminar Press, 1973.

Davidson, L.S. and J. O Ward, eds. *The Sorcery Trial of Alice Kyteler: A contemporary account (1324) together with related documents in English translation, with introduction and notes*. Binghampton, N.Y.: Medieval and Renaissance Texts and Studies, 1993.

Demos, John P. 'Underlying Themes in the Witchcraft of Seventeenth-Century New England.' *American Historical Review* 75 (1970):1311–1326.

Demos, John P. *Entertaining Satan: Witchcraft and the Culture of Early New England*. New York: Oxford University, 1982.

Dickson, M.G. *Patterns of European Sanctity: The Cult of Saints in the Later Middle Ages (with special reference to Perugia)*. Ph.D. diss., University of Edinburgh, 1974.

Douglas, Mary, ed. *Witchcraft Confessions and Accusations*. London: Tavistock, 1970.

Drake, Frederick C. 'Witchcraft in the American Colonies.' *American Quarterly* 20 (1968): 695–725.

Duerr, Hans Peter. *Dreamtime: Concerning the Boundary between Wilderness and Civilization* (1978). Translated by Felisitas Goodman. Oxford: Basil Blackwell, 1985.

Ehrenreich, Barbara and Dierdre English. *Witches, Midwives and Nurses: A History of Women Healers*. New York: Feminist Press, 1973 .

Estes, Leland. 'The Medical Origins of the European Witch Craze: A Hypothesis.' In *Articles on Witchcraft, Magic and Demonology*. Edited by Brian P. Levack. Vol 3, *Witch-hunting in Early Modern Europe: General Studies*, 293–306. New York: Garland, 1992.

Evans-Pritchard, E.E. *Witchcraft, Oracles and Magic among the Azande*. Oxford: Clarendon, 1937.

Ewen, C. L'Estrange. *Witch Hunting and Witch Trials: The Indictments for Witchcraft from the Records of 1373 Assizes held for the Home Circuit AD 1559–1736*. London: Kegan Paul, Trench, Trubner, 1929.

Fiume, Giovanna. 'The Old Vinegar Lady, or the Judicial Modernization of the Crime of Witchcraft.' In *History from Crime,* eds. Edward Muir and Guido Ruggiero, 65–87. Baltimore: John Hopkins University Press, 1994.

Frazer, James George. *The Golden Bough: A Study in Magic and Religion*. 1 Volume abridged edition. New York: MacMillan, 1922.

Garrett, Clarke. 'Women and Witches: Patterns of Analysis.' *Signs* 3 (1977): 461–470.

Bibliography

Gijswist-Hofstra, Marijke. 'Witchcraft in the Northern Netherlands.' In *Current Issues in Womens History*, ed. Arina Angerman, 75–92. London: Routledge, 1989.

Ginzburg, Carlo. 'Deciphering the Sabbath.' *Early Modern European Witchcraft: Centres and Peripheries*, ed. Bengt Ankarloo and Gustav Henningsen, 121–137. Oxford: Clarendon, 1990.

Ginzburg, Carlo. *The Night Battles: Witchcraft and Agrarian Cults in the Sixteenth and Seventeenth Centuries* (1966). Translated by John Tedeschi and Anne Tedeschi. Baltimore: John Hopkins University Press, 1983.

Ginzburg, Carlos. *Ecstasies: Deciphering the Witches' Sabbath* (1989). Translated by Raymond Rosenthal. New York: Pantheon, 1991.

Ginzburg, Carlo. *The Cheese and the Worms: The Cosmos of a Sixteenth-Century Miller*(1976). Translated by John and Anne Tedeschi. New York: Dorset Press, 1980.

Godbeer, Richard. *The Devil's Dominion: Magic and Religion in Early New England*. Cambridge: Cambridge University Press, 1992.

Gregory, Annabel. 'Witchcraft, Politics and 'Good Neighbourhood' in Early Seventeenth-Century Rye.' *Past and Present* 133 (Nov. 1991): 31–66.

Guskin, Phyllis J. 'The Context of Witchcraft: The Case of Jane Wenham (1712).' *Eighteenth Century Studies* 15 (1981): 48–71.

Harner, Michael J. ' The Roll of Hallucinogenic Plants in European Witchcraft.' In *Articles on Witchcraft, Magic and Demonology*. Edited by Brian P. Levack. Vol 3, *Witchhunting in Early Modern Europe: General Studies*, 247–272. New York: Garland, 1992.

Harris, Marvin. *Cows, Pigs, Wars and Witches: The Riddles of Culture*. New York: Random House, 1975; New York: Vintage, 1975.

Harris, Tim. 'Problematizing Popular Culture.' In *Popular Culture in England, 1500–1800*, ed. Tim Harris, 1–27. London: Macmillan, 1995.

Hastrap, Kirsten. 'Iceland: Sorcerers and Paganism.' In *Early Modern European Witchcraft: Centres and Peripheries*, ed. Bengt Ankarloo and Gustav Henningsen, 383–401. Oxford: Clarendon, 1990.

Heikkinen, Antero and Timo Kervinen. 'Finland: The Male Domination.' In *Early Modern European Witchcraft: Centres and Peripheries*, ed. Bengt Ankarloo and Gustav Henningsen, 319–338. Oxford: Clarendon, 1990.

Henningsen, Gustav. 'The Greatest Witch-trial of Them All: Navarre, 1609–14.' *History Today*, November 1980, 36.

Henningsen, Gustav. *The Witches Advocate: Basque Witchcraft and the Spanish Inquisition (1609–14)*. Reno: University of Nevada, 1980.

Hoak, Dale, 'Witch Hunting and Women in the Art of the Renaissance.' *History Today*, February 1981, 22.

Hoffer, Peter C. and N.E.H. Hull. *Murdering Mothers: Infanticide in England and New England 1558–1803*. New York: New York University Press, 1981.

Holmes, Ronald. *Witchcraft in British History*. Plymouth: Frederick Muller, 1974.

Holmes, Clive. 'Women: Witnesses and Witches' in *Past and Present* 140 (August 1993): 45–78.

Hughes, Pennethorne. *Witchcraft*. Longmans, Green, 1952; Penguin, 1965.

Johansen, Jens. Christian V. 'Denmark: The Sociology of Accusations.' In *Early Modern European Witchcraft: Centres and Peripheries*, ed. Bengt Ankarloo and Gustav Henningsen, 273–284. Oxford: Clarendon, 1990.

Kahk, Juhan. 'Estonia II: The Crusade against Idolatry.' In *Early Modern European Witchcraft: Centres and Peripheries*, ed. Bengt Ankarloo and Gustav Henningsen, 273–284. Oxford: Clarendon, 1990.

Kern, Edmund. 'Confessional Identity and Magic in the Late Sixteenth Century: Jakob Bithner and Witchcraft in Styria.' in *Sixteenth Century Journal* XXV/2 (1994): 323–340.

Kieckhefer, Richard. *European Witch Trials: Their Foundations in Popular and Learned Culture, 1300–1500*. Berkley: University of California Press, 1976.

Klaits, Joseph. *Servants of Satan: The Age of the Witch Hunts*. Bloomington: Indiana University Press, 1985.

Klaits, Joseph. 'Witchcraft Trials and Absolute Monarchy in Alsace.' In *Church, State and Society under the Bourbon Kings*, ed. Richard M. Golden, 148–172. Colorado: K.S. Lawrence, 1982.

Klaniczay, Gabor, 'Hungary: The Accusations and the Universe of Popular Magic.' In *Early Modern European Witchcraft: Centres and Peripheries*, ed. Bengt Ankarloo and Gustav Henningsen, 219–255. Oxford: Clarendon, 1990.

Levack, Brian P. *The witch-hunt in early modern Europe*. London: Longman, 1987. Also, 2nd edition, London: Longman, 1995.

Macfarlane, A. *Witchcraft in Tudor and Stuart England*. London: Routledge K. Paul, 1970.

Macfarlane, Alan. 'Witchcraft in Tudor and Stuart Essex.' In *Witchcraft Confessions and Accusations*, ed. Mary Douglas, 81–99. New York: Tavistock Publications, 1970.

Madar, Maia. 'Estonia I: Werewolves and Poisoners.' In *Early Modern European Witchcraft: Centres and Peripheries*, ed. Bengt Ankarloo and Gustav Henningsen, 257–272. Oxford: Clarendon, 1990.

Mappen, Marc ed. *Witches and Historians: Interpretations of Salem*. Huntington, N.Y.: R.E. Krieger Publ. Co., 1980.

Martin, Ruth. *Witchcraft and the Inquisition in Venice 1550–1650*. Oxford: Basil Blackwell, 1989.

Matalene, Carolyn. 'Women as Witches.' In *Articles on Witchcraft, Magic and Demonology*. Edited by Brian P. Levack. Vol 10, *Witchcraft, Women and Society*, 51–66. New York: Garland, 1992.

Midelfort, H.C. Erik. *Witch Hunting in Southwestern Germany, 1562–1684: The Social and Intellectual Foundations*. Stanford: Stanford University Press, 1972.

Midelfort, H.C. Erik. 'Heartland of the Witchcraze: Central and Northern Europe.' *History Today*, February 1981, 29.

Midelfort, H.C. Erik. 'Witchcraft and Religion in Sixteenth-Century Germany: The Formation and Consequences of an Orthodoxy.' *Archiv fur Reformantionsgeschichte* 62 (1971): 266–78.

Midelfort, H.C. Erik. 'Were there Really Witches?' In *Transition and Revolution*, ed. Robert M. Kingdon, 189–205. Minneapolis: Burgess Publ. Co., 1974.

Monter, E. William. *Witchcraft in France and Switzerland: The Borderlands During the Reformation*. London: Cornell University Press, 1976.

Monter, E. William 'Scandinavian Witchcraft in Aglo-American Perspective.' In *Early Modern European Witchcraft: Centres and Peripheries*, ed. Bengt Ankarloo and Gustav Henningsen, 425–434. Oxford: Clarendon, 1990.

Moore, R.I. *The Formation of a Persecuting Society: Power and Deviance in Western Europe, 950–1250*. Oxford: Basil Blackwell, 1987.

Muchembled, Robert. 'The Witches of the Cambrésis: The Acculturation of the Rural World in the Sixteenth and Seventeenth Centuries.' In *Religion and the People, 800–1700*, ed. Jim Obelkevich, 221–276. Chapel Hill: University of North Carolina Press, c. 1979.

Muchembled, Robert. 'Satanic Myths and Cultural Reality.' In *Early Modern European Witchcraft: Centres and Peripheries*, ed. Bengt Ankarloo and Gustav Henningsen, 139–160. Oxford: Clarendon, 1990.

Muir, Edward and Guido Ruggiero. 'Afterword: Crime and the Writing of History.' In *History from Crime*, eds. Edward Muir and Guido Ruggiero, 226–236. Baltimore: John Hopkins University Press, 1994.

Murray, Margaret A. *The God of the Witches*. London: Farber and Farber, 1931; Reprint, New York: Oxford, 1981.

Murray, Margaret Alice. *The Witch-cult in Western Europe*. Oxford: Clarendon Press, 1921.

Naess, Hans Eyvind. 'Norway: The Criminological Context.' In *Early Modern European Witchcraft: Centres and Peripheries*, ed. Bengt Ankarloo and Gustav Henningsen, 367–382. Oxford: Clarendon, 1990.

Notestein, Wallace. *A History of Witchcraft in England from 1558 to 1718*. Washington: American Historical Association, 1911. Reprint. New York, Russell and Russell, 1965.

Otten, Charlotte F. ed. *A Lycanthropy Reader: Werewolves in Western Culture*. Syracuse: Syracuse University Press, 1986.

Parker, Geoffrey. 'The European Witchcraze Revisited: Introduction', in *History Today*, November 1980, 23–24.

Parker, Geoffrey. 'Some Recent Works on the History of the Inquisition in Spain and Italy.' *Journal of Modern History* 54 (1982): 519–32.

Parrinder, Edward Geoffrey. *Witchcraft: European and African*. London: Faber and Faber, 1963; London: Faber and Faber, 1970.

Pearl, Jonathan L. 'Witchcraft in New France in the Seventeenth Century: The Social Aspect.' *Historical Reflections* 4 (1977): 191–205.

Peters, Edward. *Torture*. Oxford: Basil Blackwell, 1985.

Peters, Edward. *The Magician, the Witch, and the Law*. Philadelphia: University of Pennsylvania, 1978.

Quaife, G.R. *Godly Zeal and Furious Rage: The Witch in Early Modern Europe*. New York: St. Martin's Press, 1987.

Robbins. Rossell Hope *The Encyclopedia of Witchcraft and Demonology*, 1959 ed. London: Spring Books, 1959.

Ruether, Rosemary. 'The Persecution of Witches: A Case of Sexism and Agism?' In *Articles on Witchcraft, Magic and Demonology*. Edited by Brian P. Levack. Vol 10, *Witchcraft, Women and Society*, 251–256. New York: Garland, 1992.

Scarre, Geoffrey. *Witchcraft and Magic in Sixteenth- and Seventeenth-Century Europe*. Atlantic Highlands, New Jersey: Humanities Press International, 1987.

Sharpe, J.A. 'Witchcraft and Women in seventeenth-century England: some Northern evidence.' *Continuity and Change* 6, 2 (August 1991): 179–199.

Sharpe, J.A. *Crime in Early Modern England 1550–1750*. London: Longman, 1984.

Sharpe, J.A. *Instruments of Darkness; Witchcraft in England 1550–1750*. London: Hamish Hamilton, 1996.

Silverblatt, Irene. *Moon, Sun and Witches: Gender Ideologies and Class in Inca and Colonial Peru*. Princeton: Princeton University Press, 1987.

Soman, Alfred. 'The Parlement of Paris and the Great Witch Hunt(1565–1640).' *Sixteenth Century Journal* 9, 2 (1978): 30–44.

Starkey, Marion L. *The Devil in Massachusetts: A Modern Enquiry into the Salem Witch Trials*. New York: Alfred A. Knopf, 1949; Anchor, 1989.

Teall, John L. 'Witchcraft and Calvinism in Elizabethan England: Divine Power and Human Agency.' *Journal of the History of Ideas* 23 (1962): 21–36.

Thomas, Keith. *Religion and the Decline of Magic: Studies in Popular Beliefs in Sixteenth- and Seventeenth-Century England*. London: Wiendenfeld & Nicolson, 1971; Penguin, 1982.

Thomas, Keith. 'The Relevance of Social Anthropology to the Historical Study of English Witchcraft.' In *Witchcraft Confessions and Accusations*, ed. Mary Douglas, 47–79. New York: Tavistock, 1970.

Thompson, Janet A. *Wives, Widows, Witches and Bitches: Women in Seventeenth-Century Devon*. New York: Peter Lang, 1993.

Trevor-Roper, H.R. 'The European Witch-craze of the Sixteenth and Seventeenth Centuries' in H.R. Trevor-Roper, *Religion, the Reformation and Social Change and other Essays by H.R. Trevor-Roper* 2nd ed. London: Macmillan Press, 1972.

Ward, John O. 'Witchcraft and sorcery in the Late Roman Empire and the Early Middle Ages. An anthropological Comment.' In *Articles on Witchcraft, Magic and Demonology*.

Edited by Brian P. Levack. Vol 10, *Witchcraft, Women and Society*, 1–16. New York: Garland, 1992.

Weisman, Richard. *Witchcraft, Magic and Religion in 17th century Massachusetts*. Amherst: University of Massachusetts Press, 1984.

Wilson, David. 'Salem and The Supernatural'. CBC IDEAS Transcript, 21 and 22 December, 1992.

Secondary Sources: Scotland

Adam, Isabel. *Witch Hunt: The Great Scottish Witchcraft trials of 1697*. London: Macmillan, 1978.

Anderson, Alan and Raymond Gordon. 'The uniqueness of English witchcraft: a matter of numbers?' *British Journal of Sociology* 30 (September 1979): 359–361.

Arnott, David. *The Witches of Keil's Glen, a dramatic fragment: with other poems*. Cupar: R. Tullis, 1825.

Black, George F. *A Calendar of Cases of Witchcraft in Scotland 1510–1727*. New York: New York Public Library and Arno Press, 1938.

Boatright, Mody C. 'Witchcraft in the Novels of Sir Walter Scott', *University of Texas Studies in English* 13 (1933): 95–112.

Brodie-Innes, J.W. 'Scottish Witchcraft Trials.' In *Witches and Witch Hunters*, ed. A.E. Green. 1891. Reprint, Menston, Yorkshire: Scholars Press, 1971.

Brown, Keith M. 'The Nobility of Jacobean Scotland, 1567–1625.' In *Scotland Revisited*, ed. Jenny Wormald, 61–72. London: Collins & Brown, 1991.

Brown, Keith M. 'The Laird, his Daughter, her Husband and the Minister: Unravelling a Popular Ballad.' In *People and Power: essays in honour of T.C. Smout*, eds. Roger Mason and Normal Macdougall, 104–125. Edinburgh: John Donald, 1992.

Buckland, Raymond. *Scottish Witchcraft: The History and Magick of the Picts*. St. Paul, Minn.: Llewellyn, 1992.

Cameron, Joy. *Prisons and Punishment in Scotland: From the Middle Ages to the Present*. Edinburgh: Canongate, 1983.

Clark, Stuart 'King James's *Daemonologie*: Witchcraft and kingship,' In *The Damned Art: Essays in the Literature of Witchcraft*, ed. Sydney Anglo, 156–181. London: Routledge and Kegan Paul, 1977.

Colville, K.N. *Scottish Culture in the 17th Century (1603–60)*. Ph.D. diss., University of Edinburgh, 1930.

Cowan, Edward J. 'The darker vision of the Scottish Renaissance,' In *The Renaissance and Reformation in Scotland*, eds. I.B. Cowan and D. Shaw, 125–140. Edinburgh: Scottish Academic Press, 1983.

Cowan, Edward J. 'The Royal Witch-Hunt.' *The Sunday Mail Story of Scotland*, Vol. 2, Pt. 15, 1988, 406.

Davidson, Thomas. *Rowan Tree and Red Thread: A scottish miscellany of tales, legends and ballads: together with a description of the witches' rites and ceremonies*. Edinburgh: Oliver and Boyd, 1949.

Davies, Stephen J. 'The Courts and the Scottish Legal System 1600–1747: The Case of Stirlingshire.' In *Crime and the Law: the Social History of Crime in Western Europe since 1500*, ed. V.A.C. Gattrell, Bruce Lenman and Geoffery Parker, 120–154. London: Europa Publications, 1980.

Dawson, Jane. E.A. "The Face of Ane Perfyt Reformed Kyrk': St Andrews and the Early Scottish Reformation.' In *Humanism and Reform: the church in Europe, England and Scotland, 1400–1643: essays in honour of James K. Cameron*, ed. James Kirk, 413–435. Oxford: Basil Blackwell, 1991.

Dickinson, W. Croft. *Scotland from the Earliest Times to 1603*. Third Ed. Oxford: Clarendon, 1977. Archibald A.M. Duncan, ed.

Bibliography

Douglas, Ronald MacDonald. *The Scots Book: A Miscellany of Poems, Folklore, Prose and Letters* . . . London: Alexander Maclehose, 1935.

Donaldson, Gordon. *Scotland: James V-James VII.* Edinburgh: Oliver & Boyd, 1965; Edinburgh: Oliver & Boyd, 1978.

Dunlop, A. Ian. 'The Polity of the Scottish Church 1600–37.' *Scottish Church History Society Records* 1 (1958): 161–184.

Ferguson, John. 'Bibliographical Notes on the Witchcraft Literature of Scotland.' *Proceedings of the Edinburgh Bibliographical Society* 3 (1884). Reprinted in *Articles on Witchcraft, Magic and Demonology.* Edited by Brian P. Levack. Vol 7, *Witchcraft in Scotland*, 45–132. New York: Garland, 1992.

Foster, W. Roland. 'The Operation of Presbyteries in Scotland 1600–38.' *Scottish Church History Society Records* 15 (1966): 21–33.

Gilmore, John. *Witchcraft and the Church in Scotland.* Ph. D. diss., University of Glasgow, 1948.

Graham, Michael. *The Uses of Reform: 'Godly Discipline' and Popular Behavior in Scotland and Beyond, 1560–1610.* New York: E.J. Brill, 1996.

Graham, Ralph M. *Ecclesiastical Discipline in the Church of Scotland 1690–1730.* Ph. D. diss., Faculty of Divinity, University of Glasgow, 1964.

Hardy, John R. *The Attitude of the Church and State in Scotland to Sex and Marriage: 1560–1707.* M. Phil. diss., University of Edinburgh, 1978.

Jacobs, Joseph ed. *Celtic Fairy Tales.* David Nutt, 1892. Reprint, New York: Dover, 1968.

Kintscher, Margaret Carol. *The culpability of James VI of Scotland, later James I of England, in the North Berwick witchcraft trials of 1590–91.* M.A. diss., San Jose State University, 1991.

Larner, Christina, Christopher Hyde Lee, and Hugh McLachlan. *A Source Book of Scottish Witchcraft.* Glasgow: Sociology Department, University of Glasgow, 1977.

Larner, Christina, 'Witch Beliefs and Witch-Hunting in England and Scotland.' *History Today* (February 1981): 32.

Larner, Christina. 'James VI and I and Witchcraft.' In *The Reign of James VI and I*, ed. Alan G.R. Smith, 74–90. London: Macmillan Press, 1973.

Larner, Christina. *Enemies of God: The Witch-hunt in Scotland.* London: Chatto & Windus, 1981. Oxford: Basil Blackwell, 1983.

Larner, Christina. *Witchcraft and Religion: The Politics of Popular Belief.* Oxford: Basil Blackwell, 1984.

Larner, Christina. 'Crimen Exceptum? The Crime of Witchcraft in Europe.' In *Crime and the Law: The Social History of Crime in Western Europe since 1500*, ed. V.A.C. Gatrell, Bruce Lenman, and Geoffrey Parker, 49–75. London: Europa, 1980.

Larner, Christina. 'Two late Scottish witchcraft tracts: *Witch-Craft Proven* and *The Tryal of Witchcraft*.' In *The Damned Art: Essays in the Literature of Witchcraft*, ed. Sydney Anglo, 227–245. London: Routledge and Kegan Paul, 1977.

Legge, F. 'Witchcraft in Scotland', *The Scottish Review* 18 (1891). Reprinted in *Articles on Witchcraft, Magic and Demonology.* Edited by Brian P. Levack. Vol 7, *Witchcraft in Scotland*, 1–32. New York: Garland, 1992.

Leneman, Leah and Rosalind Mitchison, 'Acquiesence in and defiance of church discipline in early-modern Scotland.' *Scottish Church History Society Records* xxv/1 (1993): 19–39.

Leneman, Leah. ''Prophaning' The Lord's Day: Sabbath Breach in Early Modern Scotland.' *History* 74 (1989): 217–231.

Levack, Brian P. 'The Great Scottish Witch Hunt of 1661–62.' *Journal of British Studies* 20 (1984): 90–108.

Levack, Brian P. ed. *Articles on Witchcraft, Magic and Demonology.* Vol 7, *Witchcraft in Scotland.* New York: Garland, 1992.

Lynch, Michael. *Scotland: A New History.* London: Century, 1991.

MacCulloch, J.A. 'The Mingling of Fairy and Witch Beliefs in Sixteenth and Seventeenth

Century Scotland', *Folklore: The Transactions of the Folk-lore Society* xxxii (December, 1921): 229–244.

Mackay, Charles. *Memoirs of Extraordinary Popular Delusions,* Vol. 2. 1841. London: Office of the National Illustrated Library, 1852 edition.

MacLeod, Nicholas A. *Scottish Witchcraft.* Cornwall: James Pike, 1975.

MacLeod, Innes. *Discovering Galloway.* Edinburgh: John Donald, 1986.

McLachlan, H.V. and J. K. Swales, 'Lord Hale, Witches and Rape: A Comment' *British Journal of Law and Society,* 5, no. 2 (1978): 252–257.

McLachlan, Hugh and Swales, J.K. 'Scottish Witchcraft: Myth or Reality?' in *Contemporary Review* 260 (February 1992): 79–84.

Melville, R. D. 'The Use and Forms of Judicial Torture in England and Scotland.' *Scottish Historical Review.* 2, no. 7 (1905): 225–248.

Mitchison, Rosalind. *Lordship to Patronage: Scotland 1603–1745.* London: Edward Arnold, 1983.

Mitchison, Rosalind and Leah Leneman. *Sexuality and Social Control: Scotland, 1660–1780.* Oxford: Basil Blackwell, 1989.

Mullan, David G. "Uniformity in Religion': The Solemn League and Covenant(1643) and the Presbyterian Vision.' In *Later Calvinism: International Perspectives,* ed. W. Fred Graham, 249–266. Kirksville, Mo., 1994.

Mullan, David G. 'Theology in the Church of Scotland 1618–c.1640: A Calvinist Consensus?' *Sixteenth Century Journal,* XXVI/3(1995): 595–617.

Murray, M.A. 'The 'Devil' of North Berwick.' *Scottish Historical Review* 15 (1918): 310–321.

Murray, Eunice C. *Scottish Women in Bygone Days.* Glasgow: Gowans and Gray, 1930.

Neill, W.N. 'The Professional Pricker and His Test for Witchcraft.' *Scottish Historical Review* 19 (1922): 205–213.

Neilson, George ed. 'A Sermon on Witchcraft in 1697.' In *Articles on Witchcraft, Magic and Demonology.* Edited by Brian P. Levack. Vol 7, *Witchcraft in Scotland,* 390–399. New York: Garland, 1992.

Robertson, John D.M. ed. *An Orkney Anthology: The Selected Works of Ernest Walker Marwick.* Edinburgh: Scottish Academic Press, 1991.

Sharpe, Charles Kirkpatrick. *A Historical Account of the Belief in Witchcraft in Scotland.* Glasgow, 1884. Reprint, Menson, Yorkshire: Scholars Press, 1972.

Steele, Margaret. 'The 'Politick Christian': The Theological Background to the National Covenant.' In *The Scottish National Covenant in its British Context,* ed. John Morril, 31–67. Edinburgh: Edinburgh University Press, 1990.

Strawhorn, John and Ken Andrew. *Discovering Ayrshire.* Edinburgh: John Donald, 1988.

Swales, J.K. and Hugh V. McLachlan. 'Witchcraft and the status of women: a comment.' *British Journal of Sociology* 30, (1979): 349–358.

Symms, Peter Stephen Michael. *Social Control in a Sixteenth-century burgh: a study of the burgh court book of Selkirk 1503–45.* Ph. D. diss., University of Edinburgh, 1986.

Taylor, William. *The Scottish Privy Council 1603–25: Its Composition and its Work.* Ph. D. diss., University of Edinburgh, 1950.

Thomson, John Maitland. *The Public Records of Scotland.* Glasgow: Maclehose, Jackson and Co., 1922.

Truckell, A.E. 'Unpublished Witchcraft Trials – Part 1.' *Transactions of the Dumfries-shire and Galloway Natural History and Antiquarian Society* 51 (1975): 48–58.

Truckell, A.E. 'Unpublished Witchcraft Trials – Part 2.' *Transactions of the Dumfries-shire and Galloway Natural History and Antiquarian Society* 52 (1976): 95–108.

Wasser, Michael. 'Law, Politics and Witchcraft: The Curtailment of Witchcraft Prosecutions in Scotland, 1597–1628.' Unpublished paper, 1996.

Watson, Godfrey. *Bothwell and the Witches.* London: Robert Hale, 1975.

Whyte, Ian D. *Agrarian Change in Lowland Scotland in the Seventeenth Century.* Ph.D. diss., University of Edinburgh, 1974.

Whyte, Ian and Kathleen Whyte. *Discovering East Lothian*. Edinburgh: John Donald, 1988.

Whyte, Ian D. *Scotland Before the Industrial Revolution: An Economic & Social History c. 1050 – c. 1750*. Harlow: Longman, 1995.

Wormald, Jenny. *Court, Kirk and Community: Scotland 1470–1625*. Toronto: University of Toronto Press, 1981.

Yeoman, Louise Anderson. *Heart-work: Emotion, Empowerment and Authority in Covenanting Times*. Ph. D. diss., University of St. Andrews, 1991.

Secondary Sources: Fife and local history

Ballingall, G.W. *Historical Collections (with notes) regarding the Royal Burgh and Parish of Kinghorn*. Kirkcaldy: Strachan & Livingstone, 1893.

Bensen, Richard A. *South-West Fife and the Scottish Revolution: The Presbytery of Dunfermline, 1633–52*. M.Litt diss., University of Edinburgh, 1978.

Beveridge, David. *Culross and Tuliallan or Perthshire on Forth . . .* Edinburgh: William Blackwood, 1885.

Buckner, J.C.R. *Rambles in and Around Aberdour and Burntisland*. Edinburgh: J. Menzies, 1881.

Campbell, Rev. John. *Kirkcaldy Burgh and schyre: Landmarks of local history with notes on prominent personalities, old place names, old buildings, and folklore*. Kirkcaldy: Fifeshire Advertiser, 1924.

Campbell, Rev. John. *The Church and Parish of Kirkcaldy: from the earliest times till 1843*. Kirkcaldy: Alex Page, 1904.

Campbell, Rev. James. *Balmerino and its Abbey: a parish history with notices of the adjacent districts*. Edinburgh: William Blackwood and sons, 1899.

Cunningham, Andrew S. *Inverkeithing, North Queensferry Rosyth and the Naval Base*. Dunfermline: W. Clark, n.d.

Cunningham, Andrew S. *Culross: Past & Present & Torryburn & Valleyfield*. Leven: Purves and Cunningham, 1910.

Di Folco, John A. *Aspects of Seventeenth Century Social Life in Central and North Fife*. B. Phil diss., University of St. Andrews, 1975.

Fraser, James. *Memoirs of the Rev. James Fraser of Brea, AD 1639–98*. Edinburgh: Religious Tract and Book Society, 1889.

Fyfe, William Wallace. *Summer Life on Land and Water at South Queensferry*. Edinburgh: Oliver & Boyd, 1851.

Hunter, John P. 'Witches of Torryburn: The 'Inquisition' of a Fifeshire Minister'. *Scots Magazine*, 1936.

Laing, Alexander. *Lindores Abbey and Its Burgh of Newburgh*. Edinburgh: 1876.

Lamont-Brown, Raymond. *Discovering Fife*. Edinburgh: John Donald, 1988.

Lang, Theo, ed. *The Kingdom of Fife and Kinross-shire*. London: Hodder & Stoughton, 1951.

Lyon, Rev. C. J. *History of St. Andrews, Episcopal, Monastic, Academic, and Civil; Comprising the Principal part of the ecclesiastical history of Scotland . . .* Vol. 1 and 2. Edinburgh: William Tait, 1843.

MacKay, A.J.G. *A Sketch of the History of Fife and Kinross: A Study in Scottish History and Character*. Edinburgh: Wm. Blackwood, 1890.

MacKay, A.J.G. *A Century of Scottish Proverbs and Sayings: in prose and rhyme current in Fife and Chiefly of Fife Origin*. Cupar: A. Westwood, n.d.

Neale, Chris. *The 17th Century Witch Craze in West Fife: A guide to the printed sources*. Dunfermline: Dunfermline District Libraries, 1980.

Pryde, David. *The Queer Folk of Fife: Tales from the Kingdom*. Glasgow: Morison Bros., 1897.

Reid, Alan. *Kinghorn: A short history and description of a notable Fifeshire town and parish*. Kirkcaldy: L. MacBean, 1906.

Ross, William. *Glimpses of Pastoral Work in the Covenanting Times: A Record of the Labours of Andrew Donaldson, A.M. Minister at Dalgetty, Fifeshire 1644–62*. Edinburgh: Andrew Elliot, 1877.

Ross, William. *Aberdour and Inchcolme: Being Historical Notices of the Parish and Monastery in twelve lectures*. Edinburgh: David Douglas, 1885.

Sibbald, Sir Robert. *The History, Ancient and Modern, of the Sheriffdoms of Fife and Kinross . . .* Cupar: for R. Tullis, 1803.

Simpkins, J.E. *Examples of Printed Folklore concerning Fife . . . County Folklore*. Vol. VII. London: Sidgwick & Jackson, 1914.

Simpson, Eric. *Dalgety – the story of a parish*. Dalgety: Dalgety Bay Community Council, 1980.

Stephen, Rev. William. *History of Inverkeithing and Rosyth*. Aberdeen: G&W Fraser, 1921.

Stevenson, Stephanie. *Anstruther: A History*. Edinburgh: John Donald, 1989.

Stevenson, William. *The Kirk and Parish of Auchtertool*. Kirkcaldy: James Burt, 1908.

Torrie, E.P. Dennison and Russel Coleman, ed. *Historic Kirkcaldy: the archaeological implications of development*. Aberdeen: Historic Scotland and Scottish Cultural Press, 1995.

Watson, Harry D. *Kilrenny and Cellardyke: 800 Years of History*. Edinburgh: John Donald, 1986.

Wilke, James. *The History of Fife: From the Earliest Time to the Nineteenth Century*. Edinburgh: William Blackwood & Sons, 1924.

Young, Andrew. *History of Burntisland: Scottish Burgh life more particularly in the time of the Stuarts*. Kirkcaldy: Fifeshire Advertiser, 1913.

Primary Sources: Manuscript

Aberdour Kirk Session, NAS, SRO, CH2\3\1\

Burntisland Kirk Session, NAS, CH2\523\1

Crail Kirk Session, St. Andrews University Muniments department

Commission against Coke & Dick, National Library of Scotland, adv.ms.31

Culross Kirk Session, Ch2\77\2

Dunfermline Kirk Session records, SRO, CH2\592\1

Dysart Kirk Session, NAS, CH2\390\1

Falkland Kirk Session, NAS, CH2\428\1

Justiciary Court Records, NAS, JC26\13\5

Justiciary Court Records, NAS, JC2\4

Justiciary Court Records, NAS, JC26\D; JC\26\7\1

Justiciary Court Records, NAS, Culross, JC2\14

Kirkcaldy Kirk Session, Town House, Kirkcaldy

Letter to David Smyth from My Lady Methven, November 19, 1716, SRO, GD190\3\279

Letter from Allan Logan, minister in Culross, April 16, 1623, SRO, GD124\15\1214

Markinch Kirk Session, SRO, CH2\258\1

Newburgh Kirk Session, St. Andrews University Muniments department, CH2\277\1

Records of the Committee of Estates, SRO, PA11\8

Pittenweem Kirk Session, SRO, CH2\833\3

Presbytery book of Kirkcaldy, April 1630–September 1653, NAS, CH2\224\1

Presbytery of Cupar, St. Andrews University Muniments. CH2\82\1

Presbytery Book of Dunfermline, NAS, CH2\105\1

Presbytery of St. Andrew's Records, St. Andrews University Muniments Department; Ch2\msdeposit\23; vol 4, 1699–1705

St. Andrews Kirk Session, St. Andrews University Muniments Department

Synod of Fife minutes, 1639–57, NAS, CH2\154\2a

Torryburn Kirk Session, 1695–1717, SRO, CH2\355\2

Primary Sources: Published

——. *A Selection from the Ancient Minutes of the Kirk-Session of Kinghorn*. Kirkcaldy: John Crawford, 1863.

——. *A Diurnal of Remarkable Occurents*. Edinburgh: Maitland Club, 1833.

——. *Extracts from Old Minute Books of the Burgh of Kirkcaldy (1582–1792)*. ?, 1862.

The Acts of the Parliament of Scotland, vol. 6, part 2.

Calendar of State Papers, PPS, vol 2.

Registers of the Privy Council of Scotland, vol. 5, 12, 13, 14.

Registers of the Privy Council of Scotland, 2nd ser. vol. 1, 2, 3.

Registers of the Privy Council of Scotland, 3nd ser. vol. 1, 2, 3, 5, 8.

Arnot, Hugo. *A Collection and Abridgement of Celebrated Criminal Trials in Scotland from A.D. 1536, to 1784 with historical and Critical Remarks*. Edinburgh: G.W. Smellie, 1785. Reprint, Edinburgh: 1885.

Bannatyne, Richard. *Journal of the Transactions in Scotland during the contest between the adherents of Queen Mary and those of her Son, 1570, 1571, 1572, 1573*. Edinburgh: J. Ballantyne, 1806.

Calderwood, David. *The history of the Kirk of Scotland*. Thomas Thomson, ed. Edinburgh: Wodrow Society, 1842–49.

Chambers, Robert. *Domestic Annals*. Vol. 1–3. Edinburgh: W&R Chambers, 1858.

Cook, David. *Annals of Pittenweem: being notes and extracts from the Ancient Records of that burgh*. Anstruther: Lewis Russell, 1867.

Dalyell, John Graham. *The Darker Superstitions of Scotland illustrated from history and practice*. Edinburgh: Waugh & Innes, 1834.

Fleming, David Hay. *Register of the minister elders and deacons of the Christian Congreation of St. Andrews comprising the proceedings of the kirk session...1559–1600*. Edinburgh: Scottish History Society. Vol 1, 1889; Vol 2, 1890.

Hannay, Robert Kerr editor & translator. *Rentale Sancti Andree: Being the Chamberlain and Granitar Accounts of the Archbishopric in the time of Cardinal Betoun 1538–46*. Edinburgh: Scottish History Society, 2nd ser, vol 4. 1913.

Harrison, G.B. ed. King James VI, *Daemonology* (1597) and *Newes from Scotland: Declaring the damnable Life and death of Doctor Fian, a notable Sorcerer who was burned at Edenborough in January last* (1591). New York: Barnes & Noble, 1966.

Henderson, Ebenezer, ed. *Extracts from the Kirk-Session Records of Dunfermline (1640–89)*. Edinburgh: Fullarton & MacNab, 1865.

Henderson, Ebenezer. *Annals of Dunfermline*. Glasgow: –, 1879.

Hogg, Jane D. *Extracts from the Kirk Session Book of Culross – 17th Century*. Typescript. Local History Room, Dunfermline District Library.

Kinloch, George R.. *Selections from the Minute of the Synod of Fife*. Edinburgh: Abbotsford Club, 1837.

Kinloch, G.R. ed. *Selections from the Minutes of the Presbyteries of St. Andrews and Cupar 1641–98*. Edinburgh: Abbotsford club, 1837.

Kinloch, G.R. ed.. *The Diary of Mr John Lamont of Newton, 1649–71*. Edinburgh: Maitland Club, 1830.

Lyon, Rev. C. J. *History of St. Andrews, Episcopal, Monastic, Academic, and Civil; Comprising the Principal part of the ecclesiastical history of Scotland . . .* Edinburgh, William Tait, 1843. Vol. I & II.

MacBean, L. *The Kirkcaldy Burgh Records*. Kirkcaldy: n.p., 1908.

Mackenzie, Sir George. *The Laws and Customs of Scotland in Matters Criminal*. Edinburgh: ?, 1834.

Nicholl, J. *A Diary of Public transactions and other occurences chiefly in Scotland, from January 1650 to June 1667*. Edinburgh, 1836.

Peterkin, Alexander ed. *The Booke of the Universall Kirk of Scotland*. Edinburgh: Edinburgh Publishing Company, 1839.

Pitcairn, Robert. *Ancient Criminal Trials in Scotland*. Vol 1–3. Edinburgh: Bannatyne Club, 1833.

Pitcairn, Robert ed. *The autobiography and diary of Mr. James Melville*. Edinburgh: Wodrow Society, 1842.

Scott-Moncrieff, W.G. *The Records of the Proceedings of the Justiciary Court Edinburgh 1661–78*. Edinburgh: Scottish History Society, Vol. 48.

Sinclair, Sir John ed. 'Trial of William Coke and Alison Dick for Witchcraft – Extracted from the Minutes of the Kirk Session of Kirkcaldy, A.D. 1636.' In *The Statistical Account of Scotland 1791–99*. Volume X. Fife. EP Publishing, 1978 edition.

Smith, Mark C. *A Study and Annotated edition of the Register of the Minutes of the Presbytery of St. Andrew's, volume 1*. Ph. D. diss., University of St. Andrews, 1985.

Smith, J. Irvine, ed. *Selected Justiciary Cases 1624–50*. Vol III. Edinburgh: The Stair Society, 1974.

Stevenson, William, editor. *The Presbyterie Booke of Kirkcaldie: Being the record of the proceedings of that Presbytery from the 15th day of April 1630 to the 14th day of September 1653*. Kirkcaldy: James Burt, 1900.

Primary Sources: Pamphlets

——*A Just Reproof to the False Reports and Unjust Calumnies in the Foregoing Letters*. In D. Webster, *A Collection of Rare and Curious Tracts on Witchcraft and the Second Sight; with an Original Essay on Witchcraft*. Edinburgh: for D. Webster, 1820.

——*A True and Full Relation of the Witches at Pittenweem to which is added . . .* Edinburgh: 1704. In D. Webster, *A Collection of Rare and Curious Tracts on Witchcraft and the Second Sight; with an Original Essay on Witchcraft*. Edinburgh: for D. Webster, 1820.

——*A Relation of the Diabolical Practices of the Witches of the sheriffdom of Renfrew in the Kingdom of Scotland . . .* London: for Hugh Newman, 1697.

——*An Answer of a Letter from a Gentleman in Fife to a Nobleman, CONTAINING A Brief Account of the Barbarous and illegal Treatment, these poor Women accused of Witchcraft, met with from the Bailies of Pittenweem and others, with some Observations thereon; to which is added, An Account of the horrid and Barbarous Murder, in a Letter from a Gentleman in Fife, to his Friend in Edinburgh, February 5th, 1705*. 1705. In D. Webster, *A Collection of Rare and Curious Tracts on Witchcraft and the Second Sight; with an Original Essay on Witchcraft*. Edinburgh: for D. Webster, 1820.

——*Minutes and Proceedings of the Session of Torryburn, in Fifeshire, concerning witchcraft with the confession of Lillias Adie* in D. Webster, *A Collection of Rare and Curious Tracts on Witchcraft and the Second sight; with an original Essay on Witchcraft*. Edinburgh: for D. Webster, 1820.

——*Ravillat Redivivus: being a Narrative of the tryal of Mr. James Mitchell a Conventicle-preacher, who was executed the 18th of January last, for an attempt which he made on the sacred person of the Archbishop of St. Andrews*. London: Henry Hills, 1678.

——*Sadducismus Debellatus or a true Narrative of the sorceries and witchcrafts exercised by the Devil and his Instruments upon Mrs. Christian Shaw, Daughter of Mr. John Shaw, of Bargarran in the County of Renfrew in the West of Scotland, from Aug. 1696 to Apr. 1697*. London: for H. Newmann, 1698.

——*The Lawes against witches and conivration . . .* London: Printed for R.W., 1645.

——*The Trial of William Coke and Alison Dick for Witchcraft Extracted from the Minutes of the Kirk-Session of Kirkcaldy, A.D. 1636* in D. Webster *A Collection of Rare and Curious Tracts on Witchcraft and the Second sight; with an original Essay on Witchcraft*. Edinburgh: for D. Webster, 1820.

——*Witch-craft Proven, Arreign'd and Condemn'd in its Professors, Professions and Marks . . .* Glasgow: Robert Saunders, 1697.

Bibliography

Ady, Thomas. *A Candle in the Dark: shewing the Divine Cause of the distractions of the whole nation of England and of the Christian World*. London: 1655.

Forbes, William. *The Institutes of the Law of Scotland*. Vol II. Edinburgh, 1730.

Hutchison, Frances. *An Historical Essay concerning Witchcraft* . . . London, for R. Knaplock, 1718.

Kirk, Rev. Robert. *An Essay of the nature and actions of the Subterranean (and, for the most part,) Invisible People, heeretofoir going under the Names of Elves, Faunes, and Fairies, or the lyke, among the Low-Country Scots* . . . Edinburgh: James Ballantyne, 1815. (orig Ms 1691)

Kirkton, James. *A History of the Church of Scotland 1660–79*. c. 1693. Published in 1817 under the title *The secret and true history of the Church of Scotland 1660–79*. Edited by Ralph Stewart. Lewiston, N.Y.: Edwin Mellen, 1992.

Mackenzie, Sir George. *The Laws and Customs of Scotland in matters Criminal*. 1678. (Edinburgh, 1834).

Millar, J. *A History of the Witches of Renfrewshire*. (1809) A new edition. Paisley, Alex. Gardner, 1877.

Paterson, James. *A Belief in Witchcraft unsupported by Scripture*. Aberdeen: D. Chambers & Co., 1815.

Sinclair, G. *Satan's Invisible World Discovered*. Edinburgh, 1685.

Spottiswoode, *History of the Church of Scotland*. 1655; reprint, Edinburgh, 1851.

Reference Works

Scott, Hew. *Fasti Ecclesiae Scoticanae: The succession of ministers in the Church of Scotland from the Reformation*. New edition. Edinburgh: Oliver and Boyd, 1915.

Robertson, Maira. ed. *The Concise Scots Dictionary: The Scots Language in one volume from the first records to the present day*. Aberdeen: Aberdeen University Press, 1987.

A regional study of the Scottish witch-hunt: method and approach

In order to do a regional study, it is first necessary to choose a region: the next step is to locate all of the cases within that particular region. A researcher could begin by trying to read the appropriate local records. This would not be very effective in terms of time and resources as it would be possible to read court records for the entire period without discovering a single case. As well, the area of study would of necessity be very limited so that at the end of the study one would be asked the inevitable question of how this particular locality related to the broader Scottish witch-hunt. As the shape of the hunt in Scotland has not been adequately mapped, this is a very valid question. Fortunately, we already know of over three thousand cases of suspected witches from throughout Scotland thanks to the *Sourcebook of Scottish Witch-craft*. The difficulty lies in the fact that *A Sourcebook* listed these cases chronologically by the court level (High Court of Justiciary, Privy Council, Committee of Estates, etc.) from which the document originated. Primarily concerned with the central government records, the *Sourcebook* had not standardized its geographic references. (For a detailed discussion of the *Sourcebook*, in particular the process of standardizing the geographic references, see Appendix B.) It was thus necessary, after re-entering the data in a computer database, to list the cases by shire, and wherever possible village or parish. The result was not only an ability to give some shape to the hunt throughout Scotland, but also a way of locating all of the cases in the *Sourcebook* which originated from a particular region.

After discovering which cases belonged to the region under study, in this case Fife, it was then necessary to locate and read each of the individual records and to track the reference back to its source in order to get more detailed information. This represented not only a challenge, but also a different way of approaching the subject. Much of how Scottish history is written seems to arise out of the sources themselves: someone studies a particular document, then reports what he or she has found.

This, in part, may be explained by the difficulty of the palaeography (handwriting) within manuscript sources from the seventeenth century. Each 'hand' is distinct and can be very difficult to read, thus making it realistic, once having discovered how to read a particular hand, to continue working on that document. While clearly valid for many topics, a regional study required a different understanding and approach to the primary sources. The computer database was used as a way 'in' to a particular source, which was then essentially mined for information on the known case or cases. In dealing with these sources many other cases were discovered; however, it is important to recognise that this was not the primary intent of the study. There are other cases in Fife where accusations of witchcraft were made which remain buried in kirk session, presbytery, or burgh records. This is a reality that needs to be admitted and which will not be easily overcome.[1] This regional study represents an attempt to interpret the cases we know, not discover all of the cases that exist.

A study of Fife as a whole would have been impossible without the work of past generations of historians, in particular local historians. With four distinct presbyteries, a synod, and over sixty parishes, no one individual could begin to study a phenomenon like witch-hunting which spanned a century and a half were it not for the fact that local historians have transcribed session, burgh and other records. The long section in the bibliography entitled, 'Published Primary Sources' demonstrates clearly how extensive and valuable these sources are. The work of several scholars deserves particular note: William Stevenson, *The Presbyterie Booke of Kirkcaldie* and Mark Smith's *A Study and Annotated edition of the Register of the Minutes of the Presbytery of St. Andrew's, volume 1*[2] each represent complete and accurate transcriptions of the records in question and are of great value to scholars. It should also be stated that without Richard Benson's careful study of session and presbytery records in his thesis *South-West Fife and the Scottish Revolution* and his decision to list all cases of witchcraft and charming in an appendix to his thesis, we would know less about what occurred in this important area of Fife. That the current study was able to deal with all of Fife, rather than having to choose a particular region within the shire as was originally thought, is a result of the work of these and many other scholars and local historians.

By using a variety of sources from the central government and from the individual communities, a picture of the witch-hunt in Fife began to emerge. The records of the various sessions and presbyteries, of the synod of Fife, of the burghs, of the Privy Council, of the Justiciary Court, and of the Committee of Estates were consulted, wherever feasible in the original manuscripts. Printed sources which excerpted main documents, for example *Selections from the Minutes of the Presbyteries of St. Andrews and Cupar*, were checked with the original documents to see whether what was being excerpted was the particular record itself or the selection of which records to include (in the case of this volume, the selection process affected which records were chosen). Some central government sources, such as the *Records of the Privy Council* and the *Acts of the Parliament of Scotland* were used only in their printed form. The intent was to do a wide-ranging study, weaving together as much as could be gleaned from these sources into a coherent picture of the witch-hunt in Fife.

The problem of what sources are available and the kinds of information they can give is one that always haunts the historian. We tend to not only be bound to and by the sources that are available, but also often come to see the events through the 'lens' of the source we are using. In the case of the witch-hunt in Fife, this is ameliorated, somewhat, by the variety of sources that we have noted. On the whole however the main sources that have been used in this study have been those produced by the various levels of church courts – kirk session, presbytery and synod minutes. The difficulty with these records is in part one of survival. There are some frustrating gaps, situations where one would long to know how these events would be recorded by the local session. To cite only one example, the kirk session records of Inverkeithing (which, as we saw, experienced a major witch-hunt in 1661–62) do not exist prior to 1688. Of equal importance are some of the questions that are naturally raised. Were there witch-hunts in other parishes, only no records have survived which cover this period and thus we remain ignorant of the cases? And, does our reliance on these records tend to overemphasize the role played by the church in the witch-hunt? These are questions to consider as we investigate witch-hunting in Fife.

While there are problems with these, and indeed any, sources the broad range of materials consulted in this study gives us the opportunity to see not only the major hunts but also the more minor incidents of witchcraft that seem to have been a feature of life in seventeenth century Fife. This blend of central government and local records allow us to not only map out the large scale hunts and do some (admittedly limited) quantification, but also explore the more qualitative aspects of accusations of witchcraft.[3] At the same time, it is hoped that those familiar with the intense regional studies such as those done on Salem[4] will not be too disappointed. The historical literature on sixteenth and seventeenth Scotland does not allow for this kind of detailed analysis. There are simply too many basic facts which remain unknown including the population of the various parishes. Still there is a wealth of local histories and some solid regional studies of Fife.[15] With the assistance of these resources, the information obtained from the documents can be placed in some kind of overall context.

This study is essentially an historical enquiry. The *Sourcebook* and later the computer database tempted one to move into a statistical study. Yet, the data are simply not adequate (beyond some very simple comparisons based upon gender) for these findings to have much merit. It would be wonderful to know how many people were executed in Scotland, or even Fife, yet we do not. Moreover, the fact that there are more individuals for whom we have no idea as to their fate (those categorized as 'not knowns' by the *Sourcebook*) makes any conclusions based upon the scattered information we do have uncertain. This was unfortunate and somewhat disappointing. Where the information was strong was in terms of the geographical place and the date when an accusation was made. This information was used as a basis to generate chronological and geographic patterns – the historical geography (the when and where) of the witch-hunt.

To proceed in the study various approaches had to be incorporated. Studies of the witch-hunt are by their very nature inter-disciplinary. Historical geography was only one of the methodologies that had to be borrowed in the course of the study. Theology, sociology, politics, and information about the legal system of Scotland all proved important. Still, it is important to remember that it was indeed a 'borrowing from'; using insights, information, concepts from a specific discipline, while all the time being involved in an historical enquiry. This is not intended to discredit or dismiss any of these disciplines, but to clearly state the overriding approach taken in his study. This is an historical enquiry concerned with time and place, with when and why. Whereas a sociologist would want to determine which model best explains the witch-hunt, an historian is less interested in the model and more concerned about the particular details.[6] It was still necessary, however, to focus and ask what kind of history was this to be? Clearly in terms of method, the writing has been greatly influenced by Peter Burke and other historians of popular culture. Conceptually, I came to stop thinking of this as only a study of witches but under the much broader umbrella of a study of persecution. Why are some individuals targeted for persecution? Why does this occur at particular times? To this end, R.I. Moore's *The Making of a Persecuting Society* and Norman Cohn's *Europe's Inner Demons*, were influential, if not in their conclusions, at least in the questions they posed and the shape they gave to the subject.

Notes

1. John Di Folco, in his study on only part of Fife – central and North Fife – stated that it 'was physically impossible to work through all of those [unprinted church records] for the course of a century'. *Aspects of Seventeenth Century Social Life*, iv. Michael Graham, *The Uses of Reform,* includes references to cases from Anstruther Wester some of which appear to be unknown, 220–239. These cases were discovered in an unlikely source, the Anstruther Wester Parish Register, housed in the New Register House.
2. William Stevenson, ed. *The Presbyterie Booke of Kirkcaldie*. Mark C. Smith, *A Study and Annotated edition of the Register of the Minutes of the Presbytery of St. Andrew's, volume 1.*
3. J.A. Sharpe, *Crime in Early Modern Europe 1550–1750*, 36, uses this phrase. The contrast between how central government and local government sources can be used, is effectively dealt with by Sharpe.
4. Boyer and Nissenbaum, *Salem Possessed*. Godbeer, *Devil's Dominion*. The range of complementary studies on Massachusetts society which can be drawn upon makes one envious. We do not know occupations, or village tensions (as shown by court records), or many of the other aspects of village life which have been studied in New England.
5. The wealth of local histories can be seen in the section in the Bibliography 'Secondary Sources: Fife & local history'. It should be noted that the books included in this section include *only* those which make some reference to the witch-hunt. Local histories, guide books, etc. which made no mention of the subject were generally not included.
6. J.I. (Hans) Bakker, 'The Hindu-Javanese World View in Java: The Structural Roots of the Pancasila State' in *Managing Changes in Southeast Asia: Local Idenities, Global Connections*, eds. Jean DeBerhnardi et. al., 189–205, demonstrates how sociological models can be used. Also, James C. Hackler, 'Strain Theories'; Ronald Hinch, 'Conflict and Marxist Theories'; Robert A. Stebbins, 'Interactionist Theories'; and, Rick Linden, 'Social Control Theories' in *Criminology: A Canadian Perpective* 2nd edition, ed. Rick Linden (Toronto: Harcourt Brace Janovich, 1992). Each of these lenses has a value. For example, functionalist models explain the need for deviants. Interactionist theories could be used to explain why a woman might use the label of witch to her advantage. This thesis is primarily concerned with the picture, not the specific lens which can be used in interpretation.

The Source Book of Scottish Witchcraft and the creation of the Scottish Witch-Hunt Data Base

The publication in 1977 of the *Sourcebook for Scottish Witch-craft* was an important milestone for researchers into the history of the Scottish witch-hunt. This appendix will discuss the nature and strengths of the *Sourcebook*, some of the short-comings which have become clear as a result of using it extensively, and the creation of the Scottish Witch-hunt Data Base.

The *Sourcebook* focused on the central records, in the words of the compilers 'partly because they had never been used systematically before, partly because in the early days of the research project we assumed, wrongly, that in this way we could collect <u>all</u> the executions'. (Christina Larner, *et. al, Sourcebook*, vi) The compilers discussion of their use of source materials is worth reading (Ibid., vi-ix). For our discussion, several points should be noted. The first is that more cases may exist at the national level than were discovered by this project. The compilers are clear about this. There may be more cases in the unindexed boxes of pre-trial material from the High Court of Justiciary. There is also unindexed material from the Privy Council: 'This has been left unexplored by this research team. They cannot be used cost-effectively for individual cases until they have been surveyed by the archivists.' (Ibid., vii) The gaps in information were also noted. The fate of the accused is often unknown. There is also the fact that the documents do not report details of the initial interrogations: 'Never, even in the processes, do we get an account of the type of questions asked, and the way in which confessions are extracted has to be inferred.' (Ibid., viii) One final difficulty is that these records are incomplete. As noted above, the theory was that all cases after 1597 should have at least some reference to all of those accused of witchcraft and local records should have included only initial concerns or minor cases: 'In fact it is clear that an unknown number of witches were executed without going through the 'legitimate' channels'. (Ibid., viii)

This section of the introduction closed with suggestions as to what information the local records might contain.

The *Sourcebook* made the case that local materials were simply too difficult to assess at the time of the project, a conclusion fully supported by this author. Larner, Lee and McLachlan wrote:

> So far as the local material goes we have covered only samples. Our view is that while it would probably be possible to add considerably to the list of witches by intensive work on small areas, it would again probably not be cost-effective, unless the researcher were to concentrate on the major years of persecution . . . So far as other years go, however, it would be possible to read a manuscript kirk session register extending over a considerable period and find less than half a dozen cases which had any connection with witchcraft or charming. (Ibid., ix)

After researching Fife, I would only add the fact that the local records sometimes even fail to mention witches who we know existed from the central records. Clearly we have not yet uncovered all of the cases of witchcraft or charming in Scotland in this period. The *Sourcebook* lists all of the cases discovered as of its publication, an achievement that deserves recognition.

In terms of its internal organization, the *Sourcebook* listed the cases chronologically by court level: Court of Justiciary, Circuit Courts, Parliamentary Commissions, Committee of Estates and Privy Council Commissions. To this another section was added – 'Other'. These included all other references, references which often ultimately led back through a printed source to local session, presbytery, or burgh records. The 'Other' cases comprise over one quarter of the *Sourcebook* (cases 2209–3069, or 800 of 3,000). While the *Sourcebook* included some tables and sample transcripts, the true heart of the project was the listing of the cases. The information in this list was standardized. Information could include: Name, Date, Place, Sex, Marital Status, Trial Status, Fate, the source of the information, and a notation of whether this case had newly been discovered, or had been listed in Black's *A Calendar of Cases of Witchcraft in Scotland 1510–1727*. As well, a case number was assigned to each 'case'. The definition of 'case' is important: each case was an indication of a reference to witchcraft and might include more than one individual. As well, some individuals appear in the *Sourcebook* more than once, and there is some clear duplication (Ibid., xi). Spelling was taken from the original documents as much as possible. Information on the social status of the accused, available in only a few cases, was dealt with seperately (Ibid., xi).

Several of the Fields were given specific codes. For example, 'M' or 'F' (or 'U' for unknown) referred to the gender of the accused. Marital Status, Trial Status, and Fate were also alloted codes. Unfortunately, the large number of 'unknowns' which show up in some of these categories make any statistical analysis suspect. The coding for Trial Status also has some problems. The *Sourcebook* explains this as 'The level to which the case was taken', meaning (one assumes) the highest level within the judicial system, but the codes themselves seem more interested in the nature of the case:

T   taken to trial
Proc.   Preliminary proceedings taken in pre-trial processes
Men   Mentioned as a witch by an accused person
Com   Privy Council or Parliamentary Commission to named
        individuals for a local trial (Ibid., 1)

Unfortunately this confusion seems to have slipped into the coding, in particular the use of the 'Men' (mentioned) code. In the research in Fife, it was clear that sometimes this code had been used when someone had been mentioned in a document, although not necessarily by an accused or dying witch. A miscellaneous category would have been useful, but one only discovers these things after having completed a project. Unfortunately this confusion means we can not test one of Larner's arguments – that most people were accused by other suspects (i.e. 'Men' or mentioned). This argument was made in the lecture 'Natural and Unnatural Methods of Witchcraft Control', in *Witchcraft and Religion*, 138.

Discussions of the strengths and weaknesses of the *Sourcebook* can be found, not only in the introduction to the volume itself, but in *Enemies of God* (35–39) and in Bruce Lenman's review of the *Sourcebook* from the *Scottish Historical Review*, 1979 (197–200). One criticism that was not made, which indeed should have been, was the fact that the 'Place' category was so unevenly dealt with. The 'place' might be a shire, a town, a parish, or even a hamlet. Again, this is one of the errors in design which is only discovered after a project of this nature has been completed: the difficulty was that it made using the information very awkward in terms of any local or regional studies. The *Sourcebook* was also organized in such a way that it would suit some researchers (those who wanted to work on particular documentary sources, such as central records) better than others who would like to study witch-hunting chronologically, or in some other way (i.e. investigating all of the male witches).

While working on an essay for my Master's in 1981, I not only discovered the value of the *Sourcebook* but also was frustrated by how it was organized. The notion of running this data back through a computer and reshuffling it emerged. Fortunately other studies intervened for the computer technology at the time would have been less than adequate. When work began on the thesis part of the Doctorate in 1990, the first project was to re-enter the *Sourcebook* into a computer database (Borland's dBase VI version 1.0, later 1.1, were used.) The coding and the basic structure was maintained. Changes, however came to be made in the section on 'Place'. After the initial entry this category was divided into three: Shire; Village; and Hamlet. These names remain somewhat misleading. 'Village' was often, in actual fact a parish, a burgh or a town. The intent, however, was to try to see if we could at least place as many cases as possible within a particular shire. For some cases, where the shire was clearly stated, this was easy. In other situations this involved searching through Gazetteers to determine where a certain 'village' or 'hamlet' might be. Not all of the information could be placed within a particular shire. In some situations the place names were obscure; in others the name was too common. There were too many 'Newburghs' to decide to which shire it belonged. Some of these situations later resolved themselves once further research had been done. For example, the particular Newburgh from which these cases sprang was the parish in Fife (Michael Wasser was helpful in pointing out a particular case from this parish, which led to the realization there were others). Still, it was possible to place 2,766 cases out of a total of 3,089 (or 89.54%) within particular shires, thus allowing a picture to emerge as to where witch-hunting was most intense in Scotland. This research proved the groundwork for chapter 2. Spelling of place names also had to be standardized. As much as possible, modern spellings were chosen (i.e. Bruntisland became Burntisland). Within Fife, this same process was followed for the parishes, which formed the basis for the rest of the study.

In creating the database, new categories were included, mostly for the convenience of research. A new field was added to allow cases involving more than one individual to be quickly identified. Another field was added which notes which gazeteer had listed a village or hamlet as belonging to a particular shire. The other significant changes in the data included in the *Sourcebook* involved corrections and adding additional information. Many corrections were made, including incorporating the pencilled corrections noted in the copy of the *Sourcebook* held in the reading room of the Scottish Record Office (now National ???????? of Scotland). Additional cases were discovered in the course of doing intensive research on Fife. These come from the 'local records' which the compilers of the *Sourcebook* noted. Thanks to the research of Michael Wasser, who has worked extensively with the central government records, further cases have been discovered. It has not been possible to enter these into the database at this point. None of these additional cases seems to be from Fife. The information used in the thesis and this book was that which existed in the SWHDB as of June 1, 1997. This number is expected to continue to grow. For example, Michael Graham's recent book *The Uses of Reform* makes references to several witches from Anstruther West in a period when no cases were known from this particular village. At least some of these individuals (Agnes Melvill, Jonnett Foggow) are already included in the SWHDB. A careful look at the source which Graham has discovered will be needed before we can assess how many new cases are involved. This is still an exciting discovery. More such discoveries are anticipated. A new research project may soon begin in Scotland which will quickly supersede the SWHDB. If so, this is wonderful news. The easier it is for researchers to ask questions about the Scottish witch-hunt, the better.

The corrections, additions and changes have reached the stage where it no longer seems reasonable to refer to the end product as the *Sourcebook*. Instead, the name *Scottish Witch-Hunt Data Base* (SWHDB) has been chosen to reflect not only the changes, but the fact that new information can be entered and (hopefully) made available to researchers. The intent is to create an on-going list of known cases of witch-craft in Scotland which can be added to, corrected, updated and – of equal importance – sorted in different ways for the benefit of researchers. The SWHDB clearly was dependent upon the *Sourcebook*, just as the *Sourcebook* was dependent upon Black's *Calendar*. At the moment, the SWHDB continues to use the categories of the *Sourcebook*. In future, some additional categories might be added, mostly in the area of the codes. For example, cases where someone accused as a witch took their accuser before a session and charged that individual with slander are mixed in with cases where the suspect was directly charged with being a witch. Adding a category of 'sl' for slander is one possibility. It might also be helpful if we could sort out which cases involved 'charming', or break down the category of 'other' to refer to the origin being a presbytery, a session, a burgh court, or similar kinds of references. Redoing the entire *Sourcebook* would require enormous resources; finding ways of incorporating new ideas and information gradually is a more feasible approach.

This researcher's sincere thanks go to Christina Larner, Christopher Lee and Hugh McLachlan for their work in compiling and creating *A Source-book of Scottish Witchcraft*. The decision to move forward with a database that continues to expand and be used is intended to continue their efforts.

Maps, Graphs, and Tables

The Maps, Graphs, and Tables used in this book all arise out of the data from the Scottish Witch-Hunt Data Base. Moving from the SWHDB to a particular map or table involves at least one intermediary step. For example, to create the Graph 1 which shows the pattern of the witch-hunt on a national scale it was necessary to count how many cases had occurred in each year, then enter this information into a spreadsheet program. A similar process was used in creating the maps: the number of cases in each shire (or parish) was determined and then this information was transferred into the specific map. The following computer software programs were originally used in the research and production of this book:

database   dBase IV 1.1
spreadsheet   ASEASYAS 5.0
graphics   Corel 3.0, Corel Presentations 8.0

Software has exploded over the last seven years, both in terms of features and the size and speed of computer required to operate it. It has not been possible to explore whether a later version of software might have achieved a task more efficiently. In several instances 'upgrading' required more time than would have been saved. The data pertaining to specific maps is listed below.

Map 2. Scotland, 1560–1760, cases per shire

The data is in table 1. This map is unique in that the new cases discovered while doing research in Fife are *not* included. It was felt that these cases would alter the ranking of Fife in relation to the other Shires of Scotland. The assumption is that when more work is done on local records in these areas, the number of cases will also increase. The number listed under Fife in brackets (420) represents all of the cases from Fife listed in the SWHDB.

Map 3. Scotland, 1649

Unknown (63); Aberdeen (2); Ayr (2); Banff (2); Berwick (18); Bute (5); Edinburgh (31); Fife (70), 45 in the SBSW; Forfar (4); Haddington (110); Lanark (14); Linlithgow (15); Peebles (12); Renfrew (6); Roxburgh (13); Selkirk (6); Stirling (1); Wigtown (1). Total cases, 376.

Map 4. Scotland, 1650

Unknown (35); Aberdeen (3); Ayr (23); Berwick (5); Bute (1); Dumbarton (4); Dumfries (9); Edinburgh (9); Fife (6); Forfar (17); Haddington (8); Kirkcubright (1); Lanark (9); Moray (1); Peebles (13); Renfrew (5); Roxburgh (3); Selkirk (2).
Total cases, 154.

Map 5. Fife, 1560–1710

Unknown (5)- Byrehill (1); Abbotshall (1); Abdie (4); Aberdour (21); Anstruther (5); Anstruther Easter (2); Auchterdirran (1); Auchtermuchty (1); Auchtertool (1); Balmerino (2); Burntisland (18); Carnbee (1); Collessie (5);Crail (12); Creich (3); Culross (44); Cupar (3); Dalgetty (9); Dunbog (1); Dunfermline (39); Dunino (1); Dysart (31); Falkland (3); Flisk (4); Forgan (2); Inverkeithing (51); Kilmany (4); Kilrenny (2); Kinghorn (3); Kinglessie (1); Kirkcaldy (36); Largo (5); Logie (1); Markinch (1); Monimail (1); Newburgh (12); Pittenweem (28); St. Andrews (22); St. Monans (2); Torryburn (21); Wemyss (10). Total, 420

Map 6. Fife, 1649

Unknown (1); Aberdour (7); Balmerino (1); Burntisland (13); Culross (1); Dalgetty (9); Dunfermline (9); Dysart (1); Inverkeithing (28). Total, 70.

Map 7. Fife, 1624

Culross (9); Torryburn (1)

Map 8. Fife, 1630

Dysart (11); St.Andrews (1); Torryburn (1); Wemyss (1).
Total, 14.

Map 10. Fife, 1662

Auchtermuchty (1); Abdie (3); Collessie (5); Creich (1); Culross (1); Dunbog (1); Falkland (1); Flisk (4); Forgan (2); Kilmany (2); Newburgh (5). Total, 26.

Map 12. Fife, 1597

Kilrenny (1); Kirkcaldy (15); Largo (1); Pittenweem (5); Abbotshall (1); Burntisland (2); St. Andrews (1).
Total, 26.

Map 14. Fife, 1643

Anstruther (3); Anstruther easter (1); Crail (6); Culross (9); Dunfermline (18); Dysart (1); Kinghorn (2); Markinch (1); Pittenweem (5); St. Andrews (4); Torryburn (1). Total, 51.

Map 16. Fife, 1621

Crail (1); Culross (1); Inverkeithing (6); Kirkcaldy (2). Total, 10.

The Witches of Fife
(listed chronologically)

Date	Accused	Parish	Case
0/0/0	Curate of Anstruther	Anstruther	3034
0/0/0	Helen Eliot	Culross	2939
0/0/0	Margaret Reid	Kirkcaldy	3033
0/0/0	Katherine Shaw	Kirkcaldy	3053
0/0/0	Patrick Adamson	St. Andrews	3032
0/0/0	Archbishop Sharp	St. Andrews	3035
0/0/0	Grissel Anderson	Torryburn	2981
0/0/0	Euphan Stirt	Torryburn	2983
0/0/1563	Woman (1 of 4)	?	2214
0/0/1563	Woman (1 of 4)	?	2215
0/0/1563	Agnes Mullikine	Dunfermline	6
0/0/1563	Witches	St. Andrews	2220
0/0/1569	Nic Neville	St. Andrews	2219
0/0/1569	William Stewart (Lyon King of Arms)	St. Andrews	2221
28/4/1572		St. Andrews	2222
25/1/1576	Marjorye Smytht	St. Andrews	2223
26/10/1581	Bessy Robertsoune	St. Andrews	2225
28/5/1588	Alesoun Pierson	Byrehill	13
0/0/1590	Nans Murit	Abdie	3090
0/0/1590	Euphame Locoir	Crail	3091
15/3/1593	Janot Loquhour	Pittenweem	3092
10/9/1595	Elspot Gilchrist	St. Andrews	2239
10/9/1595	Jonet Lochequoir	St. Andrews	2238
10/9/1595	Agnes Melvill	St. Andrews	2237
0/0/1597	Margaret Atkin	Abbotshall	2308
0/0/1597	Janet Smyth	Burntisland	2307
5/5/1597	David Zeman	Pittenweem	3093
16/5/1597	Bettie Adie	Kilrenny	3097
9/6/1597	Jonett Foggow	Pittenweem	3095
9/6/1597	Beatrix Forgesoun	Pittenweem	3096
9/6/1597	Jonet Willeamsoun	Pittenweem	3094
13/7/1597	(Many Witches)	St. Andrews	2294
26/7/1597	Jonnett Finlasoun	Burntisland	877
3/8/1597	('The Weimen Accused')	Largo	3098
11/8/1597	Margaret Elder	Kirkcaldy	3143
11/8/1597	Issobell Rannaldsone	Kirkcaldy	3144

11/8/1597	Margaret Williamsone	Kirkcaldy	3142
17/81597	Janet Bennetie	Kirkcaldy	3148
17/8/1597	Beigis Blakatt	Kirkcaldy	3153
17/8/1597	Margaret Elder	Kirkcaldy	3156
17/8/1597	Goillis Hoggone	Kirkcaldy	3152
17/8/1597	Margaret Hoicon	Kirkcaldy	3146
17/8/1597	Isobell Jak	Kirkcaldy	3150
17/8/1597	Thomas Jamieson	Kirkcaldy	3154
17/8/1597	Isobell Jonstoun	Kirkcaldy	3155
17/8/1597	Bessie Osatt	Kirkcaldy	3149
17/8/1597	William Patersone	Kirkcaldy	3147
17/8/1597	Marion Rutherford	Kirkcaldy	3145
17/8/1597	Bessie Scott	Kirkcaldy	3151
6/10/1597	Fritte Gutter	Pittenweem	3099
0/0/1598	Janet Allane	Burntisland	2310
13/7/1598	Patrik Stewart	St. Andrews	3100
26/10/1598	Geillis Gray		3101
22/2/1599	Geillis Gray	Crail	2312
20/10/1603	Jonet Small	Largo	3102
15/12/1603	Agnes Anstruther	Dysart	3103
22/12/1603	Beatrix Traillis	Largo	3104
22/12/1603	Christen Traillis	Largo	3105
6/6/1604	Dorathie Oliphant	Kirkcaldy	2319
7/9/1610	Grissel Gairdner	Newburgh	131
4/4/1613	Agnes Anstruther	Kirkcaldy	3044
0/0/1614	Agnes Anstruther	Kirkcaldy	2339
0/0/1614	Issobell Johnestwone	Kirkcaldy	2338
27/5/1616	Helen Birrell	Kirkcaldy	3157
16/7/1618	Bessie Finlaysoune	Logie	2360
2/8/1619	Isobel Hevrie	Kirkcaldy	3158
30/1/1621	Margaret Wod	Crail	940
13/2/1621	Margaret Ent	Inverkeithing	941
13/2/1621	Bessie Chalmers	Inverkeithing	944
13/2/1621	Marioun Chatto	Inverkeithing	946
13/2/1621	Christiane Hammyltoun	Inverkeithing	942
13/2/1621	Bessie Harlaw	Inverkeithing	945
13/2/1621	Beatrice Mudie	Inverkeithing	943
13/2/1621	Alison Dick	Kirkcaldy	3159
29/3/1621	Christiane Couper	Culross	947
31/5/1621	Marioun Rutherford	Kirkcaldy	948
28/8/1622	Helen Cummyng	Aberdour	961
28/8/1622	Alesoune Hutchesoune	Aberdour	962
28/8/1622	Agnes Quarrier	Aberdour	960
28/8/1622	Agnes Robertsone	Aberdour	958
28/8/1622	Janet Robertsone	Aberdour	959
27/2/1623	Marjorie Aitkyne	Inverkeithing	965
27/2/1623	Bessie Andersone	Inverkeithing	972
27/2/1623	Christiane Balfour	Inverkeithing	971
27/2/1623	Elizabeth Broun	Inverkeithing	974
27/2/1623	Margaret Bull	Inverkeithing	970
27/2/1623	Marjory Gibsoun	Inverkeithing	977
27/2/1623	Christian Harlow	Inverkeithing	975
27/2/1623	Marioun Hendersone	Inverkeithing	973

27/2/1623	Margaret Kynnell	Inverkeithing	976
27/2/1623	Bessie Logie	Inverkeithing	969
27/2/1623	Margaret Merschell	Inverkeithing	968
27/2/1623	Jonnet Robertson	Inverkeithing	967
27/2/1623	Johne Young	Inverkeithing	966
18/3/1623	Jonet Keirie	Inverkeithing	980
1/8/1623	Thomas Greave		139
19/2/1624	Alexander Clerk	Culross	997
19/2/1624	Marjorie Rowand	Culross	998
19/2/1624	Marioun Stirk	Culross	995
19/2/1624	Jonnet Umphra	Culross	996
19/2/1624	Mayse Umphra	Culross	1000
192/1624	Jonnet Watt	Culross	1001
19/2/1624	Anna Smyth	Torryburn	999
2/3/1624	Jonet Umphra	Culross	994
30/3/1624	Helene Ezatt	Culross	1014
30/3/1624	Jonnett Tor	Culross	1013
29/7/1625	Marjorie Pattersone	Crail	1022
16/3/1626	Issobell Mawer	Wemyss	1023
4/4/1626	Helen Birrell	Kirkcaldy	3162
4/4/1626	Janet Pirie	Kirkcaldy	3160
4/4/1626	Janet Stark	Kirkcaldy	3161
13/4/1626	Helene Darumpill	Wemyss	1027
13/4/1626	Helene Dryburghe	Wemyss	1028
13/4/1626	Patrik Landrok	Wemyss	1026
13/4/1626	Jonnet Pedie	Wemyss	1025
5/5/1626	Janet	Dysart	2373
6/6/1626	Elizabeth Ross	Wemyss	1029
20/6/1626	Jonnet Dampstar	Wemyss	1030
0/9/1626	Elspett Neilsoun	Dysart	1032
21/9/1626	Annas Munk	Dysart	1031
21/11/1626	Helene Wilsoun	Dysart	1033
17/5/1627	Margaret Hendersoune	Wemyss	1064
27/9/1627	Eupham Dauling	Dysart	1065
17/11/1627	Katherene Crystie	Dysart	1066
23/4/1628	Jonnat Reany	Dunfermline	1067
4/6/1628	Effie Herring	Dunfermline	3225
4/6/1628	Bessie Stobie	Dunfermline	3227
4/6/1628	Jonet Thomson	Dunfermline	3226
24/3/1629	Alexander Drummond	Dunfermline	1159
21/1/1630	Margaret Callander	St. Andrews	1310
11/2/1630	Elspet Bladderstouns	Torryburn	1329
11/3/1630	Helen Bissat	Dysart	1337
11/3/1630	William Broun	Dysart	1336
11/3/1630	Janet Galbraith	Dysart	1335
11/3/1630	Bessie Guiddale	Dysart	1338
11/3/1630	Janet Scot	Dysart	1334
16/3/1630	Katherine Chrystie	Dysart	1340
16/3/1630	Katherine Chrystie	Dysart	1339
20/3/1630	Janet Wilkie	Wemyss	1341
21/4/1630	Janet Beverage	Dysart	1353
21/4/1630	Margaret Dasoun	Dysart	1355
21/4/1630	Alison Neving	Dysart	1354

8/7/1630	Elspet Watsoun	Dysart	1381
12/1/1632		Auchterdirran	2400
0/12/1633	William Coke	Kirkcaldy	2410
0/12/1633	Alison Dick	Kirkcaldy	2411
30/8/1634	Grissel Astrin	Culross	3167
30/8/1634	Jonet Dusone	Culross	3168
30/8/1634	Helen Rowane	Culross	3165
30/8/1634	Kath Rowane	Culross	3166
5/5/1636	William Hutchen	Kinghorn	3134
20/11/1636	Margaret Fields	Culross	3177
6/4/1637	John Patowne	Dysart	2419
12/7/1638	Marioun Grig	Dysart	2422
19/7/1638	Margaret Bannatyne	Kirkcaldy	3130
19/7/1638	Christian Wilson	Kirkcaldy	2423
27/12/1638	Janet Durie	Wemyss	2424
23/5/1639	Margaret Douglas	Kirkcaldy	3131
10/9/1640	Margaret Lindsay	Kirkcaldy	3132
0/0/1641	Katherine Mitchell	Culross	2435
7/3/1641	William Drysdale	Culross	3178
20/7/1642	Some Persons	Kinglessie	3135
10/8/1642	Margaret Wilson	Dysart	3136
0/0/1643	Margaret Brand	Dunfermline	2459
0/0/1643	Margaret Donaldson	Dunfermline	2464
0/0/1643	Katherine Elder	Dunfermline	2460
0/0/1643	Agnes Kirk	Dunfermline	2463
0/0/1643	Isobel Miller	Dunfermline	2465
3/1/1643	Margaret Cuthbertsone	Dunfermline	3169
3/1/1643	Jonnet Henrysone	Dunfermline	3170
3/1/1643	Jonet Horne	Dunfermline	3173
3/1/1643	Agnes Kinsman	Dunfermline	3171
3/1/1643	Christian Moodie	Dunfermline	3172
3/1/1643	Jonet Moodie	Dunfermline	3174
3/1/1643	Jonet Tailor	Dunfermline	3175
5/3/1643	('Others Delated')	Culross	3176
5/3/1643	Catherine Rowane	Culross	2437
2/4/1643	John Wastwater	Culross	3179
2/4/1643	Jonet Insch	Dunfermline	3181
2/4/1643	Robert Shortus	Dunfermline	3180
16/4/1643	Grissel Morris	Dunfermline	2458
14/5/1643	Marion Thomson	Culross	3182
21/5/1643	Elspeth Shearer	Culross	3183
28/5/1643	Margaret Hutton	Culross	3184
5/6/1643	Marion Burges	Culross	3185
20/6/1643	Jonett Fentoun	Dunfermline	2443
16/7/1643	('Suspects of Witchcraft')	Dunfermline	3186
0/8/1643	(Some Witches)	Anstruther	3107
16/8/1643	(Some Witches)	Anstruther	3108
16/8/1643	(Some Witches)	Anstruthereaster	3109
16/8/1643	(Some Witches)	Crail	3110
17/8/1643	Isobell Marr	Dunfermline	2444
23/8/1643	(Witch)	St. Andrews	3111
30/8/1643	(Witch)	St. Andrews	3112
30/8/1643	Isbell Dairsie	Anstruther	3037

30/8/1643	Kathren Chrystie	Dysart	3164
30/8/1643	(Apprehended Witches)	St. Andrews	3113
6/9/1643	(Witch)	Crail	3115
6/9/1643	(Witch)	Crail	3114
6/9/1643	Margaret Balfour	St. Andrews	2445
17/9/1643	Jonet Burne	Culross	3188
0/10/1643	Agnes Wallace	Crail	2466
1/10/1643	Drummond	Dunfermline	3189
11/10/1643	(Some Witches)	Crail	3117
11/10/1643	(Some Witches)	Crail	3116
31/10/1643	Jonnet Smythe	Kinghorn	2448
31/10/1643	Katherine Wallace	Kinghorn	2449
3/11/1643	(John Dawson's Wife) Duplicate?	Pittenweem	2451
3/11/1643	(Wife of John) Dawson	Pittenweem	2450
7/11/1643	Margaret Huttoun	Culross	1437
13/12/1643	Margaret Kingow	Pittenweem	2453
18/12/1643	Margaret Horsburgh	Pittenweem	2454
21/12/1643	(Wife of John) Crombie	Pittenweem	2455
31/12/1643	Janet Brown	Markinch	2457
11/1/1644	Isobell Johnson	Burntisland	3128
11/1/1644	Christine Dote	St. Monans	3041
12/1/1644	(Wife of Archibald) Wanderson	Pittenweem	2472
12/1/1644	(Wife of Thomas Wanderson	Pittenweem	2473
24/1/1644	Isbell Dairsie	Anstruther	3040
7/2/1644	Lilias Baxter	Dysart	3137
7/2/1644	Janet Rankine	Dysart	3138
7/2/6144	Margaret Myrton	St. Andrews	3042
21/2/1644		Kilrenny	3119
21/2/1644	Beatie Dote	Crail	3118
28/2/1644	Beatrix Bruce	Culross	3190
10/3/1644		Culross	3193
10/3/1644		Culross	3194
10/3/1644		Culross	3195
10/3/1644	(Witches of Torryburn')	Torryburn	3191
27/3/1644	Agnes Bennettie	Dysart	3139
27/3/1644	Margaret Cunningham	Dysart	3140
27/3/1644	Margaret Halkhead	Dysart	3141
26/5/1644	Adam Donaldson	Culross	2490
3/7/1644	(Some Witches)	Pittenweem	3120
6/8/1644	Mary Cunningham	Culross	1454
6/8/1644	Jonet Erskine	Culross	1455
7/8/1644	Jonet Wylie	Largo	3121
0/10/1644	Bessie Mason	St. Andrews	2487
2/10/1644	Margaret Young	Dysart	1459
7/11/1644	Christian Roch	Pittenweem	2482
0/0/1645	Jeane Buchane	Creich	2520
0/0/1645	Bessie Cuper	Creich	2524
0/0/1645	Sewis	St. Andrews	2521
3/10/1645	Marg Donald	Dunfermline	2523
8/11/1645	Androw Carmichae	Dunino	3122

0/0/1646	Grissel Thomson	Cupar	2530
0/0/1646	Janet Mitchells	Kilmany	2529
0/0/1646	Marie Mitchells	Kilmany	2528
28/4/1647	Isobel Thomson	Kirkcaldy	3133
0/0/1648	Helen Young	Balmerino	2533
0/0/1648	Helen Small	Monimail	2534
1/3/1648	Margaret Holden	Culross	3197
16/7/1648	William Chrictoun	Dunfermline	2535
0/0/1649	Elspeth Seith	Balmerino	2583
0/0/1649	Bessie Ma??	Dunfermline	2208
9/1/1649	('A Brewer')	Dunfermline	3197
3/4/1649	('Witches')	Inverkeithing	3198
22/4/1649	Robert Maxwell	Dalgetty	3199
29/4/1649	John Murdoche	Dunfermline	2540
8/5/1649	('Aberdour Witches')	Aberdour	3200
13/5/1649	Christian Smith	Dunfermline	3201
29/5/1649	Isabell Peacock	Dunfermline	2541
29/5/1649	Bessie Wilson	Dunfermline	2542
3/6/1649	Issobell Kelloch	Dalgetty	2543
3/6/1649	Margaret Orrock	Dalgetty	3202
3/6/1649	Issobell Scogian	Dalgetty	3224
4/6/1649	Isobell Bennet	Dalgetty	3203
27/6/1649	(Certain Persons)	Dalgetty	1934
1/7/1649	Margaret Aytoune	Inverkeithing	171
1/7/1649	Issobell Guthrie	Inverkeithing	172
1/7/1649	Issobell Leitch	Inverkeithing	187
1/7/1649	Rossina Osit	Inverkeithing	170
1/7/1649	Christine Thomsone	Inverkeithing	169
5/7/1649	(Some Witches)		3081
5/7/1649	(Some Witches)	Aberdour	1935
5/7/1649	(Some Witches)	Inverkeithing	3080
8/7/1649	Christian Garlick	Dalgetty	3205
8/7/1649	Isobell Glenn	Dalgetty	3206
10/7/1649	Emie Angus	Inverkeithing	179
10/7/1649	Margaret Blaikburne	Inverkeithing	174
10/7/1649	Barbara Chattow	Inverkeithing	177
10/7/1649	Hellen Douglas	Inverkeithing	173
10/7/1649	Marjorie Fergie	Inverkeithing	183
10/7/1649	Joannet Grege	Inverkeithing	180
10/7/1649	Mart Grege	Inverkeithing	181
10/7/1649	Issobel Mitchell	Inverkeithing	175
10/7/1649	Joannet Smetoune	Inverkeithing	184
10/7/1649	Katharine Smyth	Inverkeithing	176
10/7/1649	Hellane Stanhous	Inverkeithing	178
10/7/1649	Bessie Wilson	Inverkeithing	182
11/7/1649	Katharine Grieve	Inverkeithing	186
11/7/1649	Margaret Mairtine	Inverkeithing	185
12/7/1649	(Certain Witches)	Burntisland	1936
12/7/1649	(Certain Witches)	Dalgetty	3083
15/7/1649	Bessie Mortoun	Dunfermline	3207
15/7/1649	Marjorie Philip	Dunfermline	3208
19/7/1649	Margaret Henderson Lady Pittathrow	Inverkeithing	2600

31/7/1649	Wife of Henry Stanehouse	Aberdour	3213
31/7/1649	Wife of Thomas Smith	Aberdour	3214
31/7/1649	(The Wives of Magistrates)	Inverkeithing	1941
0/8/1649	Janet Brown	Burntisland	2550
0/8/1649	Isobel Gairdner	Burntisland	2548
0/8/1649		Burntisland	2584
0/8/1649		Burntisland	2585
0/8/1649	Issobel Bairdie	Burntisland	2596
0/8/1649	Janet Thomson	Burntisland	2549
7/8/1649	(Certain People)	Aberdour	1944
7/8/1649	(Certain People)	Inverkeithing	3085
15/8/1649	Beatrix Douglas	Inverkeithing	3209
15/8/1649	Marjorie Durie	Inverkeithing	3210
15/8/1649	Katherine Smith	Inverkeithing	3211
21/8/1649	Margaret Currie	Aberdour	3212
22/8/1649	('Dying Witches')	Aberdour	3215
28/8/1649	Marion Durie	Inverkeithing	2063
19/9/1649	Jonet Matheson	Dunfermline	3216
27/9/1649	Janet Murray	Burntisland	2095
27/9/1949	Jonet Murray	Burntisland	1512
27/9/1649	Elspet Ronaldson	Burntisland	2094
27/9/1649	Elspeth Ronaldsone	Burntisland	1511
27/9/1649	Agnes Waterson	Burntisland	2093
27/9/1649	Agnes Watersoun	Burntisland	1510
3/11/1649	Paterson Janet	Culross	3217
6/11/1649	Elizabeth Simpsone	Dysart	2166
14/4/1650	Janet Anderson	Aberdour	2695
24/4/1650	Robert Cousing	Culross	2657
7/5/1650	Marion Cunnyngham	Dunfermline	2661
26/5/1650	('A Woman')	Torryburn	3221
18/6/1650	('Delated Witches')	Aberdour	3223
26/6/1650	Elspeth Austein	Burntisland	3129
0/0/1651	Maggie	St. Monans	3218
0/0/1653	Katherine Key	Newburgh	2737
0/0/1653	Katherine Kay	Newburgh	2735
0/0/1654	Margaret Cant	Aberdour	2738
0/0/1655	Kathrene Smyth	Inverkeithing	207
0/0/1656	Agnes Pryde	Cupar	210
0/0/1656	Elspeth Scroggie	Cupar	209
12/3/1656		Inverkeithing	2748
23/6/1656	Elspeth Craiche	Culross	2749
0/0/1658	Margaret Beverage	Dysart	286
2/2/1658	John Corse	Dysart	220
0/0/1661	Margaret Carvie	Falkland	2818
0/0/1661	Barbara Horniman	Falkland	2819
0/7/1661	Susanna Alexander	Aberdour	2739
0/7/1661	Janet Bell	Aberdour	2740
0/7/1661	Marg Cant	Aberdour	2826
0/7/1661	Margaret Currie	Aberdour	2825
0/7/1661	Catharine Robertson	Aberdour	2824
0/7/1661		Newburgh	2815

0/11/1661		Newburgh	2816
19/11/1661	Kathrin Kay	Newburgh	1603
19/11/1661	Margaret Liddell	Newburgh	1604
23/1/1662	Margret Bell	Abdie	1625
23/1/1662	Elspeth Bruce	Abdie	1626
23/1/1662	Elspeth Seatoun	Abdie	1627
23/1/1662	Bessie Duncan	Creich	1637
23/1/1662	Margaret Dryburgh	Falkland	1623
23/1/1662	Jon Dougleish	Flisk	1621
23/1/1662	Jonet Edward	Flisk	1622
23/1/1662	Agnes Brounes	Kilmany	1629
23/1/1662	Jon Brounes	Kilmany	1630
23/1/1662	Helen Wentoun	Newburgh	1632
23/1/1662	Issobell Page	Newburgh	1633
23/1/1662	Margaret Philp	Newburgh	1634
23/1/1662	Cristian Anderson	Newburgh	1635
23/1/1662	Cristian Bonar	Newburgh	1636
6/2/1662	Jonat Mar	Collessie	1646
6/2/1662	Alison Melvill	Collessie	1645
6/2/1662	Elspeth Millar	Collessie	1647
6/2/1662	Jonet Staig	Collessie	1644
6/2/1662	Margaret Wishart	Collessie	1643
17/3/1662	Elspethe Craiche	Culross	2841
2/4/1662	Elspeth Anderson	Dunbog	1674
2/4/1662	Kathrin Blak	Flisk	1673
2/4/1662	Bessie Simson	Flisk	1672
7/5/1662	Jonnet Anand	Forgan	1692
7/5/1662	Elizabeth Clow	Forgan	1693
19/5/1662	Isobell Blyth	Auchtermuchty	1749
0/1/1663	(Several Persons)	Auchtertool	2863
9/5/1664	Margaret Guthrie	Carnbee	1836
0/0/1665		Culross	2873
8/9/1666	Issobell Key	St. Andrews	1842
8/9/1666	Grissel Anderson	Torryburn	1844
8/9/1666	Agnes Broun	Torryburn	1847
8/9/1666	Margaret Cowie	Torryburn	1848
8/9/1666	Margret Dobie	Torryburn	1843
8/9/1666	Elspeth Guild	Torryburn	1841
8/9/1666	Margaret Horne	Torryburn	1845
8/9/1666	Cristian May	Torryburn	1846
0/0/1667	(Witchcraft Cases)	Dunfermline	2875
0/0/1675	Grillies Robertson	Crail	2903
9/7/1675	Agnes Hendrie	Culross	609
9/7/1675	Jonet Hendrie	Culross	610
9/7/1675	Issobell Inglis	Culross	611
9/7/1675	Katherine Sands	Culross	612
25/12/1677	Currie	Dunfermline	2907
25/12/1677	Andro Currie	Dunfermline	2906
0/0/1681	Elspeth Kirkland	Aberdour	2936
29/5/1690		Kirkcaldy	3163
0/4/1701	Elizabeth Dick	Anstrosthereaster	2976
0/0/1704	Janet Cornfoot	Pittenweem	2990
0/0/1704	Isobel Adam	Pittenweem	2988

0/0/1704	Mrs. White	Pittenweem	2989
13/6/1704	Margaret Jack	Pittenweem	3127
13/6/1704	Margaret Wallace	Pittenweem	3126
14/6/1704	Janet Horseburgh	Pittenweem	3124
14/6/1704	Lillias Wallace	Pittenweem	3125
30/6/1704	Lillias Adie	Torryburn	2987
30/6/1704	Janet Whyte	Torryburn	2992
30/6/1704	Mary Wilson	Torryburn	2991
29/7/1704	Elspeth Williamson	Torryburn	2986
31/7/1704	Agnes Currie	Torryburn	3228
20/8/1704	Bessie Callender	Torryburn	3229
20/8/1704	Mary Carmichael	Torryburn	3230
0/0/1705	Thomas Brown	Pittenweem	2999
0/0/1705	Janet Corphat (or Cornfoot)	Pittenweem	3001
0/0/1705	Beatrix Laing	Pittenweem	2998
0/0/1705	Nicolas Lawson	Pittenweem	3000
20/5/1709	Betty Laing	Pittenweem	873
20/5/1709	Nicolas Lawson	Pittenweem	872

The Witch-Hunt in Haddington

Originally it was envisaged that a significant part of the research would involve a comparison between Haddington and Fife. There are some interesting comparisons. Even based upon the original data from the SBSW it was clear that Fife had many small hunts and cases where single individuals were accused while Haddington witnessed several severe hunts. Unfortunately, it is difficult to say more about this than the fact that based upon the data we currently have these two shires had a significantly different experience during the time of the witch-hunts. This becomes obvious when we consider the chronological pattern of the Haddington witch-hunt (see Graph 3 on p. 235). The geographic distribution is much more difficult to ascertain. One of the difficulties is the fact that Haddington is the name of a parish and a burgh as well as the shire. This makes it difficult to determine whether a reference to 'Haddington' refers to the shire, or the parish within the shire. There are approximately 49 cases which fall in this category. There are another 105 cases where a specific location within 'East Lothian' is unknown. The difficulties are real. The sheer number of cases makes it difficult to begin a regional study of this part of Scotland. For the moment, the prominence of Gladsmuir should be noted.

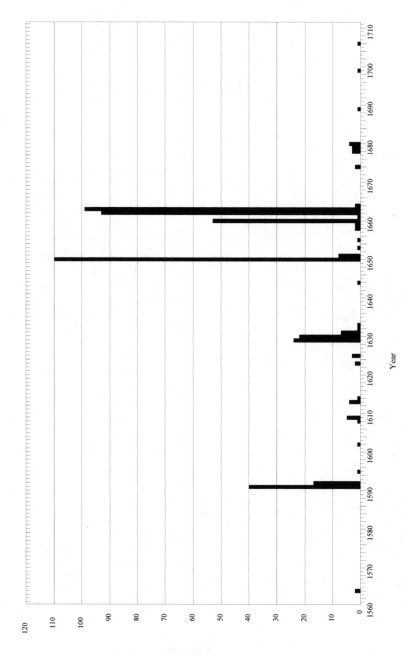

No. of cases

Year

Index